AF646896

EVOLUTION OF STRATEGY

From Sun Tzu to Clausewitz

EVOLUTION OF STRATEGY

From Sun Tzu to Clausewitz

CONTAINING THE ORIGINAL TEXTS

Commentary by

Col Harjeet Singh (Retd)

PENTAGON PRESS

EVOLUTION OF STRATEGY
From Sun Tzu to Clausewitz

First Indian Edition 2018

ISBN 978-93-86618-49-8

© Reserved

All rights reserved. No part of this publication may be reproduced, stored in a retrieval system, or transmitted, in any form or by any means, electronic, mechanical, photocopying, recording, or otherwise, without first obtaining written permission of the copyright owner.

Published in India by
PENTAGON PRESS
206, Peacock Lane
Shahpur Jat
New Delhi-110049
Phones: 011-64706243, 26491568
Telefax: 011-26490600
email: rajan@pentagon-press.com
website: www.pentagon-press.com

Printed at Aegean Offset Printers, Greater Noida, U.P.

CONTENTS

PREFACE

"The self is the friend of a man who masters himself through the self, but for a man without self-mastery, the self is like an enemy at war."

— The Bhagwad Gita

All wars result from political decisions and express a political intent, whether it may be appropriate or not, for implementing the policy it serves. War, or any kind of conflict, is waged and won through a strategy. While the philosophical inquiry into the subject of war leaves more questions unanswered, there have been efforts throughout the ages to determine better ways to wage war. Cynical as it may sound, it is an indisputable fact of history that man has made immense efforts to find ways and means to indulge in mass killing of his fellow beings. An ancestor in the dim past would have discovered the usefulness of a sharp stone to fell his opponent, but since then, there has been a consistent, constant and deliberate attempt to get the better of the other in combat. From the simple stone to a sharpened one; from a sharpened stone to one attached to a wooden shaft, to a sling, to weapons made of copper, bronze, iron to gunpowder and finally to the nuclear bomb. From the simple and straight forward frontal combat to deceiving the opponent, lying in wait, attacking from behind, jumping at him in the darkness and all other stratagems of warfare are being constantly refined. Thus, perhaps, 'strategy' has developed over the ages.

Strategy that could bring victory in war, or failure of which brought defeat has occurred to the thinkers over the ages. However, there are common grounds, some common precepts, and standard practices that seem to bring about victory. There have been several endeavours to define its concepts and crystallize them; and advocated it to those who would listen. Some, possibly much, has been lost in the tide of history. But many ideas remain, and have been a matter of study by all military minds. This, therefore, is an attempt to study a few of those thinkers who wrote about war.

Does such a study serve any purpose? It would, if mankind found the universal answer, or panacea to win or end wars. It should, if they had found the 'open sesame' to win battles. It could, if military leaders could even agree on the 'principles of war', so favourite a subject of all staff colleges. But that has not happened. All the same, several writers have influenced the thought process of generals and, at times, kings and statesmen. From them has emerged the word 'strategy'.

Strategy was defined by Clausewitz to be the use of armed force to achieve the military objectives and, by extension, the political purpose of a war. To the armed forces, it has implied a system of expediency to achieve a desired objective, based on the resources available to implement a state policy. It is this operational meaning which is of greater significance to the military professional. The context of strategy, therefore, changes with the issues and type of conflict a state is involved in. There are many military, as well as non-military factors, which shape the way that warfare is conducted. It is linked to the nature of society, military institutions and policies.

Here then is an attempt to study evolution of strategy. A study of this nature is beset with problems. Warfare may be as old as mankind, but its study is not. Much of what is written is disjointed. Great generals did not put down their thoughts. One wonders if Caesar even heard of Sun Tzu. Hannibal did not write down the thoughts he had when he conceived the strategy which every general worth his salt has tried to emulate. In spite of what Napoleon said, till lately the study of strategy has not been considered to be an academic discipline. Though every king or head of state had to learn skills of fighting (and presumably in that process the stratagem to conduct war) few theoreticians applied themselves to writing text books on it. It was an exclusive preserve of the military, and they did whatever they thought had to be done.

It would be totally pretentious to claim to fill that void in this book. Perhaps a body of historians may one day attempt it. This study is limited only to the examination of a few well known authors, whose writings have survived, and highlights some of their thoughts. It is not likely to add to the vast body of literature on warfare but would, hopefully, add to the understanding of a subject that has defied comprehension and scientific categorisation.

A few words on the choice of the strategists. Five have been chosen to represent the spectrum from early days to the time when one can say that modern warfare, or war as we know it today, started. Hence Sun Tzu, conceivably the oldest of them all; Vegetius whose influence lasted for over a millennium; Frederick the Great, who influenced the formation of the great war machine which later became the German Armies of the First and Second World Wars; and Napoleon, whose influence on later captains need not be highlighted. Clausewitz completes the pantheon.

There could be many others. In fact, very justifiable criticism can be levelled against this study by pointing out the omission of great captains and thinkers like Xenephon (Gustavus Adolphus was believed to have been an ardent student of Xenephon), Belisarius, Gustavus Adolphus himself, Jomini, Machiavelli, whose treatise on war should be read even now, and Marshall Saxe. The work of Ardant du Picq is also significant - the author of two original and insightful studies, *Ancient Battle* and *Modern Battle*, compiled as the classic *Battle Studies*. The question that motivated his work was how soldiers would fight in the age of mass firepower and mass armies. He set out to discover the essence of battle performance in individual and group psychology. Du Picq believed that face-to-face fighting was unnatural to man and only made possible from ancient times by the combination of discipline, cohesive organisation, and thoughtful tactics. Nevertheless, the selection is not arbitrary but aimed to provide coherence to the idea of military strategy.

"All warfare starts in the mind."

CHAPTER 1

WHAT IS STRATEGY?

"Strategy is more than a science: it is the application of knowledge to practical life, the development of thought capable of modifying the original guiding idea in the light of ever changing situations; it is the art of acting under the pressure of the most difficult conditions."

— Helmuth von Moltke, 1800-91

What is strategy? There are far too many definitions—each to its own light. It is usually taken to be something connected with the military; or in some other connotations and nuances, something concerning statecraft and warfare. This is no longer so. Now everyone talks of strategy. The sales manager promoting the sale of his company's product talks of 'strategy'. Political parties work out a 'strategy' to capture votes. Strategy today is a fashionable word, much bandied about for all kinds of things. Somewhat irrelevantly, there is another fashionable word—concept. Today everyone seems to talk about 'concept' or 'conceptualizes', leaving one to wonder as to who does the actual work.

Here, of course, we shall not go into the commercial application of the word strategy but in its military connotation. The word covers a very wide range of activities. It could imply the plans a country has against another in the sphere of politico-military activities; it could also be used by a general to bring his troops to the battlefield in a superior or planned manner. The problem is not just semantics; it is one of understanding and using competently, one of the most essential tools of the military profession. Though seeking a precise and a universally acceptable definition of military strategy may not be a feasible proposition, there is definitely a need to have a general and common understanding on a conceptual approach to military strategy. It necessitates an understanding of the description of the basic elements that constitute military strategy and comprehending the analysis as to how these elements are inter-related.

The word strategy derives from the Greek *strategos*, a civil-military official elected by the citizens of Athens to assume leadership in time of war. Most attempts at definition have turned upon a contrast with 'tactics', the art of making arrangements, or of putting things in position. For centuries it was considered that strategy referred to military measures taken beyond the range of the enemy's weapons, while tactics referred to those taken within that range. The original etymology belies the tendency to assume that strategy refers simply to the conduct of military operations on a large scale. Its most essential meaning underpins the intellectual and practical reconciliation of military means and political ends.

In recent times, as the ends of policy have become more complex and diverse, it has become common for strategy to encompass non-military means as well; though one might argue that it has always been so. Expressions like national strategy and grand strategy typically refer to the full range of methods by which states act internationally, including non-coercive diplomacy, trade, peacetime alliances, and so on, as well as the actual use or threat of force. In this context, the adoption of the world strategy by private organisations to refer to any deliberate, long term plan has blurred its conceptual distinctiveness.

As applied to the conduct of states, a strategy is a course of action in which the use of force is not excluded as a matter of principle. Strategic action can be readily distinguished, for instance, from actions governed by market relationships, which are essentially rule-bound and, as a consequence, susceptible to an abstract analysis that has eluded theorists of war. For all its competitive pressures, the market place is a far less confounding environment than the battlefield. The latter is the domain of force and fraud, which admit no limits in principle, nor any sort of mutually transparent rationality to help ensure that the conduct of one antagonist is understandable to the others.

If strategy is made necessary by the inherent chaos of the international system, it is made possible by the human capacity to anticipate and organize against adversity; to detect in the conclusion of a pact of friendship between former rivals, or the arranged marriage of an obscure princess to a neighbouring prince, or the discovery of new and fertile lands overseas, or a thousand other contingent events – some remote or proximate threat, to which a forceful response may someday be required. Such responses may be simple or elaborate, cunning or bold, bellicose or pacific; but all are shaped by deeply rooted geographic, social, economic, and cultural facts, as well as by whatever immediate interests are thought to be at stake. If strategy is, proverbially, a realm of uncertainty, it is because it must account for fundamentally unpredictable behaviour, shaped by assumptions that are rarely fully understood, even by those most directly concerned.

All the expedients of strategy nevertheless share a common purpose; to reach military results that alter the political calculations of the belligerents. If there is a central idea around which serious strategic analysis must revolve, it is victory. However, the latter is to an extent, unfashionable, because it is too prone to be interpreted in purely military terms and to attribute undue importance to events on the battlefield. Victory is difficult to define *per se*. The capture of a town, the successful defence of a hill, or the defeat of an enemy army will undeniably be victories, in a military context. Yet military victory can be strategically barren if it fails to alter the political context in which the military action was carried out. This disconnect can be demoralizing to soldiers, and is a common source of civil-military discord. More than a few of history's most skilful soldiers - Napoleon, Lee, the German High Command of both world wars, have single-mindedly pursued tactical success all the way to strategic ruin; while others less gifted by prevailing military standards – Washington, Blucher, Giap – have achieved strategic decisions favourable to their cause despite tactical results that were deemed mediocre.

Strategic possibilities are always influenced by the means employed to raise the armed forces intended to achieve them. The ancient phalanx and the medieval armies were brought to the battlefield by a complex web of social relationships that were only partly military in character. Such armies were capable of tremendous violence when brought into contact with each other – a formidable task in itself – but they were also temporary organisations, called into existence by immediate threats or opportunities, or in response to some cultural imperative (personal, honour, civil obligations, etc). Such armies had exceedingly limited capabilities, and could engage in sustained combat for only a few hours at a time, before losing cohesion. The strategic pursuit or exploitation necessary to capitalize upon tactical success did not exist, and wars were accordingly decided, as often as not, by simple exhaustion, or impatience with futility.

The standing armies of the past possessed greater military efficiency – they could train regularly, and their officers were drawn from the feudal elite. They were more professional in outlook – but their strategic significance lay chiefly in the fact that they existed all year round, and were firmly at the disposal of the ruler. Although it would be wrong to imagine that anything like strategic planning existed before the 19th century, standing armies allowed rulers to estimate their own strength, and that of potential allies and opponents, more consistently, and so (in theory at least) to integrate military means and political ends more effectively.

Nevertheless, if military action had far reaching results, it was a reflection of the political base upon which armies, and the rulers that employed them, rested. For most rulers the perils of defeat were more striking than the hope of victory.

Strategic considerations are different for navies, and they have usually achieved their strategic effects more directly than armies, by attacking an adversary's seaborne trade or overseas possessions, or by supporting harassing operations against his coast. However, it has been historically rare for such measures to achieve decisive results by themselves. The simultaneous application of land and sea power was accomplished by strategic alliances; and brings into focus the importance of diplomacy.

The strategic possibilities of the modern era have been largely defined by mass social mobilisation and technological change. By the middle of the 19th century, it was clear that the modern battlefield could only be mastered by mass armies far larger than any country could afford to maintain in peacetime. Regular armies became training organisations for large bodies of conscripts, whose rapid mobilisation and dispersed deployment became central to the military art. Although railways and the telegraph made rapid mobilisation possible, it gave rise to the need for intensive, continuous military planning. Also, once concentrated for battle, the difficulties of moving, supplying and manoeuvring large armies quickly enhanced the importance of logistics.

The modern strategists governing ideal of swift, decisive results, achieved by rapidly evolving, intensely violent, well controlled manoeuvres, has remained elusive, largely because it rests upon a foundation of what has proven to be an unjustified social pessimism. The impact of industrialisation on naval warfare has been equally complex. The emergence of an integrated global economy has increased the value of seaborne trade, a target that navies are best suited to attack. Few countries produce all the necessities of life within their own borders, and increase their dependence on freedom of the seas. The promise that naval power could dominate events on land, or render the fighting of armies redundant is now ephemeral.

Technology has also become a big factor in warfare, though it is rare for any state to remain at a technological disadvantage to its competitors for long. Military advantages based upon technical means are notable mainly for their evanescence – which only heightens the need to keep up. They have made the arms race a distinctive feature of the modern strategic environment.

No new technology has had more far reaching strategic consequences than the airplane, and the ballistic missiles that have followed in its wake. Air power has offered a technological proficiency that renders it an important method of warfighting. Airplanes have made modern warfare swift and efficient. The effects of tactical air power and as an independent, strategic weapon seemed unlimited. By providing a means of striking directly at the social and political fabric of the adversary, strategic air power captured the quintessence of what strategy was always supposed to mean – the optimum effective application of military force for political ends. By dissolving all meaningful distinction between armed forces and the civil societies they protected, war in the air has made war as conventionally understood a thing of the past. In airspace, strategy and tactics has become one.

With the advent of nuclear weapons, to the potential of strategic air power has considerably attenuated. Nevertheless, the unique possibilities afforded by war in the air continue to exert enormous sway. Strategic air power, i.e. the independent use (or threat) of air strikes to achieve direct political effects – dominates both ends of the conflict spectrum. Nuclear deterrence remains the ultimate guarantee of security for most of the large countries in the world, who either possess such weapons themselves or have allies that do. At the same time precision guided munitions and stealth technology have made air weapons the preferred instruments for the conduct of low intensity conflict and coercive diplomacy by advanced societies.

The quest for decisiveness is at the heart of strategic decision making. We can now revert to the question of what is strategy. Any strategy consists of three elements i.e. ends, ways and means. Converted into an equation it amounts to: Strategy = Ends + Ways + Means. Keeping this concept as a guide we can develop a similar equation for military strategy:

Military Strategy = Military Strategic Objectives
+
Military Strategic Concepts
+
Military Resources

"Ends" can be expressed as military strategic objectives. "Ways" are concerned with the various methods of applying military force. In essence this becomes an examination of courses of action, designed to achieve the military strategic objectives. These courses of action are termed military strategic concepts. "Means" refer to the military resources which are required to accomplish the mission (manpower, material, finances, logistics, etc.) This leads us to the conclusion that military strategy equals military strategic objectives plus military strategic concepts plus military resources.

This conceptual approach very broadly is applicable to all levels of war; strategic, operational and tactical. From a corps commander down to platoon leaders: they are all concerned with ways to employ means to achieve objectives. It applies to the Navy and Air Force as well.

To elaborate on the point, the broad and basic strategy of the Allies during the Second World War was to tackle Germany and Italy first, then Japan. This was discussed at great length during the Quebec conference. That then was the grand strategy. If we define strategy to encompass level as high as that, one would be left with many gaps. But then the military has used the word 'strategy; in many other contexts. Montgomery devised a "strategy" to defeat Rommel's columns in the hills of Alam Halfa (Battle of El Alamein). Von Schlieffen in First World War had designed a strategy which according to many, if followed in its original conception, might have had brought about the defeat of the Anglo-French Armies (and perhaps spared that generation the agony of mass slaughter). One need not quote from Napoleon's campaigns to show how he had worked out "strategy".

But much of the above can also be called tactics. Rommel's defeat in Alam Halfa was a tactical defeat (though it did change the entire course of campaign in the Western African Desert. On the other hand, given the help that he had sought, he might have been able to turn the defeat into victory. Do Field Marshall Slim's plans for the reconquest of Burma (the famous hammer and anvil manoeuvre) come under word strategy or tactics? By itself, Slim's plans and moves were brilliant, and much admired by all military historians. But was it strategy or was it tactics?

One can go on to another plane. Mao Zedong devised a strategy for revolutionary warfare and framed some rules for it. Later General Giap adopted it brilliantly, first to liberate North Vietnam and then to unify Vietnam. Perhaps one could argue that Mao's thoughts – or strategy of mass uprising and revolutionary war was not perhaps all that original. Sun Tzu wrote something about it, and may be it was Spartacus who first practiced it, albeit on a small scale. One may need to remember that peasant's revolt – in today's terms 'guerrilla warfare' – is nothing new. Caesar periodically had to send troops to various parts of Europe to subdue armed uprisings. And Napoleon's problems in Spain are far too well known to recount here. Hence the question: does all this come under the purview of strategy?

These examples abound. Historical parallels are easy to draw. It would have been a comparatively easy task if a continuous history of strategic thought existed, where easy categorisations could be made in distinguishing various aspects of strategy, or better still, various facets of it.[1] What does appear, in spite of conflicting definitions made by different writers, is that an attempt can be made at arriving at a spectrum as to where strategy starts and ends, and where tactics starts and ends. Since various authors have tackled various hues of this spectrum, there is a need to define the spectrum itself.

The word strategy, in a strictly military sense, means "the art of the general". While Machiavelli was probably the first thinker on the larger aspects of war and the methods of conducting it, the majority of the great captains like Frederick the Great, and de Saxe considered strategy to be what today would be termed as tactics or grand tactics or the "strategy" of the battlefield. This somewhat narrow definition continued even during the Napoleonic wars, although Napoleon himself had included political and economic moves to increase the chances of victory. However, Napoleon and most of his predecessors had combined the offices of military commander and leader of the State. Their decisions on the battlefield or in the councils of State were complementary to each other and they could shape their strategy whether for statecraft or the battlefield in the manner they liked.

All nations have traditional and established objectives, often assumed and rarely written. A fairly well understood meaning of military strategy, since nation states came into being, has been national security or defence of territorial integrity of the country. But the entire concept of security, in modern times, has been expanded to include political, economic, ideological, and even psychological fields. Thus at the highest level, the methods of accomplishing policy goals, particularly as they pertain to war, have come to be called the national strategy. It includes manoeuvres in such diverse and differing fields as political, commercial and technological. Therefore, ever present is the question of whether strategy is the positioning of armed forces in times of war, or the composite activities of a government in every sphere of its endeavour in times of war, or in other periods of international tension, activities in order to achieve its national objectives.

To a military man, strategy should mean preparation for, and conduct of war. For the purpose of this text, the definition adopted by Liddell Hart would do: "The art of distributing and applying military means to fulfil the ends of policy".[2] All military strategists have emphasized the relationship between war and politics. From this we may construe that all military forces must be given appropriate missions, within their capabilities. Liddell hart explained that: "In discussing the subject of the 'objective' in war it is essential to be clear about, and to keep clear in our minds, the distinction between the political and the military objective. The two are different but not separate. For nations do not wage war for war's sake, but in the pursuance of policy. The military objective is only the means to a political end. Hence the military objective should be governed by the political objective, subject to the basic condition that policy does not demand – what is, practically – impossible".[3]

Liddell Hart of course made further elaborations. According to him there is also a grand strategy or higher strategy. The role of grand strategy is 'to coordinate and direct all the resources of a nation, or band of nations, towards attainment of the political object of the war – the goal defined by fundamental policy".

If we accept the above definition of strategy, what would be tactics? Tactics now becomes translation of strategy to actual plans to win a battle. By the same analogy as of strategy, grand tactics will be at the level of Corps and division, while tactics (or minor tactics) will be at the level of units and sub units. There is naturally overlap between each of the terms. The spectrum could be diagrammatically shown like this:

One can therefore draw the spectrum from grand strategy, derived form national policy and goals; leading on to strategy; which should lead on to grand tactics and finally to tactics or minor tactics. This book, generally speaking, covers the middle two i.e. strategy and grand tactics, as there is much overlap between the two.

There are two levels of military strategy (The levels refer to the time dimension):

- Operational (Short Range)
- Long Range

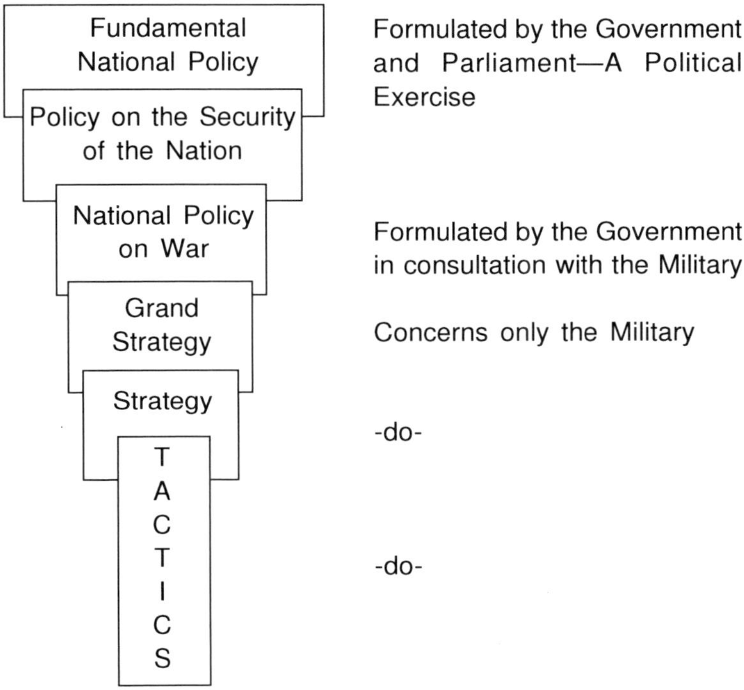

Strategies based on existing military capabilities are operational strategies—these strategies are used as a foundation (basis) for the formulation of specific plans for action in the short–range time period. Longer range strategies may be based on appreciated future threats, objectives and requirements; and are therefore not as constrained by current force posture. In fact they may determine improvements required in military capabilities. In the case of great powers, there could be other strategies that may be regional or even global, concerning themselves with specific threat scenarios.

Military Strategic objectives and military strategic concepts of a military strategy determine requirements for resources. These are, in turn, influenced by the availability of resources. If we fail to consider military resources as an element of military strategy, we may be faced with what has come to be called a strategy-capability mismatch i.e. the existence of inadequate military capabilities to implement strategic concepts and to accomplish the strategic objectives of a military strategy. This mismatch is usually the case when developing a long range strategy requiring improved military force structure capabilities. However, this mismatch may be disastrous if it is concerned with an operational strategy upon which contingency plans and military operations are based. That is why operational strategies must be based on existing capabilities.

Military resources determine capabilities. They may include conventional and unconventional forces, strategic and nuclear forces (where the countries have NBC capability or face a NBC threat), defensive and offensive forces, active and reserve forces, war material, weapons systems manpower and so on. The total force package must be well balanced with fighting arms, supporting arms and logistics support elements adequately equipped and sustained.

Depending upon the type of strategy being developed, the forces that are being considered for employing may or may not currently exist. In short range (operational) the forces must exist. In longer range strategies, the strategic concepts determine the type of forces that should exist and the way they should be employed.

In the examination of military strategic objectives, the objective should be military in nature. While Clausewitz, Lenin, and Mao have all emphasized the integral relationship of war and politics, military force must be given appropriate missions within their capabilities. (This is, generally, not a problem lower level). Liddell Hart has stressed that: "In war it is essential to be clear about and to keep clear in our minds, the distinction between the political and the military objective".

In defining military strategy, the ultimate objectives are those of national policy. Sometimes policy guidance itself is difficult to find or if it is there, it is unclear or ambiguous. National policy also concerns itself with all the basic elements of national power: political, economic, diplomatic, psychological, military and so on. Therefore, it is quite natural that national policies in these various fields are often overlapping, and may even be contradictory. There are seldom "purely military" or "purely political" objectives. At times national leaders may choose to use the military element of power, in pursuit of national policy objectives, that are primarily political or economic in nature. This can cause problems. Sometimes military force is not the appropriate tool. Military commanders may then have difficulty in deriving feasible military objectives from the objectives of national policy.

A military strategic concept can be defined as the course of action accepted as the result of an assessment of the strategic situation. Military strategic concepts may combine a wide range of options, e.g. forward defence (i.e. forward-basing or forward deployment), strategic reserves, reinforcements, show of force, pre-positioned stocks, and so on. The determination of strategic concepts is of major importance. A word of caution; strategic concepts should not be confused with strategy. Strategic concepts must always be considered in relation to military strategic objectives and the resources.

Military Strategy is one of the main tools, a very vital tool for ensuring national security. Under ideal circumstances military objectives and strategic concepts determine force structure and deployment of military forces. However, military objectives and strategic concepts are necessarily affected by the capabilities and limitations of the military forces in being. Also, a military strategy may not be a declared one, or the actual military strategy may be totally different from the declared one. Some strategists even feel that it is unwise or even dangerous to enunciate openly a military strategy.

NOTES

1. An interesting study would be to enter into the field of evolution of strategy for nuclear warfare: from massive retaliation to mutually assured destruction from nuclear symmetry or nuclear asymmetry. Curiously, this area is totally dominated by "egg heads" and not "brass hats". Till the advent of nuclear weapons, the study of strategy and tactics had been, by and large, confined to the military, serving or ex-soldiers; but for reasons not fully analysed the academic world entered into the field of nuclear war in a big way in the 1950s. This perhaps happened because, almost universally, generals are taught to draw "lessons" from the past and apply them to the future; they did not quite know what to do with this new weapon, with which no war has been fought, and hopefully, will not be fought.
2. Some other definitions of the word are given below:
   (a) "Generalship or the art of conducting a campaign and maneouvering an army – Chambers Dictionary.
   (b) "Generalship, art of war, management of an army or armies in a campaign, art of moving and disposing troops or ships so as to impose upon the enemy the place and time and conditions for fighting preferred by oneself – Oxford Dictionary.
   (c) Clauzewitz gave a number of definitions; rather, he did not quite "define" it, but explained it in many places. But the following two would indicate the general line of his thoughts: "Tactics is the theory of use of military forces in combat, strategy is the theory of the use of combat for the object of the war" and "The art of the employment of battle as a means to gain the object of war".
   (d) "Practical adoption of the means placed at a general's disposal to attainment of the object in view"—Moltke.
   (e) "The theatre of war is the province of strategy, the field of battle the province of tactics—Sir Edward Hamley
   (f) Tactics is the art of handling troops in the battlefield; strategy is the art of bringing forces to the battle field in a favourable position.—Field Marshal Wavell
3. Hart, B.H. Liddell, *Strategy*, New York: Praeger Publishers, 1975, p. 351.

CHAPTER 2

SUN TZU: ART OF WAR

"All men can see the tactics whereby I conquer, but what none can see is the strategy out of which victory is evolved"

— SUN TZU

Sun Tzu was a Chinese general, military theorist, and philosopher. He is the author of the world's first and potentially most long lived work of military theory, ***Art of War***, also known as The Thirteen Chapters. In the 1980s, it was adopted by Tokyo, Wall Street, and the City of London as a text for students of business strategy.

Sun Tzu probably wrote his opus in the period of the Warring States in the 5th century BC. It has been suggested that the work might be by Sun Wu and date from the late 6th century BC, but there are repeated reference to crossbows, invented in China around 400 BC. Furthermore, there is no mention of cavalry by Sun Tzu, which appeared around 320 BC, only of chariots. We can, therefore, be reasonably sure that this first and most universal work on the art of war dates around 500 BC.

It is difficult not to be amazed by the writings of Sun Tzu. Not much is known about him – he is believed to have been a native of the Chou States and a general or ruler of Wu. There are no detailed records of what type of battles he fought, what weapons were used, what victories he achieved, or which territories he conquered. But this much can be surmised – the weapons must have been swords and lances and daggers, bows and arrows, and chariots, and the basic form of conducting war could not have been greatly different to that elsewhere in the world during that period. Nevertheless, the concepts and principles embodied in the ***Art of War*** are the distilled wisdom of a great soldier, which have influenced Chinese military thinking for millennia, and still echo in myriad applications today.

The ***Art of War*** by Sun Tzu undeniably retains its original value as an extremely comprehensible body of work. To the military commander able to adapt the postulates of Sun Tzu to modern warfare even now, two and a half thousand years after their formulation, it remains an invaluable guide. It was the greatest military classic of the Chinese, and greatly valued by the Japanese, even more so than the Chinese. Somewhat surprisingly, Sun Tzu remained relatively unknown to the West till about 19th century.

Like many great works of military thought, the Art of War is a mixture of profound philosophy and detailed and dated tactical prescriptions. The opening sentences are clear enough: "The art of war is of vital importance to the State. It is a matter of life and death, a road either to safety or to ruin. Hence it is a subject of inquiry which can on no account be neglected". Probably its most lasting observation is to do with information warfare. "All war is based on deception. Therefore when capable, feign incapacity; when active, inactivity. When near, make it appear that you are away; when far away, that you are near". Sun Tzu was the first to enunciate the indirect approach in war; indeed, he coined the phrase. "He who was master of both the direct and the indirect approach would be victorious", is a reflection of the interaction of regular and partisan forces which was a characteristic of war in Sun-Tzu's age. Mao Zedong and the Vietnamese followed this tradition. Sun Tzu likened an army to water, for just as flowing water avoids the heights and hastens to the lowlands, so an army avoids strength and strikes weakness.

Sun-Tzu was the first to set out what we would now recognize as principles of war; moral influence, weather, terrain, command, and doctrine. The first meant the trust of people in their leaders. By command, he meant the qualities and ability of the general and by doctrine he meant organisation, command and control, and logistics.

Written in the aphoristic form of classical Chinese literature, it is a difficult, nearly impracticable treatise to make a summary of. Each sentence, each maxim has to be read, understood and pondered upon. Indeed there have been many commentaries on Sun Tzu, not to mention their usefulness as quotations in the business arena. But the relevance of most of his postulates in today's battlefield is truly amazing. For example, Sun Tzu said "In all fighting the direct method may be used for joining battle, but indirect methods will be needed to secure victory". Readers will realize that the basic idea of Sun Tzu was practiced by many, perhaps intuitively, but was developed into a full treatise nearly two thousand years later, when it came to be called as the "Strategy of Indirect Approach".[1]

Further, in the writings of Sun Tzu, one perceives the concept of a "holding force" and "enveloping force". Both for tactics and strategy, Sun Tzu places high value on manoeuvre – a lesson periodically forgotten and re-learnt again and again. Witness also the battles of all great captains, who won their battles by using the principle of manoeuvre.[2] Sun Tzu advises avoidance of battle unless all considerations are favourable, nor does he forget the importance of deception. "All warfare is based on deception", he writes. "When able to attack, the general must seem unable, when using his forces, he should appear inactive. Tactical dispositions should mask strength with readiness. And conversely, the skilful opponent should be judged not by appearance, but by the more precise information obtained from spies.

Special mention could be made of some other aspects covered by Sun Tzu. A surprisingly modern thought is the importance given by Sun Tzu to "Estimation and Calculations". Sun Tzu claimed that he could forecast victory or defeat by the seven items of his estimate. If Sun Tzu were a modern writer, he probably would have called them 'Principles of War'.[3] His attention to terrain is also in keeping with modern thoughts and practice, e.g. "The natural formation of the country is the soldiers' best ally". He dwells on discipline and loyalty, and in fact, enunciates what can be termed as the foundation of morale and leadership" when he writes, "Regard your soldiers as your children, and they will follow you to the deepest valleys; look upon them as your own beloved sons, and they will stand by you unto death". He advocates that men must be gradually disciplined, and having done so, discipline must be strictly enforced i.e. "if soldiers are punished before they have grown attached to you, they will not prove submissive. If, when they have become attached to you, punishments are not enforced, they will be useless"

The book has thirteen chapters. The first broadly lays down the basic considerations. Sun Tzu contends that the art of war is governed by five constant factors: namely the Moral Law, Heaven, Earth, Commander, Method and Discipline. The wise general was asked to "calculate" these five factors, as applicable to the contestants, in order to arrive at the plans. He also emphasized here on the value of deception, which is the essence of warfare. The importance of weighing all options and preparing thoroughly, and initiating action when there is a high probability of success are axiomatic. Sun Tzu's dictum: "Attack where they are unprepared, go forth where they will not expect it", is a watchword of Chinese military thought even today.

The second chapter concerns maintenance of the Army by the State or the general. He brings out how expensive it is to maintain an army. Wisely, albeit surprisingly, he seemed to have thought of very small items and expenses as well. To quote "... the expenditure at home including entertainment of guests, small items such as glue and paint, and sums spent on chariots and armour, will reach the total of thousand ounces silver per day. Such is the cost of raising an army of 100,000 men". Thus he advocates a short war,[4] so that there is no "second levy, neither are his supply wagons loaded more than twice". He also states that a wise general makes a point of foraging on the enemy. "One cartload of the enemy's provision is equivalent of twenty of one's own". And he sums up the chapter with: "In war, then, let your great object be victory, not a lengthy campaign". The single important idea that is propagated is that protracted warfare is inimical to the state, and third parties can get involved in the conflict

The next chapter deals with stratagems, more specifically, "Attack by Stratagem". It is almost impossible to summarize the chapter as each of the postulates or aphorisms have to be read carefully, but attention needs to be drawn to some important ones. Sun Tzu states: "Hence to fight and conquer in all your battles is not supreme excellence; supreme excellence consists in breaking the enemy's resistance without fighting".[5] Thus, the highest ideal is to subjugate the enemy without fighting, by frustrating their plans, thwarting their preparations, and undermining their alliances. Should fighting become necessary, the best commanders will be those who can conquer their enemies with minimal destruction to both sides. It is, therefore, important to attack the enemy's plans rather than the actual enemy forces. Sun Tzu makes a powerful plea to avoid siege warfare, gives a formula for 'relative strength'; and finally gives five 'essentials' for victory. This highlights the importance of understanding one's own capabilities and deficiencies.

The next chapter deals with tactics or to be more exact "Tactical Dispositions". The postulations here are very broad and generalized, and are basically a continuation of the previous chapter. Here Sun Tzu addresses himself to the question of defeat versus victory in the background of "security", in which he highlights that "security against defeat implies defensive tactics, ability to defeat the enemy means taking the offensive. Standing on the defensive indicates insufficient strength; attacking a superabundance of strength". The concept of appropriate force levels and co-relating them to the task and terrain at hand are extremely relevant. Significantly, Sun Tzu also highlights command and control measures to exploit the potential of the army.

The fifth chapter is headed "Energy". Sun Tzu's conception of energy is the selection of weak points vis-a-vis strong points and exploiting the weak points by a combination of command (good decisions), control (timings of moves) and manoeuvre (both direct and indirect). He illustrates the effectiveness of combination vividly: "There are not more than five musical notes, yet he combination of these five notes give rise to more melodies than can be heard..." The application of unorthodox measures is considered to be complementary to the orthodox ones.

The next two chapters (6 and 7) are elaborations on the concepts of weak and strong points and manoeuvring. Both are comparatively long chapters. Much of the advice pertains to gaining advantage over the enemy; e.g., arrive first on the battle field, be well supplied so that the enemy can be starved out, surprise the enemy by doing the unexpected, keep the enemy divided while keeping your forces concentrated, fight on a ground of your own choosing and so on. Another piece of wisdom is: "do not repeat the tactics which have gained you one victory, but let your methods be regulated by the infinite variety of circumstances". His entreaties on manoeuvring harp on blending and harmonizing the different elements. He advises the general not to overdo, not to be overambitious by illustrating vividly the effect of long forced marches. "Ponder and deliberate before you make a move", says Sun Tzu. (How true, even if one would consider it to be a bit trite). There is also very practical advice: "When you plunder a countryside, let the spoil be divided amongst your men; when you capture new territory, cut it up into allotments for the benefit of the soldiery" or, "in night fighting, then, make much use of signal fires and drums and in fighting by day, of flags and banners, as a means of influencing the ears and eyes of your army".

Advice on Tactics continues in Chapter 8, headed "Variation in Tactics". Much of it pertains to seizing an opportunity (advantage as Sun Tzu calls it), and understanding what can be done and what should not be done. Worth quoting are the five faults that may affect a general: "(1) Recklessness, which leads to destruction, (2) Cowardice, which leads to capture; (3) A hasty temper that can be provoked by insult; (4) A delicacy of honour that is sensitive to shame; and (5) Over solicitude for his men, which exposes him to worry and trouble". An aspect that is highlighted is the importance of being flexible and varying tactics to suit circumstances, thus avoiding becoming predictable. Modern day theorists feel that a cardinal rule is to never change a winning strategy. However, Sun Tzu's dictum is to not repeat a winning strategy.

Chapter 9 is another long one, containing more practical advice. It is headed "The Army on the March", but as in the case of other chapters, contains much more. The rules laid down and advice given pertains to encamping the army as also observing signs of the enemy. For instance, "the rising of birds in their flight is a sign of an ambuscade; when there is dust rising in high columns, it is the sign of chariots advancing (modern cavalry men would also confirm that). There are also some very piquant observations: "peace proposals unaccompanied by a sworn covenant indicate a plot; and, when there is much running about, it means that the critical moment has come". Also, "one who seeks peace without setting any prior conditions is executing a stratagem". Another important enunciation of Sun Tzu was that doubts about a commander's orders must never be permitted to arise. This appears to be a great variation from the contemporary military age where orders are directives are reinterpreted and redefined, almost from the time they are issued.

Sun Tzu must be the first military thinker who saw the importance of terrain. Though some aspects of terrain appear in almost all the chapters the tenth and eleventh chapters are devoted to terrain. Sun Tzu divides terrain in six categories and it must be the first attempt to do so. The six kinds of terrain, according to Sun Tzu, are; accessible ground, entangling grounds, temporizing ground, narrow passes, precipitous height and positions at a great distance form the enemy. What follows are the definitions of these categorisations and instruction as to how to make the best use of them, or what to avoid. The tenth chapter also covers another area; calamities, not arising from natural causes but for which the general is responsible". These are: fight, insubordination, collapse, rain, disorganisation and rout. Sun Tzu elaborates as to when and how such calamities might occur.

The theme of ground reappears in the next chapter where Sun Tzu states: "the art of war recognizes nine varieties of ground"; (1) dispersive ground (2) facile ground (3) contentious ground (4) open ground (5) ground of intersecting highways (6) serious ground (7) difficult ground (8) hemmed in ground, and (9) desperate ground. The eleventh chapter is actually headed as The Nine Situations, and Sun Tzu describes what kind of situation would bring about the aforesaid ground conditions. Alternatively, it can be also said that Sun Tzu defined the various ground conditions. For example: "When the army has penetrated into the hearts of a hostile country, leaving a number of fortified cities in the rear it is serious ground", or" ground which is reached through narrow gorges, and from which we can retire only by tortuous paths, so that a small number of the enemy would suffice to crush a large body of our men, this is hemmed in ground:". The chapter also gives principles to be observed by an invading force, somewhat dispersed throughout the chapter. In both the chapters Sun Tzu gives valuable advice on management also.

Rather surprisingly, Sun Tzu devotes an entire chapter, albeit a short one, to "The Attack by Fire". Not that the chapter, as in others, does not contain many other aspects; it does appear that Sun Tzu gave considerable thought to use of "fire" in warfare. It is to be remembered that his was a time when gun powder was unknown and the weapons of war consisted of swords, spears, bows and arrows, chariots and the like. Use of fire in defence, especially defending fortifications, of course is ancient. Pouring down burning hot oil, or throwing a burning torch from the ramparts of a fort on to the attacking force must be as old as warfare itself. But Sun Tzu talks of attack by fire. He enunciates five ways to attack by fire: "The first is to burn soldiers in their camps, the second is to burn stores, the third is to burn their baggage trains, the fourth is to burn arsenals and magazines and fifth is to hurl dropping fire amongst the enemy".

The last chapter deals with spies. It is headed "The Use of Spies". Sun Tzu establishes the need for foreknowledge: "Thus, what enables the wise sovereign and the good general to strike and conquer and achieve things beyond the reach of ordinary men is foreknowledge". He continues: "hence the use of spies, of whom there are five classes: (1) local spies (2) inward spies (3) converted spies (4) doomed spies, and (5) surviving spies". His definition of doomed and surviving spies is interesting: "Having doomed spies, doing certain things openly for the purpose of deception, and allowing our own spies to know of them and report them to the enemy".[6] And surviving spies, "finally are those who bring back news from the enemy's camp:" He further elaborates on the methods of converting an enemy's spies, and the use of doomed spies to convey false information to the enemy.

In summation, it is appropriate to narrate a fairly well known and much quoted incident, which could be apocryphal. Sun Tzu was asked by the King of Wu to prove his theories by testing them on women. Sun Tzu readily agreed and assembled all the concubines of the court, and appointed two of the King's favourite ones as the commanders. He explained them various drill movements and started giving orders. The girls only giggled. Sun Tzu said: "If the instructions are not clear and if the explanations are not trustworthy, it is the general's fault". Sun Tzu then explained the instructions and again repeated the orders. When they again failed to obey, Sun Tzu said: "If the orders have been explained and instructed, and if the troops yet do not perform, it is the fault of the officers." He then ordered the two leaders to be beheaded – much to the chagrin of the king and protest of the court. When the king asked Sun Tzu to forgive the concubines, Sun Tzu said: "I have already received my commission as commanding general. According to the rules for generals, when in command of the army, even if the ruler issues orders to him, the general does not have to accept them." He then had them beheaded. After that, there was no more disobedience – the rest of the women's company obeyed all the orders given.

NOTES

1. The strategy of indirect approach has come to be associated with that great thinker and writer, Capt B.H. Liddell Hart. A keen student of warfare, who was able to foresee the effect of mechanisation on future wars, his concepts on strategy (to be later named as Strategy of Indirect Approach and Expanding Torrent) were the outcome of technological innovations of the First World War.
2. Manoeuvre and its counterpart, mobility, has been indeed a major factor in winning battles. Few decisive battles seem to have been won by a static force. On the other hand, a static mentality has usually led to defeat. Alexander won the decisive battle of Arbela (or Gaugamela) where his cavalry was able to overcome the Persians who were much superior in number. It was the heavy cavalry of Hannibal which was able to entrap the Roman Army at the battle of Cannae. Gustavus Adolphus was able to bring back mobility on the battlefield by reorganisation of the cavalry. On the other hand, static defence's like the Maginot Line of the Second World War or the Bar Lev Line in the Yom Kippur War of 1973 failed.
3. In later times, it was Jomini who was able to discern and formulate the basic elements which could be said to be the principles of war.

4 All wars after the Second World War have tended to be short. In fact, a classification needs to be made between long and short wars. Historically, there have been many long wars, i.e. Punic wars, Hundred Years War (1337-1453), War of the Roses (1455-87), Thirty Years War (1618-48), Napoleonic Wars, not to speak of the First and Second World Wars. Most of the wars, except the First and Second World Wars, were not continuous. There were prolonged periods of belligerent posturing – what today might be called cold war – but not continuous engagements as in the First and Second World Wars. It is also relevant that such wars did not become the 'end' of all activities. "War' was one of the activities undertaken by the king or the country. The concept of total war came much later, introduced by Machiavelli.

5 The discerning reader will immediately see its application by Hitler; and its disregard by the Allies in the Second World War. Hitler was able to annex Austria and

Czechoslovakia without shedding a drop of blood; he also conquered the better part of Europe including Poland, Holland, Norway and France, speedily and with the least amount of bloodshed. On the other hand, the Allies, especially the Americans, in their mistaken interpretation of Clausewitz, fought to defeat the German Armed Forces in battle, rather than work towards the capitulation of the Nazi Government. This must be seen in the background of the fact that Allies knew of the growing resistance to Nazi rule.

6. The game of double bluff and moles is not really new.

THE ART OF WAR

SUN TZU

I. LAYING PLANS

Sun Tzu said: The art of war is of vital importance to the State. It is a matter of life and death, a road either to safety or to ruin. Hence it is a subject of inquiry which can on no account be neglected.

The art of war, then, is governed by five constant factors, to be taken into account in one's deliberations, when seeking to determine the conditions obtaining in the field. These are:

- The Moral Law
- Heaven
- Earth
- The Commander
- Method and Discipline

The Moral Law causes the people to be in complete accord with their ruler, so that they will follow him regardless of their lives, undismayed by any danger.

Heaven signifies night and day, cold and heat, times and seasons.

Earth comprises distances, great and small; danger and security; open ground and narrow passes; the chances of life and death.

The Commander stands for the virtues of wisdom, sincerely, benevolence, courage and strictness.

By Method and Discipline are to be understood the marshaling of the army in its proper subdivisions, the graduations of rank among the officers, the maintenance of roads by which supplies may reach the army, and the control of military expenditure.

These five heads should be familiar to every general: he who knows them will be victorious; he who knows them not will fail. Therefore, in your deliberations, when seeking to determine the military conditions, let them be made the basis of a comparison, in this wise:—

- Which of the two sovereigns is imbued with the Moral law?
- Which of the two generals has most ability?
- With whom lie the advantages derived from Heaven and Earth?
- On which side is discipline most rigorously enforced?
- Which army is stronger?
- On which side are officers and men more highly trained?

- In which army is there the greater constancy both in reward and punishment?

By means of these seven considerations I can forecast victory or defeat.

The general that hearkens to my counsel and acts upon it will conquer: let such a one be retained in command! The general that hearkens not to my counsel nor acts upon it will suffer defeat:—let such a one be dismissed!

While heeding the profit of my counsel, avail yourself also of any helpful circumstances over and beyond the ordinary rules. According as circumstances are favourable, one should modify one's plans.

All warfare is based on deception.

Hence, when able to attack, we must seem unable; when using our forces, we must seem inactive; when we are near, we must make the enemy believe we are far away; when far away, we must make him believe we are near.

Hold out baits to entice the enemy. Feign disorder, and crush him.

If he is secure at all points, be prepared for him. If he is in superior strength, evade him.

If your opponent is of choleric temper, seek to irritate him. Pretend to be weak, that he may grow arrogant.

If he is taking his ease, give him no rest. If his forces are united, separate them.

Attack him where he is unprepared, appear where you are not expected.

These military devices, leading to victory, must not be divulged beforehand.

Now the general who wins a battle makes many calculations in his temple before the battle is fought. The general who loses a battle makes but few calculations beforehand. Thus do many calculations lead to victory and few calculations to defeat: but what about making no calculations at all! It is by attention to this point that I can foresee who is likely to win or lose.

II. WAGING WAR

Sun Tzu said: In the operations of war, where there are in the field a thousand swift chariots, as many heavy chariots, and a hundred thousand mail-clad soldiers, with provisions enough to carry them a thousand li, the expenditure at home and at the front, including entertainment of guests, small items such as glue and paint, and sums spent on chariots and armour, will reach the total of a thousand ounces of silver per day. Such is the cost of raising an army of 100,000 men.

When you engage in actual fighting, if victory is long in coming, the soldier's weapons will grow dull and their ardour will be dampened. If you lay siege to a town, you will exhaust your strength. Again, if the campaign is protracted, the resources of the State will not be equal to the strain.

Now, when your weapons are dulled, your ardour dampened, your strength exhausted and your treasure spent, other chieftains will spring up to take advantage of your extremity. Then no man, however wise, will be able to avert the consequences that must ensue.

Thus, though we have heard of stupid haste in war, cleverness has never been seen associated with long delays.

There is no instance of a country having benefited from prolonged warfare.

It is only one who is thoroughly acquainted with the evils of war that can thoroughly understand the profitable way of carrying it on.

The skilful soldier does not raise a second levy, neither are his supply-wagons loaded more than twice. Bring war material with you from home, but forage on the enemy. Thus the army will have food enough for its needs.

Poverty of the State exchequer causes an army to be maintained by contributions from a distance. Contributing to maintain an army at a distance causes the people to be impoverished.

On the other hand, the proximity of an army causes prices to go up; and high prices cause the people's substance to be drained away. When their substance is drained away, the peasantry will be afflicted by heavy exactions.

With this loss of substance and exhaustion of strength, the homes of the people will be stripped bare, and three-tenths of their income will be dissipated; while government expenses for broken chariots, worn-out horses, breast-plates and helmets, bows and arrows, spears and shields, protective mantles, draught-oxen and heavy wagons, will amount to four-tenths of its total revenue.

Hence a wise general makes a point of foraging on the enemy. One cartload of the enemy's provisions is equivalent to twenty of one's own, and likewise a single picul of his fodder is equivalent to twenty from one's own store.

Now in order to kill the enemy, our soldier's must be roused to anger; that there may be advantage from defeating the enemy, they must have their rewards.

Therefore in chariot fighting, when ten or more chariots have been taken, those should be rewarded who took the first. Our own flags should be substituted for those of the enemy, and the chariots mingled and used in conjunction with ours. The captured soldiers should be kindly treated and kept.

This is called, using the conquered foe to augment one's own strength.

In war, then, let your great object be victory, not lengthy campaigns.

Thus it may be known that the leader of armies is the arbiter of the people's fate, the man on whom it depends whether the nation shall be in peace or in peril.

III. ATTACK BY STRATAGEM

Sun Tzu said: In the practical art of war, the best thing of all is to take the enemy's country whole and intact; to shatter and destroy it is not so good. So, too, it is better to capture an army entire than to destroy it, to capture a regiment, a detachment or a company entire than to destroy them.

Hence to fight and conquer in all your battles is not supreme excellence; supreme excellence consists in breaking the enemy's resistance without fighting.

Thus the highest form of generalship is to thwart the enemy's plans; the next best is to prevent the junction of the enemy's forces; the next in order is to attack the enemy's army in the field; and the worst policy of all is to besiege walled cities.

The rule is, not to besiege walled cities if it can possibly be avoided. The preparation of earthworks, movable shelters, and various implements of war, will take up three whole months; and the piling up of mounds over against the walls will take three months more.

The general, unable to control his irritation, will launch his men to the assault like swarming ants, with the result that one-third of his men are slain, while the town still remains untaken. Such are the disastrous effects of a siege.

Therefore the skilful leader subdues the enemy's troops without any fighting; he captures their cities without laying siege to them; he overthrows their kingdom without lengthy operations in the field.

With his forces intact he will dispute the mastery of the Empire, and thus, without losing a man, his triumph will be complete. This is the method of attacking by stratagem.

It is the rule in war, if our forces are ten to the enemy's one, to surround him; if five to one, to attack him; if twice as numerous, to divide our army into two.

If equally matched, we can offer battle; if slightly inferior in numbers, we can avoid the enemy; if quite unequal in every way, we can flee from him.

Hence, though an obstinate fight may be made by a small force, in the end it must be captured by the larger force.

Now the general is the pillar of the State; if the pillar is complete at all points; the State will be strong; if the pillar is defective, the State will be weak.

There are three ways in which a ruler can bring misfortune upon his army:

- By commanding the army to advance or to retreat, being ignorant of the fact that it cannot obey. This is called hobbling the army.
- By attempting to govern an army in the same way as he runs the civil administration, being ignorant of the conditions which obtain in an army. This causes restlessness in the soldier's minds.
- By employing the officers of his army without discrimination, through ignorance of the military principle of adaptation to circumstances. This shakes the confidence of the soldiers.

When the army is restless and distrustful, trouble is sure to come from the other feudal princes. This is simply bringing anarchy into the army, and flinging victory away.

Thus we may know that there are five essentials for victory:

- He will win who knows when to fight and when not to fight.
- He will win who knows how to handle both superior and inferior forces.
- He will win whose army is animated by the same spirit throughout all its ranks.
- He will win who, prepared himself, waits to take the enemy unprepared.
- He will win who has military capacity and is not interfered with by the sovereign.

Hence the saying: If you know the enemy and know yourself, you need not fear the result of a hundred battles. If you know yourself but not the enemy, for every victory gained you will also suffer a defeat. If you know neither the enemy nor yourself, you will succumb in every battle.

IV. TACTICAL DISPOSITIONS

Sun Tzu said: The good fighters of old first put themselves beyond the possibility of defeat, and then waited for an opportunity of defeating the enemy.

To secure ourselves against defeat lies in our own hands, but the opportunity of defeating the enemy is provided by the enemy himself. Thus the good fighter is able to secure himself against defeat, but cannot make certain of defeating the enemy. Hence the saying: One may know how to conquer without being able to do it.

Security against defeat implies defensive tactics; ability to defeat the enemy means taking the offensive.

Standing on the defensive indicates insufficient strength; attacking, a superabundance of strength.

The general who is skilled in defence hides in the most secret recesses of the earth; he who is skilled in attack flashes forth from the topmost heights of heaven. Thus on the one hand we have ability to protect ourselves; on the other, a victory that is complete.

To see victory only when it is within the ken of the common masses is not the acme of excellence.

Neither is it the acme of excellence if you fight and conquer and the whole Empire says, "Well done!"

To lift an autumn hare is no sign of great strength; to see the sun and moon is no sign of sharp sight; to hear the noise of thunder is no sign of a quick ear.

What the ancients called a clever fighter is one who not only wins, but excels in winning with ease. Hence his victories bring him neither reputation for wisdom nor credit for courage.

He wins his battles by making no mistakes. Making no mistakes is what establishes the certainty of victory, for it means conquering an enemy that is already defeated.

Hence the skilful fighter puts himself into a position which makes defeat impossible, and does not miss the moment for defeating the enemy.

Thus it is that in war the victorious strategist only seeks battle after the victory has been won, whereas he who is destined to defeat first fights and afterwards looks for victory.

The consummate leader cultivates the moral law, and strictly adheres to method and discipline; thus it is in his power to control success.

In respect of military method, we have, firstly, Measurement; secondly, Estimation of quantity; thirdly, Calculation; fourthly, Balancing of chances; fifthly, Victory.

Measurement owes its existence to Earth; Estimation of quantity to Measurement; Calculation to Estimation of quantity; Balancing of chances to Calculation; and Victory to Balancing of chances.

A victorious army opposed to a routed one, is as a pound's weight placed in the scale against a single grain. The onrush of a conquering force is like the bursting of pent-up waters into a chasm a thousand fathoms deep.

V. ENERGY

Sun Tzu said: The control of a large force is the same principle as the control of a few men: it is merely a question of dividing up their numbers.

Fighting with a large army under your command is no way different from fighting with a small one: it is merely a question of instituting signs and signals.

To ensure that your whole host may withstand the brunt of the enemy's attack and remain unshaken— this is effected by manoeuvres direct and indirect.

That the impact of your army may be like a grindstone dashed against an egg—this is effected by the science of weak points and strong.

In all fighting, the direct method may be used for joining battle, but indirect methods will be needed in order to secure victory.

Indirect tactics, efficiently applied, are inexhaustible as Heaven and Earth, unending as the flow of rivers and streams; like the sun and moon, they end but to begin anew; like the four seasons, they pass away to return once more.

There are not more than five musical notes, yet the combinations of these five give rise to more melodies than can ever be heard.

There are not more than five primary colours (blue, yellow, red, white, and black), yet in combination they produce more hues than can ever been seen.

There are not more than five cardinal tastes (sour, acrid, salt, sweet, bitter), yet combinations of them yield more flavours than can ever be tasted.

In battle, there are not more than two methods of attack—the direct and the indirect; yet these two in combination give rise to an endless series of manoeuvres.

The direct and the indirect lead on to each other in turn. It is like moving in a circle—you never come to an end. Who can exhaust the possibilities of their combination?

The onset of troops is like the rush of a torrent which will even roll stones along in its course.

The quality of decision is like the well-timed swoop of a falcon which enables it to strike and destroy its victim.

Therefore the good fighter will be terrible in his onset, and prompt in his decision.

Energy may be likened to the bending of a crossbow; decision, to the releasing of a trigger.

Amid the turmoil and tumult of battle, there may be seeming disorder and yet no real disorder at all; amid confusion and chaos, your array may be without head or tail, yet it will be proof against defeat.

Simulated disorder postulates perfect discipline, simulated fear postulates courage; simulated weakness postulates strength.

Hiding order beneath the cloak of disorder is simply a question of subdivision; concealing courage under a show of timidity presupposes a fund of latent energy; masking strength with weakness is to be effected by tactical dispositions.

Thus one who is skilful at keeping the enemy on the move maintains deceitful appearances, according to which the enemy will act. He sacrifices something, that the enemy may snatch at it.

By holding out baits, he keeps him on the march; then with a body of picked men he lies in wait for him.

The clever combatant looks to the effect of combined energy, and does not require too much from individuals. Hence his ability to pick out the right men and utilize combined energy.

When he utilizes combined energy, his fighting men become as it were like unto rolling logs or stones. For it is the nature of a log or stone to remain motionless on level ground, and to move when on a slope; if four-cornered, to come to a standstill, but if round-shaped, to go rolling down.

Thus the energy developed by good fighting men is as the momentum of a round stone rolled down a mountain thousands of feet in height. So much on the subject of energy.

VI. WEAK POINTS AND STRONG

Sun Tzu said: Whoever is first in the field and awaits the coming of the enemy, will be fresh for the fight; whoever is second in the field and has to hasten to battle will arrive exhausted. Therefore the clever combatant imposes his will on the enemy, but does not allow the enemy's will to be imposed on him.

By holding out advantages to him, he can cause the enemy to approach of his own accord; or, by inflicting damage, he can make it impossible for the enemy to draw near.

If the enemy is taking his ease, he can harass him; if well supplied with food, he can starve him out; if quietly encamped, he can force him to move.

Appear at points which the enemy must hasten to defend; march swiftly to places where you are not expected.

An army may march great distances without distress, if it marches through country where the enemy is not.

You can be sure of succeeding in your attacks if you only attack places which are undefended. You can ensure the safety of your defence if you only hold positions that cannot be attacked.

Hence that general is skilful in attack whose opponent does not know what to defend; and he is skilful in defence whose opponent does not know what to attack.

O divine art of subtlety and secrecy! Through you we learn to be invisible, through you inaudible; and hence we can hold the enemy's fate in our hands.

You may advance and be absolutely irresistible, if you make for the enemy's weak points; you may retire and be safe from pursuit if your movements are more rapid than those of the enemy.

If we wish to fight, the enemy can be forced to an engagement even though he be sheltered behind a high rampart and a deep ditch. All we need do is attack some other place that he will be obliged to relieve.

If we do not wish to fight, we can prevent the enemy from engaging us even though the lines of our encampment be merely traced out on the ground. All we need do is to throw something odd and unaccountable in his way.

By discovering the enemy's dispositions and remaining invisible ourselves, we can keep our forces concentrated, while the enemy's must be divided.

We can form a single united body, while the enemy must split up into fractions. Hence there will be a whole pitted against separate parts of a whole, which means that we shall be many to the enemy's few.

And if we are able thus to attack an inferior force with a superior one, our opponents will be in dire straits.

The spot where we intend to fight must not be made known; for then the enemy will have to prepare against a possible attack at several different points; and his forces being thus distributed in many directions, the numbers we shall have to face at any given point will be proportionately few.

For should the enemy strengthen his front, he will weaken his rear; should he strengthen his rear, he will weaken his front; should he strengthen his left, he will weaken his right; should he strengthen his right, he will weaken his left. If he sends reinforcements everywhere, he will everywhere be weak.

Numerical weakness comes from having to prepare against possible attacks; numerical strength, from compelling our adversary to make these preparations against us.

Knowing the place and the time of the coming battle, we may concentrate from the greatest distances in order to fight.

But if neither time nor place be known, then the left wing will be impotent to succour the right, the right equally impotent to succour the left, the van unable to relieve the rear, or the rear to support the van. How much more so if the furthest portions of the army are anything under a hundred li apart, and even the nearest are separated by several li!

Though according to my estimate the soldiers of Yueh exceed our own in number, that shall advantage them nothing in the matter of victory. I say then that victory can be achieved.

Though the enemy be stronger in numbers, we may prevent him from fighting.

Scheme so as to discover his plans and the likelihood of their success.

Rouse him, and learn the principle of his activity or inactivity. Force him to reveal himself, so as to find out his vulnerable spots.

Carefully compare the opposing army with your own, so that you may know where strength is superabundant and where it is deficient.

In making tactical dispositions, the highest pitch you can attain is to conceal them; conceal your dispositions, and you will be safe from the prying of the subtlest spies, from the machinations of the wisest brains.

How victory may be produced for them out of the enemy's own tactics—that is what the multitude cannot comprehend.

All men can see the tactics whereby I conquer, but what none can see is the strategy out of which victory is evolved.

Do not repeat the tactics which have gained you one victory, but let your methods be regulated by the infinite variety of circumstances.

Military tactics are like unto water; for water in its natural course runs away from high places and hastens downwards.

So in war, the way is to avoid what is strong and to strike at what is weak.

Water shapes its course according to the nature of the ground over which it flows; the soldier works out his victory in relation to the foe whom he is facing.

Therefore, just as water retains no constant shape, so in warfare there are no constant conditions.

He who can modify his tactics in relation to his opponent and thereby succeed in winning, may be called a heaven-born captain.

The five elements (water, fire, wood, metal, earth) are not always equally predominant; the four seasons make way for each other in turn. There are short days and long; the moon has its periods of waning and waxing.

VII. MANEOUVERING

Sun Tzu said: In war, the general receives his commands from the sovereign.

Having collected an army and concentrated his forces, he must blend and harmonize the different elements thereof before pitching his camp.

After that, comes tactical manoeuvring, than which there is nothing more difficult. The difficulty of tactical manoeuvring consists in turning the devious into the direct, and misfortune into gain.

Thus, to take a long and circuitous route, after enticing the enemy out of the way, and though starting after him, to contrive to reach the goal before him, shows knowledge of the artifice of deviation.

Manoeuvring with an army is advantageous; with an undisciplined multitude, most dangerous.

If you set a fully equipped army on the march in order to snatch an advantage, the chances are that you will be too late. On the other hand, to detach a flying column for the purpose involves the sacrifice of its baggage and stores.

Thus, if you order your men to roll up their buff-coats, and make forced marches without halting day or night, covering double the usual distance at a stretch, doing a hundred li in order to wrest an advantage, the leaders of all your three divisions will fall into the hands of the enemy.

The stronger men will be in front; the jaded ones will fall behind, and on this plan only one-tenth of your army will reach its destination.

If you march fifty li in order to outmanoeuvre the enemy, you will lose the leader of your first division, and only half your force will reach the goal.

If you march thirty li with the same object, two-thirds of your army will arrive.

We may take it then that an army without its baggage-train is lost; without provisions it is lost; without bases of supply it is lost.

We cannot enter into alliances until we are acquainted with the designs of our neighbours.

We are not fit to lead an army on the march unless we are familiar with the face of the country—its mountains and forests, its pitfalls and precipices, its marshes and swamps.

We shall be unable to turn natural advantage to account unless we make use of local guides.

In war, practice deception, and you will succeed.

Whether to concentrate or to divide your troops, must be decided by circumstances.

Let your rapidity be that of the wind, your compactness that of the forest.

In raiding and plundering be like fire, is immovability like a mountain.

Let your plans be dark and impenetrable as night, and when you move, fall like a thunderbolt.

When you plunder a countryside, let the spoil be divided amongst your men; when you capture new territory, cut it up into allotments for the benefit of the soldiery.

Ponder and deliberate before you make a move.

He will conquer who has learnt the artifice of deviation. Such is the art of manoeuvring.

The Book of Army Management says: On the field of battle, the spoken word does not carry far enough: hence the institution of gongs and drums. Nor can ordinary objects be seen clearly enough: hence the institution of banners and flags.

Gongs and drums, banners and flags, are means whereby the ears and eyes of the host may be focused on one particular point.

The host thus forming a single united body, is it impossible either for the brave to advance alone, or for the cowardly to retreat alone. This is the art of handling large masses of men.

In night-fighting, then, make much use of signal-fires and drums, and in fighting by day, of flags and banners, as a means of influencing the ears and eyes of your army.

A whole army may be robbed of its spirit; a commander-in-chief may be robbed of his presence of mind.

Now a soldier's spirit is keenest in the morning; by noonday it has begun to flag; and in the evening, his mind is bent only on returning to camp.

A clever general, therefore, avoids an army when its spirit is keen, but attacks it when it is sluggish and inclined to return. This is the art of studying moods.

Disciplined and calm, to await the appearance of disorder and hubbub amongst the enemy:—this is the art of retaining self-possession.

To be near the goal while the enemy is still far from it, to wait at ease while the enemy is toiling and struggling, to be well-fed while the enemy is famished:—this is the art of husbanding one's strength.

To refrain from intercepting an enemy whose banners are in perfect order, to refrain from attacking an army drawn up in calm and confident array:—this is the art of studying circumstances.

It is a military axiom not to advance uphill against the enemy, nor to oppose him when he comes downhill.

Do not pursue an enemy who simulates flight; do not attack soldiers whose temper is keen.

Do not swallow bait offered by the enemy. Do not interfere with an army that is returning home.

When you surround an army, leave an outlet free. Do not press a desperate foe too hard.

Such is the art of warfare.

VIII. VARIATION IN TACTICS

Sun Tzu said: In war, the general receives his commands from the sovereign, collects his army and concentrates his forces

When in difficult country, do not encamp. In country where high roads intersect, join hands with your allies. Do not linger in dangerously isolated positions. In hemmed-in situations, you must resort to stratagem. In desperate position, you must fight.

There are roads which must not be followed, armies which must be not attacked, towns which must be besieged, positions which must not be contested, commands of the sovereign which must not be obeyed.

The general who thoroughly understands the advantages that accompany variation of tactics knows how to handle his troops.

The general who does not understand these, may be well acquainted with the configuration of the country, yet he will not be able to turn his knowledge to practical account.

So, the student of war who is unversed in the art of war of varying his plans, even though he is acquainted with the Five Advantages, will fail to make the best use of his men.

Hence in the wise leader's plans, considerations of advantage and of disadvantage will be blended together.

If our expectation of advantage be tempered in this way, we may succeed in accomplishing the essential part of our schemes.

If, on the other hand, in the midst of difficulties we are always ready to seize an advantage, we may extricate ourselves from misfortune.

Reduce the hostile chiefs by inflicting damage on them; and make trouble for them, and keep them constantly engaged; hold out specious allurements, and make them rush to any given point.

The art of war teaches us to rely not on the likelihood of the enemy's not coming, but on our own readiness to receive him; not on the chance of his not attacking, but rather on the fact that we have made our position unassailable.

There are five dangerous faults which may affect a general:

- Recklessness, which leads to destruction;
- Cowardice, which leads to capture;
- A hasty temper, which can be provoked by insults;
- A delicacy of honour which is sensitive to shame;
- Over-solicitude for his men, which exposes him to worry and trouble

These are the five besetting sins of a general, ruinous to the conduct of war.

When an army is overthrown and its leader slain, the cause will surely be found among these five dangerous faults. Let them be a subject of meditation.

IX. THE ARMY ON THE MARCH

Sun Tzu said: We come now to the question of encamping the army, and observing signs of the enemy. Pass quickly over mountains, and keep in the neighbourhood of valleys.

Camp in high places, facing the sun. Do not climb heights in order to fight. So much for mountain warfare.

After crossing a river, you should get far away from it.

When an invading force crosses a river in its onward march, do not advance to meet it in mid-stream. It will be best to let half the army get across, and then deliver your attack.

If you are anxious to fight, you should not go to meet the invader near a river which he has to cross.

Moor your craft higher up than the enemy, and facing the sun. Do not move up-stream to meet the enemy. So much for river warfare.

In crossing salt-marshes, your sole concern should be to get over them quickly, without any delay.

If forced to fight in a salt-marsh, you should have water and grass near you, and get your back to a clump of trees. So much for operations in salt-marches.

In dry, level country, take up an easily accessible position with rising ground to your right and on your rear, so that the danger may be in front, and safety lie behind. So much for campaigning in flat country.

These are the four useful branches of military knowledge which enabled the Yellow Emperor to vanquish four sovereigns.

All armies prefer high ground to low and sunny places to dark.

If you are careful of your men, and camp on hard ground, the army will be free from disease of every kind, and this will spell victory.

When you come to a hill or a bank, occupy the sunny side, with the slope on your right rear. Thus you will at once act for the benefit of your soldiers and utilize the natural advantages of the ground.

When, in consequence of heavy rains up-country, a river which you wish to ford is swollen and flecked with foam, you must wait until it subsides.

Country in which there are precipitous cliffs with torrents running between, deep natural hollows, confined places, tangled thickets, quagmires and crevasses, should be left with all possible speed and not approached.

While we keep away from such places, we should get the enemy to approach them; while we face them, we should let the enemy have them on his rear.

If in the neighbourhood of your camp there should be any hilly country, ponds surrounded by aquatic grass, hollow basins filled with reeds, or woods with thick undergrowth, they must be carefully routed out and searched; for these are places where men in ambush or insidious spies are likely to be lurking.

When the enemy is close at hand and remains quiet, he is relying on the natural strength of his position.

When he keeps aloof and tries to provoke a battle, he is anxious for the other side to advance.

If his place of encampment is easy of access, he is tendering a bait.

Movement amongst the trees of a forest shows that the enemy is advancing. The appearance of a number of screens in the midst of thick grass means that the enemy wants to make us suspicious.

The rising of birds in their flight is the sign of an ambuscade. Startled beasts indicate that a sudden attack is coming.

When there is dust rising in a high column, it is the sign of chariots advancing; when the dust is low, but spread over a wide area, it betokens the approach of infantry. When it branches out in different directions, it shows that parties have been sent to collect firewood. A few clouds of dust moving to and fro signify that the army is encamping.

Humble words and increased preparations are signs that the enemy is about to advance. Violent language and driving forward as if to the attack are signs that he will retreat.

When the light chariots come out first and take up a position on the wings, it is a sign that the enemy is forming for battle.

Peace proposals unaccompanied by a sworn covenant indicate a plot.

When there is much running about and the soldiers fall into rank, it means that the critical moment has come.

When some are seen advancing and some retreating, it is a lure.

When the soldiers stand leaning on their spears, they are faint from want of food.

If those who are sent to draw water begin by drinking themselves, the army is suffering from thirst.

If the enemy sees an advantage to be gained and makes no effort to secure it, the soldiers are exhausted.

If birds gather on any spot, it is unoccupied. Clamour by night betokens nervousness.

If there is disturbance in the camp, the general's authority is weak. If the banners and flags are shifted about, sedition is afoot. If the officers are angry, it means that the men are weary.

When an army feeds its horses with grain and kills its cattle for food, and when the men do not hang their cooking-pots over the camp-fires, showing that they will not return to their tents, you may know that they are determined to fight to the death.

The sight of men whispering together in small knots or speaking in subdued tones points to disaffection amongst the rank and file.

Too frequent rewards signify that the enemy is at the end of his resources; too many punishments betray a condition of dire distress.

To begin by bluster, but afterwards to take fright at the enemy's numbers, shows a supreme lack of intelligence.

When envoys are sent with compliments in their mouths, it is a sign that the enemy wishes for a truce.

If the enemy's troops march up angrily and remain facing ours for a long time without either joining battle or taking themselves off again, the situation is one that demands great vigilance and circumspection.

If our troops are no more in number than the enemy, that is amply sufficient; it only means that no direct attack can be made. What we can do is simply to concentrate all our available strength, keep a close watch on the enemy, and obtain reinforcements.

He who exercises no forethought but makes light of his opponents is sure to be captured by them.

If soldiers are punished before they have grown attached to you, they will not prove submissive; and, unless submissive, then will be practically useless. If, when the soldiers have become attached to you, punishments are not enforced, they will still be unless.

Therefore soldiers must be treated in the first instance with humanity, but kept under control by means of iron discipline. This is a certain road to victory.

If in training soldiers commands are habitually enforced, the army will be well-disciplined; if not, its discipline will be bad.

If a general shows confidence in his men but always insists on his orders being obeyed, the gain will be mutual.

X. TERRAIN

Sun Tzu said: We may distinguish six kinds of terrain:

- Accessible ground
- Entangling ground
- Temporizing ground
- Narrow passes
- Precipitous heights
- Positions at a great distance from the enemy

Ground which can be freely traversed by both sides is called accessible.

With regard to ground of this nature, be before the enemy in occupying the raised and sunny spots, and carefully guard your line of supplies. Then you will be able to fight with advantage.

Ground which can be abandoned but is hard to re-occupy is called entangling.

From a position of this sort, if the enemy is unprepared, you may sally forth and defeat him. But if the enemy is prepared for your coming, and you fail to defeat him, then, return being impossible, disaster will ensue.

When the position is such that neither side will gain by making the first move, it is called temporizing ground. In a position of this sort, even though the enemy should offer us an attractive bait, it will be advisable not to stir forth, but rather to retreat, thus enticing the enemy in his turn; then, when part of his army has come out, we may deliver our attack with advantage.

With regard to narrow passes, if you can occupy them first, let them be strongly garrisoned and await the advent of the enemy. Should the army forestall you in occupying a pass, do not go after him if the pass is fully garrisoned, but only if it is weakly garrisoned.

With regard to precipitous heights, if you are beforehand with your adversary, you should occupy the raised and sunny spots, and there wait for him to come up.

If the enemy has occupied them before you, do not follow him, but retreat and try to entice him away.

If you are situated at a great distance from the enemy, and the strength of the two armies is equal, it is not easy to provoke a battle, and fighting will be to your disadvantage.

These six are the principles connected with Earth. The general who has attained a responsible post must be careful to study them.

Now an army is exposed to six calamities, not arising from natural causes, but from faults for which the general is responsible. These are:

- Flight
- Insubordination
- Collapse
- Ruin
- Disorganisation
- Rout

Other conditions being equal, if one force is hurled against another ten times its size, the result will be the flight of the former.

When the common soldiers are too strong and their officers too weak, the result is insubordination. When the officers are too strong and the common soldiers too weak, the result is collapse.

When the higher officers are angry and insubordinate, and on meeting the enemy give battle on their own account from a feeling of resentment, before the commander-in-chief can tell whether or no he is in a position to fight, the result is ruin.

When the general is weak and without authority; when his orders are not clear and distinct; when there are no fixes duties assigned to officers and men, and the ranks are formed in a slovenly haphazard manner, the result is utter disorganisation.

When a general, unable to estimate the enemy's strength, allows an inferior force to engage a larger one, or hurls a weak detachment against a powerful one, and neglects to place picked soldiers in the front rank, the result must be rout.

These are six ways of courting defeat, which must be carefully noted by the general who has attained a responsible post.

The natural formation of the country is the soldier's best ally; but a power of estimating the adversary, of controlling the forces of victory, and of shrewdly calculating difficulties, dangers and distances, constitutes the test of a great general.

He who knows these things, and in fighting puts his knowledge into practice, will win his battles. He who knows them not, nor practices them, will surely be defeated.

If fighting is sure to result in victory, then you must fight, even though the ruler forbid it; if fighting will not result in victory, then you must not fight even at the ruler's bidding.

The general who advances without coveting fame and retreats without fearing disgrace, whose only thought is to protect his country and do good service for his sovereign, is the jewel of the kingdom.

Regard your soldiers as your children, and they will follow you into the deepest valleys; look upon them as your own beloved sons, and they will stand by you even unto death.

If, however, you are indulgent, but unable to make your authority felt; kind-hearted, but unable to enforce your commands; and incapable, moreover, of quelling disorder: then your soldiers must be likened to spoilt children; they are useless for any practical purpose.

If we know that our own men are in a condition to attack, but are unaware that the enemy is not open to attack, we have gone only halfway towards victory.

If we know that the enemy is open to attack, but are unaware that our own men are not in a condition to attack, we have gone only halfway towards victory.

If we know that the enemy is open to attack, and also know that our men are in a condition to attack, but are unaware that the nature of the ground makes fighting impracticable, we have still gone only halfway towards victory.

Hence the experienced soldier, once in motion, is never bewildered; once he has broken camp, he is never at a loss.

Hence the saying: If you know the enemy and know yourself, your victory will not stand in doubt; if you know Heaven and know Earth, you may make your victory complete.

XI. THE NINE SITUATIONS

Sun Tzu said: The art of war recognizes nine varieties of ground:

- Dispersive ground
- Facile ground
- Contentious ground
- Open ground
- Ground of intersecting highways
- Serious ground
- Difficult ground
- Hemmed-in ground
- Desperate ground

When a chieftain is fighting in his own territory, it is dispersive ground.

When he has penetrated into hostile territory, but to no great distance, it is facile ground.

Ground the possession of which imports great advantage to either side, is contentious ground.

Ground on which each side has liberty of movement is open ground.

Ground which forms the key to three contiguous states, so that he who occupies it first has most of the Empire at his command, is a ground of intersecting highways.

When an army has penetrated into the heart of a hostile country, leaving a number of fortified cities in its rear, it is serious ground.

Mountain forests, rugged steeps, marshes and fens—all country that is hard to traverse: this is difficult ground.

Ground which is reached through narrow gorges, and from which we can only retire by tortuous paths, so that a small number of the enemy would suffice to crush a large body of our men: this is hemmed in ground.

Ground on which we can only be saved from destruction by fighting without delay, is desperate ground.

On dispersive ground, therefore, fight not. On facile ground, halt not. On contentious ground, attack not.

On open ground, do not try to block the enemy's way. On the ground of intersecting highways, join hands with your allies.

On serious ground, gather in plunder. In difficult ground, keep steadily on the march.

On hemmed-in ground, resort to stratagem. On desperate ground, fight.

Those who were called skilful leaders of old knew how to drive a wedge between the enemy's front and rear; to prevent co-operation between his large and small divisions; to hinder the good troops from rescuing the bad, the officers from rallying their men.

When the enemy's men were united, they managed to keep them in disorder.

When it was to their advantage, they made a forward move; when otherwise, they stopped still.

If asked how to cope with a great host of the enemy in orderly array and on the point of marching to the attack, I should say: "Begin by seizing something which your opponent holds dear; then he will be amenable to your will."

Rapidity is the essence of war: take advantage of the enemy's unreadiness, make your way by unexpected routes, and attack unguarded spots.

The following are the principles to be observed by an invading force: The further you penetrate into a country, the greater will be the solidarity of your troops, and thus the defenders will not prevail against you.

Make forays in fertile country in order to supply your army with food.

Carefully study the well-being of your men, and do not overtax them. Concentrate your energy and hoard your strength. Keep your army continually on the move, and devise unfathomable plans.

Throw your soldiers into positions whence there is no escape, and they will prefer death to flight. If they will face death, there is nothing they may not achieve. Officers and men alike will put forth their uttermost strength.

Soldiers when in desperate straits lose the sense of fear. If there is no place of refuge, they will stand firm. If they are in hostile country, they will show a stubborn front. If there is no help for it, they will fight hard.

Thus, without waiting to be marshaled, the soldiers will be constantly on the qui vive; without waiting to be asked, they will do your will; without restrictions, they will be faithful; without giving orders, they can be trusted.

Prohibit the taking of omens, and do away with superstitious doubts. Then, until death itself comes, no calamity need be feared.

If our soldiers are not overburdened with money, it is not because they have a distaste for riches; if their lives are not unduly long, it is not because they are disinclined to longevity.

On the day they are ordered out to battle, your soldiers may weep, those sitting up bedewing their garments, and those lying down letting the tears run down their cheeks. But let them once be brought to bay, and they will display the courage of a Chu or a Kuei.

The skilful tactician may be likened to the *shuaijan*. Now the *shuaijan* is a snake that is found in the Ch'ang mountains. Strike at its head, and you will be attacked by its tail; strike at its tail, and you will be attacked by its head; strike at its middle, and you will be attacked by head and tail both.

Asked if an army can be made to imitate the *shuaijan*, I should answer, Yes. For the men of Wu and the men of Yueh are enemies; yet if they are crossing a river in the same boat and are caught by a storm, they will come to each other's assistance just as the left hand helps the right.

Hence it is not enough to put one's trust in the tethering of horses, and the burying of chariot wheels in the ground

The principle on which to manage an army is to set up one standard of courage which all must reach.

How to make the best of both strong and weak—that is a question involving the proper use of ground.

Thus the skilful general conducts his army just as though he were leading a single man, willy-nilly, by the hand.

It is the business of a general to be quiet and thus ensure secrecy; upright and just, and thus maintain order.

He must be able to mystify his officers and men by false reports and appearances, and thus keep them in total ignorance.

By altering his arrangements and changing his plans, he keeps the enemy without definite knowledge. By shifting his camp and taking circuitous routes, he prevents the enemy from anticipating his purpose.

At the critical moment, the leader of an army acts like one who has climbed up a height and then kicks away the ladder behind him. He carries his men deep into hostile territory before he shows his hand.

He burns his boats and breaks his cooking-pots; like a shepherd driving a flock of sheep, he drives his men this way and that, and nothing knows whither he is going.

To muster his host and bring it into danger:—this may be termed the business of the general.

The different measures suited to the nine varieties of ground; the expediency of aggressive or defensive tactics; and the fundamental laws of human nature: these are things that must most certainly be studied.

When invading hostile territory, the general principle is, that penetrating deeply brings cohesion; penetrating but a short way means dispersion.

When you leave your own country behind, and take your army across neighbourhood territory, you find yourself on critical ground. When there are means of communication on all four sides, the ground is one of intersecting highways.

When you penetrate deeply into a country, it is serious ground. When you penetrate but a little way, it is facile ground.

When you have the enemy's strongholds on your rear, and narrow passes in front, it is hemmed-in ground. When there is no place of refuge at all, it is desperate ground.

Therefore, on dispersive ground, I would inspire my men with unity of purpose. On facile ground, I would see that there is close connection between all parts of my army.

On contentious ground, I would hurry up my rear.

On open ground, I would keep a vigilant eye on my defences. On ground of intersecting highways, I would consolidate my alliances.

On serious ground, I would try to ensure a continuous stream of supplies. On difficult ground, I would keep pushing on along the road.

On hemmed-in ground, I would block any way of retreat. On desperate ground, I would proclaim to my soldiers the hopelessness of saving their lives.

For it is the soldier's disposition to offer an obstinate resistance when surrounded, to fight hard when he cannot help himself, and to obey promptly when he has fallen into danger.

We cannot enter into alliance with neighbouring princes until we are acquainted with their designs. We are not fit to lead an army on the march unless we are familiar with the face of the country—its mountains and forests, its pitfalls and precipices, its marshes and swamps. We shall be unable to turn natural advantages to account unless we make use of local guides.

To be ignored of any one of the following four or five principles does not befit a warlike prince.

When a warlike prince attacks a powerful state, his generalship shows itself in preventing the concentration of the enemy's forces. He overawes his opponents, and their allies are prevented from joining against him.

Hence he does not strive to ally himself with all and sundry, nor does he foster the power of other states. He carries out his own secret designs, keeping his antagonists in awe. Thus he is able to capture their cities and overthrow their kingdoms.

Bestow rewards without regard to rule, issue orders without regard to previous arrangements; and you will be able to handle a whole army as though you had to do with but a single man.

Confront your soldiers with the deed itself; never let them know your design. When the outlook is bright, bring it before their eyes; but tell them nothing when the situation is gloomy.

Place your army in deadly peril, and it will survive; plunge it into desperate straits, and it will come off in safety.

For it is precisely when a force has fallen into harm's way that is capable of striking a blow for victory.

Success in warfare is gained by carefully accommodating ourselves to the enemy's purpose.

By persistently hanging on the enemy's flank, we shall succeed in the long run in killing the commander-in-chief. This is called ability to accomplish a thing by sheer cunning.

On the day that you take up your command, block the frontier passes, destroy the official tallies, and stop the passage of all emissaries.

Be stern in the council-chamber, so that you may control the situation.

If the enemy leaves a door open, you must rush in.

Forestall your opponent by seizing what he holds dear, and subtly contrive to time his arrival on the ground.

Walk in the path defined by rule, and accommodate yourself to the enemy until you can fight a decisive battle.

At first, then, exhibit the coyness of a maiden, until the enemy gives you an opening; afterwards emulate the rapidity of a running hare, and it will be too late for the enemy to oppose you.

XII. THE ATTACK BY FIRE

Sun Tzu said: There are five ways of attacking with fire:

- The first is to burn soldiers in their camp
- Second is to burn stores
- Third is to burn baggage trains
- Fourth is to burn arsenals and magazines
- Fifth is to hurl dropping fire amongst the enemy

In order to carry out an attack, we must have means available. The material for raising fire should always be kept in readiness.

There is a proper season for making attacks with fire, and special days for starting a conflagration.

The proper season is when the weather is very dry; the special days are those when the moon is in the constellations of the Sieve, the Wall, the Wing or the Cross-bar; for these four are all days of rising wind.

In attacking with fire, one should be prepared to meet five possible developments:

When fire breaks out inside to enemy's camp, respond at once with an attack from without.

If there is an outbreak of fire, but the enemy's soldiers remain quiet, bide your time and do not attack.

When the force of the flames has reached its height, follow it up with an attack, if that is practicable; if not, stay where you are.

If it is possible to make an assault with fire from without, do not wait for it to break out within, but deliver your attack at a favourable moment.

When you start a fire, be to windward of it. Do not attack from the leeward.

A wind that rises in the daytime lasts long, but a night breeze soon falls.

In every army, the five developments connected with fire must be known, the movements of the stars calculated, and a watch kept for the proper days.

Hence those who use fire as an aid to the attack show intelligence; those who use water as an aid to the attack gain an accession of strength.

By means of water, an enemy may be intercepted, but not robbed of all his belongings.

Unhappy is the fate of one who tries to win his battles and succeed in his attacks without cultivating the spirit of enterprise; for the result is waste of time and general stagnation.

Hence the saying: The enlightened ruler lays his plans well ahead; the good general cultivates his resources.

Move not unless you see an advantage; use not your troops unless there is something to be gained; fight not unless the position is critical.

No ruler should put troops into the field merely to gratify his own spleen; no general should fight a battle simply out of pique.

If it is to your advantage, make a forward move; if not, stay where you are.

Anger may in time change to gladness; vexation may be succeeded by content.

But a kingdom that has once been destroyed can never come again into being; nor can the dead ever be brought back to life.

Hence the enlightened ruler is heedful, and the good general full of caution. This is the way to keep a country at peace and an army intact.

XIII. THE USE OF SPIES

Sun Tzu said: Raising a host of a hundred thousand men and marching them great distances entails heavy loss on the people and a drain on the resources of the State. The daily expenditure will amount to a thousand ounces of silver. There will be commotion at home and abroad, and men will drop down exhausted on the highways. As many as seven hundred thousand families will be impeded in their labour.

Hostile armies may face each other for years, striving for the victory which is decided in a single day. This being so, to remain in ignorance of the enemy's condition simply because one grudges the outlay of a hundred ounces of silver in honours and emoluments, is the height of inhumanity.

One who acts thus is no leader of men, no present help to his sovereign, no master of victory.

Thus, what enables the wise sovereign and the good general to strike and conquer, and achieve things beyond the reach of ordinary men, is foreknowledge.

Now this foreknowledge cannot be elicited from spirits; it cannot be obtained inductively from experience, nor by any deductive calculation.

Knowledge of the enemy's dispositions can only be obtained from other men.

Hence the use of spies, of whom there are five classes:

- Local spies
- Inward spies
- Converted spies
- Doomed spies
- Surviving spies

When these five kinds of spy are all at work, none can discover the secret system. This is called "divine manipulation of the threads." It is the sovereign's most precious faculty.

Having local spies means employing the services of the inhabitants of a district.

Having inward spies, making use of officials of the enemy.

Having converted spies, getting hold of the enemy's spies and using them for our own purposes.

Having doomed spies, doing certain things openly for purposes of deception, and allowing our spies to know of them and report them to the enemy.

Surviving spies, finally, are those who bring back news from the enemy's camp.

Hence it is that which none in the whole army are more intimate relations to be maintained than with spies. None should be more liberally rewarded. In no other business should greater secrecy be preserved.

Spies cannot be usefully employed without a certain intuitive sagacity.

They cannot be properly managed without benevolence and straightforwardness.

Without subtle ingenuity of mind, one cannot make certain of the truth of their reports.

Be subtle! be subtle! and use your spies for every kind of business.

If a secret piece of news is divulged by a spy before the time is ripe, he must be put to death together with the man to whom the secret was told.

Whether the object be to crush an army, to storm a city, or to assassinate an individual, it is always necessary to begin by finding out the names of the attendants, the aides-de-camp, and door-keepers and sentries of the general in command. Our spies must be commissioned to ascertain these.

The enemy's spies who have come to spy on us must be sought out, tempted with bribes, led away and comfortably housed. Thus they will become converted spies and available for our service.

It is through the information brought by the converted spy that we are able to acquire and employ local and inward spies.

It is owing to his information, again, that we can cause the doomed spy to carry false tidings to the enemy.

Lastly, it is by his information that the surviving spy can be used on appointed occasions.

The end and aim of spying in all its five varieties is knowledge of the enemy; and this knowledge can only be derived, in the first instance, from the converted spy. Hence it is essential that the converted spy be treated with the utmost liberality.

Of old, the rise of the Yin dynasty was due to I Chih who had served under the Hsia. Likewise, the rise of the Chou dynasty was due to Lu Ya who had served under the Yin.

Hence it is only the enlightened ruler and the wise general who will use the highest intelligence of the army for purposes of spying and thereby they achieve great results. Spies are a most important element in war, because on them depends an army's ability to move.

CHAPTER 3

VEGETIUS: DE RE MILITARI

"Qui desiderat pacem, praeparet bellum."
(Let him who wants peace, prepare for war)
— Vegetius

It is somewhat surprising that perhaps the most influential military treatise in the western world from the Roman times to the early 19th century is relatively unknown and comparatively unread. It is known as De re Militari or Epitoma rei militari. Its impression on organisation, traditions and disciplines of Western armies are evident even today. Flavius Vegetius Renatus was a Roman of high rank. Little is known of his life, but it is apparent from his writings that he had not had extensive practical experience as a soldier. He had collected and synthesized (in fact he says so himself) ancient manuscripts and regulations, military customs and practices. His principles sources were Cato the elder, Cornelius Celsus, Paternus, and the regulations and ordinances of Augustus, Trajan and Hadrian. His work is the only Roman military manual to survive complete. It describes how military affairs might be best regulated.

Western military theory and strategy has its roots in De Re Militari, which was written between 384-389 A.D. Vegetius' treatise was both a plea and a plan to revitalize the Eastern Roman army after its disastrous defeat by Gothic horsemen at the Battle of Adrianople (378 A.D.).[1] Unfortunately, Vegetius' military remedies were too narrow in scope to save an already tottering empire. It is somewhat strange, even paradoxical that the book was written for the Romans; but was little used by them. Possibly, the decay of Roman Armies had progressed far too much for Vegetius' pleas for stricter discipline and drill to be followed.

Some of the recommendations of Vegetius were probably impracticable. He advocated the revival of the ancient organisation of the famous Roman Legions.[2] But by his time, the cavalry had already adopted the armour of foot soldiers and had become the principle arm of battle. The heavily armoured foot soldier was becoming immobile, and thus the flexibility of Roman legions as opposed to the Greek Phalanx was being lost. Light infantry, unable to resist the shock action of cavalry, was turning more and more to missiles. It is indeed a strange quirk of history that when the crossbow and gun powder deprived the cavalry of their shock effect, the tactics of Vegetius again became the ideal of armies. Indeed, De Re Militari, became the bible of the armies of the Western world.

De re Militari was a practical and authoritative guide to medieval warfare in Europe. The reason for its popularity was its user-friendly compendium of ancient thinking on war, including extracts from the writings of earlier military commentators.

Machiavelli used Vegetius as a foundation for his own treatise, The Art of War, written in 1521. Not only did the structure of Machiavelli's work mimic De re Militari, but portions of the latter text, including the principles of war found at the end of Book III, were reproduced without modification by Machiavelli. Machiavelli sought to adapt the old laws of Roman warfare to the new realities of 16th century Italy. He argued that this was possible because human history was immutable, and not necessarily unique. The classical military legacy of Rome represented a homogenous historical experience that provided infallible and general rules of war that – if applied properly – reduced the relative impact of chance. In other words, military history was an educational tool; it provided lessons that rationalized war.

De re Militari is dedicated to Emperor Valentinian. (There are some doubts as to which Valentinian, as there were three Roman emperors of that name). It can be surmised, however, that it was possibly Valentinian II; from the mention made in the book of a defeat of Roman Armies by Goths, but no mention of the sack of Rome by Alaric, the King of the Goths, during the reign of Valentinian III. Vegetius was basically a reformer whose main attempt appears to have been to restore the past glory of Roman armies. He constantly lauds the military virtues of the "ancients", and gives example of the ancients to his contemporaries. His small book was easy to read, presumably not to frighten his readers with an arduous text. Vegetius reconstructs the recruitment and organisation, field strategy and tactics, siege and naval warfare, by using many sources of different dates. It did not influence imperial policy, but it gained wide readership in later centuries.

The treatise contains five books. Of particular value are the 26 chapters on strategy, tactics, and the principles of war (or military procedure) contained in Book III. It is not intended to dwell on the fourth and fifth books. Both are very brief and deal with attack and defence of fortified positions and naval operations. These are of interest only to military antiquarians and are of little relevance to strategy.

The first and second books are of interest, not from the point of view of development of strategy, but generally on the development of armies. His first book is devoted to the selection, training and discipline of recruits. Vegetius unendingly emphasized the importance of discipline and drill. He starts the book by declaring "victory in war does not depend entirely upon numbers or mere courage; only skill and discipline will ensure it". He insists upon utmost meticulousness in drill: "No part of drill is more essential in action than for soldiers to keep their ranks with greatest exactness.[3] His description of the many arms which the Roman soldier had to learn reminds one of the needs of today's infantry soldiers.[4] Recruits, he advocated, had to be hardened to march twenty miles in half a summer's day, normally, and twenty four miles as forced marches. Vegetius also mentions that the military mark[5] should not be given to a recruit, as soon as he is enlisted.

Vegetius urged that young soldiers in particular should be obliged frequently to carry loads of up to sixty pounds (exclusive of their arms), and to march with it at a military pace. This is because on strenuous campaigns they often will face the necessity of carrying their provisions as well as their arms. This could be considered a fore-runner of the concept of logistics and moving self-contained for about 10 days. This concept has hardly altered over the centuries.

The second book deals with organisation and officers of the legion. The organisation of legion was given in detail, as were the "supporting arms". Each legion needed to have fifty five *ballistas*, ten *onagri*, with its pontoon equipment,[6] boats and "whatever is necessary for every kind of service that the encampments may have all the strength and conveniences of a fortified city". Trains of workmen were to be provided to perform all the duties now performed by various services in the armies of the World today. He did not forget the importance of military music and had a paragraph on it.

The third book contains advice on strategy and tactics. Not that it does not contain other material too; indeed, the 'books' are not laid out in any clear cut division of tactics, strategy, administration, discipline and so on. The third book actually starts with a discourse on the numbers which should compose an Army. It continues with advice on how to preserve the health of the army;[7] on forage and provisions and methods to prevent mutiny in an army. Of greater interest are his maxims on "marches in the neighbours of the enemy".

Vegetius placed adequate importance on knowledge of ground: "In the first place he should have an exact description of the country that is the seat of war, in which the distances of places specified by the number of miles, the nature of roads, the shortest routes, by roads, mountains and rivers should be correctly inserted". He adequately emphasizes on maintaining security, (secrecy or concealment from the enemy). He expounds as to how should the army organize its march: "The general before he puts his troops in motion should send out detachments of trusty and experienced soldiers well mounted to reconnoitre the places through which he has to pass, in front, in rear and on the right and left, lest he should fall into ambuscades. The night is more advantageous for your spies do their work than in the day"... Cavalry should march off first, then the infantry, the baggage, bat horses, servants and carriages follow in the centre, and part of the best cavalry and infantry come in the rear"... The part where the enemy is most expected must be reinforced with some of the best cavalry, light infantry and foot archers".

These maxims continue to find place, with terms suitably modernized, in current usage, in all text books on advance to contact or offensive operations. He does not ignore defence either and has some exceptionally relevant dictums as to how an army on the march should defend itself. Vegetius explains three methods of entrenching a camp, even it is for a night and advocates throwing up a slight parapet of turf and planting it with a row of palisades or caltrops[8] of wood.

Vegetius also gives advice on how to cross a river and very detailed instructions on how to encamp an army. It included details like where the tents of the first centuries or cohorts are pitched, and the dragons[9] and other ensigns planted. He has some very relevant and valuable advice on when to accept a "general engagement".[10] "Every plan, therefore, is to be considered, every expedient tried and every method taken before matters are brought to this last extremity".

Good officers decline general engagements where the danger is common and prefer the employment of strategies and finesse to destroy the enemy as much as possible in detail and intimidate them without exposing our own forces".[11] He follows with advice on preparation required for a general engagement; choice of the field of battle; order of battle, proper distance and intervals that should be maintained; disposition of the cavalry, use of reserves, and the post of the general. Some of his maxims are worth quoting, because of their aptness even in the modern day battle field, as also for the fact that they have been followed by most of the great captains of the past e.g. "Victory depends much on the nature of the field of battle"... the highest ground is the best". One can see here the formation of the basic concept of vital ground. "If your cavalry is not equal to the enemy's it is proper, after the ancient custom, to intermingle it with light infantry armed with small shields and trained to this kind of service". Its modern day application needs no elaboration. Vegetius also entreated upon formation of reserves and locating them suitably. "Some should be posted in rear of the wings, and some near the centre, to be ready to fly immediately to the assistance of any part of the line which is hard pressed, to prevent it form being pierced, to supply the vacancies made therein during action and thereby keep up the courage of their fellow soldiers and check the impetuosity of the enemy."[12] Later, he also advocates placing the reserves under the second-in-command.

Vegetius had clear and unambiguous advice on the position of the General. "The post of the Commander-in-Chief is generally on the right between the cavalry and infantry, for from this place he can best direct the motion of the whole army. It is also the best spot to give his orders to both horse and foot, and to animate them equally by his presence". The point to note is that Vegetius saw the function of Commander-in-Chief to direct rather than personally indulge in combat.[13] Vegetius continues with directions on manoeuvres in action, where he emphasizes on protecting the wings (flanks) and obtaining surprise. He further goes on to recommend seven different types of formation to be adopted by armies marching up to attack. He considered the "oblique" to the best disposition.[14]

Special mention must be made of the next aspect dealt with. "The flight of an enemy should not be prevented but facilitated". Discerning readers will immediately spot the importance of this dictum. Vegetius propounds that where no hope remains, fear itself will arm an enemy and despair inspires courage. "When men find they must inevitably perish, they willingly resolve to die with their comrades and with their arms in their hands". This dictum is a valid one even today.[15] Advice on how to retreat and employment of armed chariots and elephants follow. The book ends with a list of "general maxims", which are basically a summary of those propounded earlier. Most of them are eminently quotable and applicable even today.

Medieval warfare had many elements that are involved in military strategy. They include the coordination and direction of armies and allies on a large scale, the planning of appropriate logistical arrangements and of supply routes, and the matching of fighting methods to the overall objectives of war. It is a common view that none of this was possible in the Middle Ages, that tactics and personal prowess were all that mattered in war, and that armies could not be effectively controlled by commanders who did not even possess maps. In fact, there was much thought given to strategy. De Re Militari was widely read throughout the Middle Ages and commanders put its broad concepts into practice.

There is much evidence that campaigns were planned in quite a modern sense. The Crusades saw consideration of such eminently strategic matters as whether or not to move against Damascus or against Egypt, and whether an alliance could be made with the Mongols to coordinate military efforts. Richard the Lionheart's participation in the Third Crusade shows a strategic mind at work, with much care taken to maintain supply routes, and a refusal to be diverted by the romantic goal of Jerusalem. Fighting methods were matched to overall objectives. The widespread destruction of territory was not aimless violence; medieval commanders deliberately used fire and sword as a highly effective way of compelling opponents to negotiate and come to terms.

NOTES

1. Most military historians believe that this battle established the cavalry as the dominant arm of European warfare for the next millennium. Fought on 9 August 378, gothic warriors shattered the elite infantry of the eastern Roman empire, a defeat that crippled the imperial army and is often regarded as one of history's most decisive battles. The role played by cavalry was decisive, but there was no innovation in tactics or armament. (Adrianpole is south-west of modern Istanbul)
2. The Romans also started with the Greek phalanx. But somewhere around 400 BC they adopted a more open order. The Greek phalanx moved in one mass. The Roman legion was divided into three sections, the hestati or young soldiers, the principles or the men of mature age, and the triari or the veterans. Each section was divided into ten maniples or companies. This heavy infantry was equipped with helmet, shield, cuirass, short sword and a pike (later, due to heavy armament the pike was given only to the triarii). The hestati and principles also carried two javelins. Attached to heavy infantry were light infantry and cavalry. Heavy infantry adopted a chess board like formation, which allowed maniples in the rear to come up to the front easily and quickly, as also to accept penetration by the enemy columns and still defeat them. Also see the note below for weapons of a Roman soldier.

3. Vegetius advice on drill and discipline will be termed old fashioned in the day of modern "management". But, the relevance of drilling to reach perfection at the level he was talking about (drills to be followed in battle, not the barrack square) are probably as relevant today as they have always been. Note also the importance given to "drill" by Sun Tzu.
4. Roman soldiers had to learn the use of :
   (a) Spathase —large sword
   (b) Semispathae—a small sword, little larger than a dagger.
   (c) Martiobarbuli—small javelins or loaded javelins – five small javelins were carried in sockets made in the shield. They were thrown at the first charge.
   (d) Pilum or speculum—A long javelin with a shaft of 5½ ft and triangular head of iron nine inches long. (Soldiers were particularly exercised in this weapon as, when skilfully thrown, it could penetrate the shields of foot soldier or cuirasses of the horse).
   (e) Verriculum or Verutum—A smaller javelin with a shaft three and half feet long and a head of five inches.
   (f) Fistibalus—A sling for throwing missiles, usually stones. Common slings were also used.
   (g) Marubalistae or Arcubalistae—Bows and arrows. Slings and bows and arrows were used mostly by the light infantry and archers.
5. This mark was imprinted on the hands of the soldiers, either with a hot iron, or in some other manner. It was indelible.
6. *Ballista* was a machine for throwing darts. *Onagri* was a machine for throwing stones; it was drawn by oxen. Pontoon equipment mainly consisted of small boats hollowed out of single piece of timber, with long cables or chains to fasten them together.
7. Many and most have to be followed very strictly even today. For instance:
   "The water must be wholesome and not marshy".
   "The troops should never encamp with tents".
   "It is the duty of officers of legion, the tribunes and even of the commander in chief to take care that the sick soldiers are supplied with proper diet and diligently attended by the physicians".
8. An instrument with four points so designed that when any three of them are on the ground the fourth projects upward. These are extensively used today for antitank barriers.
9. The dragon was the particular ensign of each cohort.
10. The aspect is actually covered under the heading "Motives for the plan of operation of campaign".
11. It is also interesting to note Vegetius' advice to the Commander-in-Chief in this context; "A Commander-in-Chief, therefore, whose power and dignity are so great and to whose fidelity and bravery the fortunes of his countrymen, the defence of their cities, the lives of the soldiers, the glory of the state, are entrusted, should not only consult the good of the army in general, but extend, his care to every private solider in it".

12. Vegetius ascribes the concept of having a reserve to the Lacednemonians which was later picked up by the Carthagians. The Romans obviously learnt it from the Carthagians during the Punic wars.
13. That the general should lead and direct rather than indulge in personal combat was realized first by Alexander the Great. Alexander was believed to have been fond of personal combat, but realized the importance of the general staying behind to "see" the whole army. But the romance of personal bravery has persisted, as it perhaps does even today. Patton is an example.
14. Frederick the Great had adopted the "oblique" formation very effectively in the Battle of Leuthen (1757) against the Austrians. Traditionally the oblique order has come to be associated with Frederick the Great. See the next chapter.
15. Vegetius formulated this maxim from Scipio. In fact he quotes Scipio: "A golden bridge should be made for a flying enemy". Much of the controversy over this percept comes from Clauzewitz's argument that victory can be achieved only by destruction of the opposing forces.

DE RI MILITARI

To the Emperor Valentinian

It has been an old custom for authors to offer to their Princes the fruits of their studies in belles letters, from a persuasion that no work can be published with propriety but under the auspices of the Emperor, and that the knowledge of a Prince should be more general, and of the most important kind, as its influence is felt so keenly by all his subjects. We have many instances of the favourable reception which Augustus and his illustrious successors conferred on the works presented to them; and this encouragement of the Sovereign made the sciences flourish. The consideration of Your Majesty's superior indulgence for attempts of this sort, induced me to follow this example, and makes me at the same time almost forget my own inability when compared with the ancient writers. One advantage, however, I derive from the nature of this work, as it requires no elegance of expression, or extraordinary share of genius, but only great care and fidelity in collecting and explaining, for public use, the instructions and observations of our old historians of military affairs, or those who wrote expressly concerning them.

My design in this treatise is to exhibit in some order the peculiar customs and usages of the ancients in the choice and discipline of their new levies. Nor do I presume to offer this work to Your Majesty from a supposition that you are not acquainted with every part of its contents; but that you may see that the same salutary dispositions and regulations which your own wisdom prompts You to establish for the happiness of the Empire, were formerly observed by the founders thereof; and that Your Majesty may find with ease in this abridgement whatever is most useful on so necessary and important a subject.

BOOK I: THE SELECTION AND TRAINING OF NEW LEVIES

THE ROMAN DISCIPLINE THE CAUSE OF THEIR GREATNESS

Victory in war does not depend entirely upon numbers or mere courage; only skill and discipline will insure it. We find that the Romans owed the conquest of the world to no other cause than continual military training, exact observance of discipline in their camps and unwearied cultivation of the other arts of war. Without these, what chance would the inconsiderable numbers of the Roman armies have had against the multitudes of the Gauls? Or with what success would their small size have been opposed to the prodigious stature of the Germans? The Spaniards surpassed us not only in numbers, but in physical strength. We were always inferior to the Africans in wealth and unequal to them in deception and stratagem. And the Greeks, indisputably, were far superior to us in skill in arts and all kinds of knowledge.

But to all these advantages the Romans opposed unusual care in the choice of their levies and in their military training. They thoroughly understood the importance of hardening them by continual practice, and of training them to every manoeuvre that might happen in the line and in action. Nor were they less strict in punishing idleness and sloth. The courage of a soldier is heightened by his knowledge of his profession, and he only wants an opportunity to execute what he is convinced he has been perfectly taught. A handful of men, inured to war, proceed to certain victory, while on the contrary numerous armies of raw and undisciplined troops are but multitudes of men dragged to slaughter.

THE SELECTION OF RECRUITS

To treat our subject with some method, we shall first examine what provinces or nations are to be preferred for supplying the armies with recruits. It is certain that every country produces both brave men and cowards; but it is equally as certain that some nations are naturally more warlike than others, and that courage, as well as strength of body, depends greatly upon the influence of the different climates.

We shall next examine whether the city or the country produces the best and most capable soldiers. No one, I imagine, can doubt that the peasants are the most fit to carry arms for they from their infancy have been exposed to all kinds of weather and have been brought up to the hardest labour. They are able to endure the greatest heat of the sun, are unacquainted with the use of baths, and are strangers to the other luxuries of life. They are simple, content with little, inured to all kinds of fatigue, and prepared in some measure for a military life by their continual employment in their country-work, in handling the spade, digging trenches and carrying burdens. In cases of necessity, however, they are sometimes obliged to make levies in the cities. And these men, as soon as enlisted, should be taught to work on entrenchments, to march in ranks, to carry heavy burdens, and to bear the sun and dust. Their meals should be coarse and moderate; they should be accustomed to lie sometimes in the open air and sometimes in tents. After this, they should be instructed in the use of their arms. And if any long expedition is planned, they should be encamped as far as possible from the temptations of the city. By these precautions their minds, as well as their bodies, will properly be prepared for the service.

I realize that in the first ages of the Republic, the Romans always raised their armies in the city itself, but this was at a time when there were no pleasures, no luxuries to enervate them. The Tiber was then their only bath, and in it they refreshed themselves after their exercises and fatigues in the field by swimming. In those days the same man was both soldier and farmer, but a farmer who, when occasion arose, laid aside his tools and put on the sword. The truth of this is confirmed by the instance of Quintius Cincinnatus, who was following the plow when they came to offer him the dictatorship. The chief strength of our armies, then, should be recruited from the country. For it is certain that the less a man is acquainted with the sweets of life, the less reason he has to be afraid of death.

THE PROPER AGE FOR RECRUITS

If we follow the ancient practice, the proper time for enlisting youth into the army is at their entrance into the age of puberty. At this time instructions of every kind are more quickly imbibed and more lastingly imprinted on the mind. Besides this, the indispensable military exercises of running and leaping must be acquired before the limbs are too much stiffened by age. It is activity, improved by continual practice, which forms the useful and good soldier. Formerly, says Sallust, the Roman youth, as soon as they were of an age to carry arms, were trained in the strictest manner in their camps to all the fatigues and exercises of war. For it is certainly better that a soldier, perfectly disciplined, should, through emulation, repine at his not being yet arrived at a proper age for action, than have the mortification of knowing it is past. A sufficient time is also required for his instruction in the different branches of the service. It is no easy matter to train the horse or foot archer, or to form the legionary soldier to every part of the drill, to teach him not to quit his post, to keep ranks, to take a proper aim and throw his missile weapons with force, to dig trenches, to plant palisades, how to manage his shield, glance off the blows of the enemy, and how to parry a stroke with dexterity. A soldier, thus perfect in his business, so far from showing any backwardness to engage, will be eager for an opportunity of signaling himself.

THEIR SIZE

We find the ancients very fond of procuring the tallest men they could for the service, since the standard for the cavalry of the wings and for the infantry of the first legionary cohorts was fixed at six feet, or at least five feet ten inches. These requirements might easily be kept up in those times when such numbers followed the profession of arms and before it was the fashion for the flower of Roman youth to devote themselves to the civil offices of state. But when necessity requires it, the height of a man is not to be regarded so much as his strength; and for this we have the authority of Homer, who tells us that the deficiency of stature in Tydeus was amply compensated by his vigour and courage.

SIGNS OF DESIRABLE QUALITIES

Those employed to superintend new levies should be particularly careful in examining the features of their faces, their eyes, and the make of their limbs, to enable them to form a true judgment and choose such as are most likely to prove good soldiers. Experience assures us that there are in men, as well as in horses and dogs, certain signs by which their virtues may be discovered. The young soldier, therefore, ought to have a lively eye, should carry his head erect, his chest should be broad, his shoulders muscular and brawny, his fingers long, his arms strong, his waist small, his shape easy, his legs and feet rather nervous than fleshy. When all these marks are found in a recruit, a little height may be dispensed with, since it is of much more importance that a soldier should be strong than tall.

TRADES PROPER FOR NEW LEVIES

In choosing recruits regard should be given to their trade. Fishermen, fowlers, confectioners, weavers, and in general all whose professions more properly belong to women should, in my opinion, by no means be admitted into the service. On the contrary, smiths, carpenters, butchers, and huntsmen are the most proper to be taken into it. On the careful choice of soldiers depends the welfare of the Republic, and the very essence of the Roman Empire and its power is so inseparably connected with this charge, that it is of the highest importance not to be entrusted indiscriminately, but only to persons whose fidelity can be relied on. The ancients considered Sertorius' care in this point as one of the most eminent of his military qualifications. The soldiery to whom the defence of the Empire is consigned and in whose hands is the fortune of war, should, if possible, be of reputable families and unexceptionable in their manners. Such sentiments as may be expected in these men will make good soldiers. A sense of honour, by preventing them from behaving ill, will make them victorious.

But what good can be expected from a man by nature a coward, though ever so well disciplined or though he has served ever so many campaigns? An army raised without proper regard to the choice of its recruits was never yet made good by length of time; and we are now convinced by fatal experience that this is the source of all our misfortunes. So many defeats can only be imputed to the effects of a long peace which has made us negligent and careless in the choice of our levies and to the inclination so prevalent among the better sort in preferring the civil posts of the government to the profession of arms and to the shameful conduct of the superintendents, who, through interest or connivance, accept many men which those who are obliged to furnish substitutes for the army choose to send, and admit such men into the service as the masters themselves would not even keep for servants. Thus it appears that a trust of such importance should be committed to none but men of merit and integrity.

THE MILITARY MARK

The recruit, however, should not receive the military mark as soon as enlisted. He must first be tried if fit for service; whether he has sufficient activity and strength; if he has capacity to learn his duty; and whether he has the proper degree of military courage. For many, though promising enough in appearance, are found very unfit upon trial. These are to be rejected and replaced by better men; for it is not numbers, but bravery which carries the day.

After their examination, the recruits should then receive the military mark, and be taught the use of their arms by constant and daily exercise. But this essential custom has been abolished by the relaxation introduced by a long peace. We cannot now expect to find a man to teach what he never learned himself. The only method, therefore, that remains of recovering the ancient customs is by books, and by consulting the old historians. But they are of little service to us in this respect, as they only relate the exploits and events of wars, and take no notice of the objects of our present enquiries, which they considered as universally known.

INITIAL TRAINING

The first thing the soldiers are to be taught is the military step, which can only be acquired by constant practice of marching quick and together. Nor is anything of more consequence either on the march or in the line than that they should keep their ranks with the greatest exactness. For troops who march in an irregular and disorderly manner are always in great danger of being defeated. They should march with the common military step twenty miles in five summer-hours, and with the full step, which is quicker, twenty-four miles in the same number of hours. If they exceed this pace, they no longer march but run, and no certain rate can be assigned.

But the young recruits in particular must be exercised in running, in order to charge the enemy with great vigour; occupy, on occasion, an advantageous post with greater expedition, and prevent the enemy in their designs upon the same; that they may, when sent to reconnoitre, advance with speed, return with greater celerity and more easily come up with the enemy in a pursuit.

Leaping is another very necessary exercise, to enable them to pass ditches or embarrassing eminences of any kind without trouble or difficulty. There is also another very material advantage to be derived from these exercises in time of action; for a soldier who advances with his javelin, running and leaping, dazzles the eyes of his adversary, strikes him with terror, and gives him the fatal stroke before he has time to put himself on his defence. Sallust, speaking of the excellence of Pompey the Great in these particulars, tells us that he disputed the superiority in leaping with the most active, in running with the most swift, and in exercises of strength with the most robust. Nor would he ever have been able to have opposed Serrorius with success, if he had not prepared both himself and his soldiers for action by continual exercises of this sort.

TO LEARN TO SWIM

Every young soldier, without exception, should in the summer months be taught to swim; for it is sometimes impossible to pass rivers on bridges, but the flying and pursuing army both are often obliged to swim over them. A sudden melting of snow or fall of rain often makes them overflow their banks, and in such a situation, the danger is as great from ignorance in swimming as from the enemy. The ancient Romans, therefore, perfected in every branch of the military art by a continued series of wars and perils, chose the Field of Mars as the most commodious for their exercises on account of its vicinity to the Tiber, that the youth might therein wash off the sweat and dust, and refresh themselves after their fatigues by swimming. The cavalry also as well as the infantry, and even the horses and the servants of the army should be accustomed to this exercise, as they are all equally liable to the same accidents.

THE POST EXERCISE

We are informed by the writings of the ancients that, among their other exercises, they had that of the post. They gave their recruits round bucklers woven with willows, twice as heavy as those used on real service, and wooden swords double the weight of the common ones. They exercised them with these at the post both morning and afternoon.

This is an invention of the greatest use, not only to soldiers, but also to gladiators. No man of either profession ever distinguished himself in the circus or field of battle, who was not perfect in this kind of exercise. Every soldier, therefore, fixed a post firmly in the ground, about the height of six feet. Against this, as against a real enemy, the recruit was exercised with the above mentioned arms, as it were with the common shield and sword, sometimes aiming At the head or face, sometimes at the sides, at others endeavouring to strike at the thighs or legs. He was instructed in what manner to advance and retire, and in short how to take every advantage of his adversary; but was thus above all particularly cautioned not to lay himself open to his antagonist while aiming his stroke at him.

NOT TO CUT, BUT TO THRUST WITH THE SWORD

They were likewise taught not to cut but to thrust with their swords. For the Romans not only made a jest of those who fought with the edge of that weapon, but always found them an easy conquest. A stroke with the edges, though made with ever so much force, seldom kills, as the vital parts of the body are defended both by the bones and armour. On the contrary, a stab, though it penetrates but two inches, is generally fatal. Besides in the attitude of striking, it is impossible to avoid exposing the right arm and side; but on the other hand, the body is covered while a thrust is given, and the adversary receives the point before he sees the sword. This was the method of fighting principally used by the Romans, and their reason for exercising recruits with arms of such a weight at first was, that when they came to carry the common ones so much lighter, the greater difference might enable them to act with greater security and alacrity in time of action.

THE DRILL CALLED ARMATURA

The new levies also should be taught by the masters at arms the system of drill called *armatura*, as it is still partly kept up among us. Experience even at this time convinces us that soldiers, perfect therein, are of the most service in engagements. And they afford certain proofs of the importance and effects of discipline in the difference we see between those properly trained in this branch of drill and the other troops. The old Romans were so conscious of its usefulness that they rewarded the masters at arms with a double allowance of provision. The soldiers who were backward in this drill were punished by having their allowance in barley. Nor did they receive it as usual, in wheat, until they had, in the presence of the prefect, tribunes, or other principal officers of the legion, showed sufficient proofs of their knowledge of every part of their study.

No state can either be happy or secure that is remiss and negligent in the discipline of its troops. It is not profusion of riches or excess of luxury that can influence our enemies to court or respect us. This can only be effected by the terror of our arms. It is an observation of Cato that misconduct in the common affairs of life may be retrieved, but that it is quite otherwise in war, where errors are fatal and without remedy, and are followed by immediate punishment. For the consequences of engaging an enemy, without skill or courage, is that part of the army is left on the field of battle, and those who remain receive such an impression from their defeat that they dare not afterwards look the enemy in the face.

THE USE OF MISSILE WEAPONS

Besides the aforementioned exercise of the recruits at the post, they were furnished with javelins of greater weight than common, which they were taught to throw at the same post. And the masters at arms were very careful to instruct them how to cast them with a proper aim and force. This practice strengthens the arm and makes the soldier a good marksman.

THE USE OF THE BOW

A third or fourth of the youngest and fittest soldiers should also be exercised at the post with bows and arrows made for that purpose only. The masters for this branch must be chosen with care and must apply themselves diligently to teach the men to hold the bow in a proper position, to bend it with strength, to keep the left hand steady, to draw the right with skill, to direct both the attention and the eye to the object, and to take their aim with equal certainty either on foot or on horseback. But this is not to be acquired without great application, nor to be retained without daily exercise and practice.

The utility of good archers in action is evidently demonstrated by Cato in his treatise on military discipline. To the institution of a body of troops of this sort Claudius owed his victory over an enemy who, till that time, had constantly been superior to him. Scipio Africanus, before his battle with the Numantines, who had made a Roman army ignominiously pass under the yoke, thought he could have no likelihood of success except by mingling a number of select archers with every century.

THE SLING

Recruits are to be taught the art of throwing stones both with the hand and sling. The inhabitants of the Balearic Islands are said to have been the inventors of slings, and to have managed them with surprising dexterity, owing to the manner of bringing up their children. The children were not allowed to have their food by their mothers till they had first struck it with their sling. Soldiers, notwithstanding their defensive armour, are often more annoyed by the round stones from the sling than by all the arrows of the enemy. Stones kill without mangling the body, and the contusion is mortal without loss of blood. It is universally known the ancients employed slingers in all their engagements. There is the greater reason for instructing all troops, without exception, in this exercise, as the sling cannot be reckoned any encumbrance, and often is of the greatest service, especially when they are obliged to engage in stony places, to defend a mountain or an eminence, or to repulse an enemy at the attack of a castle or city.

THE LOADED JAVELIN

The exercise of the loaded javelins, called *martiobarbuli*, must not be omitted. We formerly had two legions in lllyricum, consisting of six thousand men each, which from their extraordinary dexterity and skill in the use of these weapons were distinguished by the same appellation. They supported for a long time the weight of all the wars and distinguished themselves so remarkably that the Emperors Diocletian and Maximian on their accession honoured them with the titles of Jovian and Herculean and preferred them before all the other legions. Every soldier carries five of these javelins in the hollow of his shield. And thus the legionary soldiers seem to supply the place of archers, for they wound both the men and horses of the enemy before they come within reach of the common missile weapons.

TO BE TAUGHT TO VAULT

The ancients strictly obliged both the veteran soldiers and recruits to a constant practice of vaulting. It has indeed reached our times, although little regard is paid to it at present. They had wooden horses for that purpose placed in winter under cover and in summer in the field. The young soldiers were taught to vault on them at first without arms, afterwards completely armed. And such was their attention to this exercise that they were accustomed to mount and dismount on either side indifferently, with their drawn swords or lances in their hands. By assiduous practice in the leisure of peace, their cavalry was brought to such perfection of discipline that they mounted their horses in an instant even amidst the confusion of sudden and unexpected alarms.

AND TO CARRY BURDENS

To accustom soldiers to carry burdens is also an essential part of discipline. Recruits in particular should be obliged frequently to carry a weight of not less than sixty pounds (exclusive of their arms), and to march with it in the ranks. This is because on difficult expeditions they often find themselves under the necessity of carrying their provisions as well as their arms. Nor will they find this troublesome when inured to it by custom, which makes everything easy. Our troops in ancient times were a proof of this, and Virgil has remarked it in the following lines:

The Roman soldiers, bred in war's alarms,
Bending with unjust loads and heavy arms,
Cheerful their toilsome marches undergo,
And pitch their sudden camp before the foe.

THE ARMS OF THE ANCIENTS

The manner of arming the troops comes next under consideration. But the method of the ancients no longer is followed. For though after the example of the Goths, the Alans and the Huns, we have made some improvements in the arms of the cavalry, yet it is plain the infantry are entirely defenceless. From the foundation of the city till the reign of the Emperor Gratian, the foot wore cuirasses and helmets. But negligence and sloth having by degrees introduced a total relaxation of discipline, the soldiers began to think their armour too heavy, as they seldom put it on. They first requested leave from the Emperor to lay aside the cuirass and afterwards the helmet. In consequence of this, our troops in their engagements with the Goths were often overwhelmed with their showers of arrows. Nor was the necessity of obliging the infantry to resume their cuirasses and helmets discovered, notwithstanding such repeated defeats, which brought on the destruction of so many great cities.

Troops, defenceless and exposed to all the weapons of the enemy, are more disposed to fly than fight. What can be expected from a foot-archer without cuirass or helmet, who cannot hold at once his bow and shield; or from the ensigns whose bodies are naked, and who cannot at the same time carry a shield and the colours? The foot soldier finds the weight of a cuirass and even of a helmet intolerable. This is because he is so seldom exercised and rarely puts them on.

But the case would be quite different, were they even heavier than they are, if by constant practice he had been accustomed to wear them. But it seems these very men, who cannot support the weight of the ancient armour, think nothing of exposing themselves without defence to wounds and death, or, which is worse, to the shame of being made prisoners, or of betraying their country by flight; and thus to avoid an inconsiderable share of exercise and fatigue, suffer themselves ignominiously to be cut in pieces. With what propriety could the ancients call the infantry a wall, but that in some measure they resembled it by the complete armour of the legionary soldiers who had shields, helmets, cuirasses, and greaves of iron on the right leg; and the archers who had gauntlets on the left arm. These were the defensive arms of the legionary soldiers. Those who fought in the first line of their respective legions were called *principes*, in the second *hastati,* and in third *triarii.*

The *triarii,* according to their method of discipline, rested in time of action on one knee, under cover of their shields, so that in this position they might be less exposed to the darts of the enemy than if they stood upright; and also, when there was a necessity for bringing them up, that they might be fresh, in full vigour and charge with the greater impetuosity. There have been many instances of their gaining a complete victory after the entire defeat of both the *principes* and *hastati.*

The ancients had likewise a body of light infantry, slingers, and *ferentarii* (the light troops), who were generally posted on the wings and began the engagement. The most active and best disciplined men were selected for this service; and as their number was not very great, they easily retired in case of a repulse through the intervals of the legion, without thus occasioning the least disorder in the line.

The Pamonian leather caps worn by our soldiers were formerly introduced with a different design. The ancients obliged the men to wear them at all times so that being constantly accustomed to have the head covered they might be less sensible of the weight of the helmet.

As to the missile weapons of the infantry, they were javelins headed with a triangular sharp iron, eleven inches or a foot long, and were called piles. When once fixed in the shield it was impossible to draw them out, and when thrown with force and skill, they penetrated the cuirass without difficulty. At present they are seldom used by us, but are the principal weapon of the barbarian heavy-armed foot. They are called *bebrae*, and every man carries two or three of them to battle.

It must be observed that when the soldiers engage with the javelin, the left foot should be advanced, for, by this attitude the force required to throw it is considerably increased. On the contrary, when they are close enough to use their piles and swords, the right foot should be advanced, so that the body may present less aim to the enemy, and the right arm be nearer and in a more advantageous position for striking. Hence it appears that it is as necessary to provide soldiers with defensive arms of every kind as to instruct them in the use of offensive ones. For it is certain a man will fight with greater courage and confidence when he finds himself properly armed for defence.

ENTRENCHED CAMPS

Recruits are to be instructed in the manner of entrenching camps, there being no part of discipline so necessary and useful as this. For in a camp, well chosen and entrenched, the troops both day and night lie secure within their works, even though in view of the enemy. It seems to resemble a fortified city which they can build for their safety wherever they please. But this valuable art is now entirely lost, for it is long since any of our camps have been fortified either with trenches or palisades. By this neglect our forces have been often surprised by day and night by the enemy's cavalry and suffered very severe losses. The importance of this custom appears not only from the danger to which troops are perpetually exposed who encamp without such precautions, but from the distressful situation of an army that, after receiving a check in the field, finds itself without retreat and consequently at the mercy of the enemy. A camp, especially in the neighbourhood of an enemy, must be chosen with great care. Its situation should be strong by nature, and there should be plenty of wood, forage and water. If the army is to continue in it any considerable time, attention must be had to the salubrity of the place. The camp must not be commanded by any higher grounds from whence it might be insulted or annoyed by the enemy, nor must the location be liable to floods which would expose the army to great danger. The dimensions of the camps must be determined by the number of troops and quantity of baggage, that a large army may have room enough, and that a small one may not be obliged to extend itself beyond its proper ground. The form of the camps must be determined by the site of the country, in conformity to which they must be square, triangular or oval. The Praetorian gate should either front the east or the enemy. In a temporary camp it should face the route by which the army is to march. Within this gate the tents of the first centuries or cohorts are pitched, and the dragons and other ensigns planted.

The Decumane gate is directly opposite to the Praetorian in the rear of the camp, and through this the soldiers are conducted to the place appointed for punishment or execution.

There are two methods of entrenching a camp. When the danger is not imminent, they carry a slight ditch round the whole circuit, only nine feet broad and seven deep. With the turf taken from this they make a kind of wall or breastwork three feet high on the inner side of the ditch. But where there is reason to be apprehensive of attempts of the enemy, the camp must be surrounded with a regular ditch twelve feet broad and nine feet deep perpendicular from the surface of the ground. A parapet is then raised on the side next the camp, of the height of four feet, with hurdles and fascines properly covered and secured by the earth taken out of the ditch. From these dimensions the interior height of the entrenchment will be found to be thirteen feet, and the breadth of the ditch twelve. On the top of the whole are planted strong palisades which the soldiers carry constantly with them for this purpose. A sufficient number of spades, pickaxes, wicker baskets and tools of all kinds are to be provided for these works.

There is no difficulty in carrying on the fortifications of a camp when no enemy is in sight. But if the enemy is near, all the cavalry and half the infantry are to be drawn up in order of battle to cover the rest of the troops at work on the entrenchments and be ready to receive the enemy if they offer to attack. The centuries are employed by turns on the work and are regularly called to the relief by a crier till the whole is completed. It is then inspected and measured by the centurions, who punish such as have been indolent or negligent. This is a very important point in the discipline of young soldiers, who when properly trained to it will be able in an emergency to fortify their camp with skill and expedition.

EVOLUTIONS

No part of drill is more essential in action than for soldiers to keep their ranks with the greatest exactness, without opening or closing too much. Troops too much crowded can never fight as they ought, and only embarrass one another. If their order is too open and loose, they give the enemy an opportunity of penetrating. Whenever this happens and they are attacked in the rear, universal disorder and confusion are inevitable. Recruits should therefore be constantly in the field, drawn up by the roll and formed at first into a single rank. They should learn to dress in a straight line and to keep an equal and just distance between man and man. They must then be ordered to double the rank, which they must perform very quickly, and instantly cover their file leaders. In the next place, they are to double again and form four deep. And then the triangle or, as it is commonly called, the wedge, a disposition found very serviceable in action. They must be taught to form the circle or orb; for well-disciplined troops, after being broken by the enemy, have thrown themselves into this position and have thereby prevented the total rout of the army. These evolutions, often practiced in the field of exercise, will be found easy in execution on actual service.

MONTHLY MARCHES

It was a constant custom among the old Romans, confirmed by the Ordinances of Augustus and Hadrian, to exercise both cavalry and infantry three times in a month by marches of a certain length. The foot were obliged to march completely armed the distance of ten miles from the camp and return, in the most exact order and with the military step which they changed and quickened on some part of the march. Their cavalry likewise, in troops and properly armed, performed the same marches and were exercised at the same time in their peculiar movement and evolutions; sometimes, as if pursuing the enemy, sometimes retreating and returning again with greater impetuosity to the charge. They made these marches not in plain and even ground only, but both cavalry and infantry were ordered into difficult and uneven places and to ascend or descend mountains, to prepare them for all kinds of accidents and familiarize them with the different manoeuvres that the various situations of a country may require.

CONCLUSION

These military maxims and instructions, invincible Emperor, as a proof of my devotion and zeal for your service, I have carefully collected from the works of all the ancient authors on the subject. My design herein is to point out the certain method of forming good and serviceable armies, which can only be accomplished by an exact imitation of the ancients in their care in the choice and discipline of their levies. Men are not degenerated in point of courage, nor are the countries that produced the Lacedaemonians, the Athenians, the Marsians, the Samnites, the Peligni and even the Romans themselves, yet exhausted. Did not the Epirots acquire in former times a great reputation in war? Did not the Macedonians and Thessalians, after conquering the Persians, penetrate even into India? And it is well known that the warlike dispositions of the Dacians, Moesians and Thracians gave rise to the fable that Mars was born among them.

To pretend to enumerate the different nations so formidable of old, all which now are subject to the Romans, would be tedious. But the security established by long peace has altered their dispositions, drawn them off from military to civil pursuits and infused into them a love of idleness and ease. Hence a relaxation of military discipline insensibly ensued, then a neglect of it, and it sunk at last into entire oblivion. Now will it appear surprising that this alteration should have happened in latter times, if we consider that the peace, which lasted about twenty years or somewhat more after the first Punic war, enervated the Romans, before everywhere victorious, by idleness and neglect of discipline to such a degree, that in the second Punic war they were not able to keep the field against Hannibal. At last, after the defeat of many consuls and the loss of many officers and armies, they were convinced that the revival of discipline was the only road to victory and thereby recovered their superiority. The necessity, therefore, of discipline cannot be too often inculcated, as well as the strict attention requisite in the choice and training of new levies. It is also certain that it is a much less expense to a State to train its own subjects to arms than to take foreigners into its pay.

PREFACE TO BOOK II

To the Emperor Valentinian

Such a continued series of victories and triumphs proved incontestably Your Majesty's full and perfect knowledge of the military discipline of the ancients. Success in any profession is the most certain mark of skill in it. By a greatness of mind above human comprehension Your Majesty condescends to seek instruction from the ancients, notwithstanding your own recent exploits surpass antiquity itself. On receiving Your Majesty's orders to continue this abridgement, not so much for your instruction as convenience, I knew not how to reconcile my devotion to Your commands with the respect due to Your Majesty. Would it not be the greatest height of presumption to pretend to mention the art of war to the Lord and Master of the world and the

Conqueror of all the barbarous nations, unless it were to describe his own actions? But disobedience to the will of so great a Prince would be both highly criminal and dangerous. My obedience, therefore, made me presumptuous, from the apprehensions of appearing more so by a contrary conduct. And in this I was not a little encouraged by the late instance of Your Majesty's indulgence. My treatise on the choice and discipline of new levies met with a favourable reception from Your Majesty, and since a work succeeded so well, composed of my own accord, I can have no fears for one undertaken by your own express commands.

BOOK II: THE ORGANISATION OF THE LEGION

THE MILITARY ESTABLISHMENT

The military establishment consists of three parts, the cavalry, infantry and marine. The wings of cavalry were so called from their similitude to wings in their extension on both sides of the main body for its protection. They are now called vexillations from the kind of standards peculiar to them. The legionary horse are bodies particularly annexed to each legion, and of a different kind; and on their model were organized the cavalry called Ocreati, from the light boots they wear. The fleet consists of two divisions, the one of men of war called Liburnae, and the other of armed sloops. The cavalry are designed for plains. Fleets are employed for the protection of seas and rivers. The infantry are proper for the defence of eminences, for the garrisons of cities and are equally serviceable in plain and in uneven ground. The latter, therefore, from their facility of acting everywhere, are certainly the most useful and necessary troops to a state exclusively of the consideration of their being maintained at a less expense. The infantry are divided into two corps, the legions and auxiliaries, the latter of which are furnished by allies or confederates. The peculiar strength of the Romans always consisted in the excellent organisation of their legions. They were so denominated *ab eligendo*, from the care and exactness used in the choice of the soldiers. The number of legionary troops in an army is generally much more considerable than that of the auxiliaries.

DIFFERENCE BETWEEN THE LEGIONS AND AUXILIARIES

The Macedonians, the Greeks and the Dardanians formed their troops into phalanxes of eight thousand men each. The Gauls, Celtiberians and many other barbarous nations divided their armies into bodies of six thousand each. The Romans have their legions usually six thousand strong, sometimes more.

We shall now explain the difference between the legions and the auxiliaries. The latter are hired corps of foreigners assembled from different parts of the Empire, made up of different numbers, without knowledge of one another or any tie of affection. Each nation has its own peculiar discipline, customs and manner of fighting. Little can be expected from forces so dissimilar in every respect, since it is one of the most essential points in military undertakings that the whole army should be put in motion and governed by one and the same order. But it is almost impossible for men to act in concert under such varying and unsettled circumstances. They are, however, when properly trained and disciplined, of material service and are always joined as light troops with the legions in the line. And though the legions do not place their principal dependence on them, yet they look on them as a very considerable addition to their strength.

But the complete Roman legion, in its own peculiar cohorts, contains within itself the heavy-armed foot, i.e.: the *principes, hastati, triarii*, and *antefignani*, the light-armed foot, consisting of the *ferentarii,* archers, slingers, and *balistarii*, together with the legionary cavalry incorporated with it. These bodies, all actuated with the same spirit, are united inseparably in their various dispositions for forming, encamping and fighting. Thus the legion is compact and perfect in all its parts and, without any foreign assistance, has always been superior to any force that could be brought against it. The Roman greatness is a proof of the excellence of their legions, for with them they always defeated whatever numbers of the enemy they thought fit, or their circumstances gave them an opportunity to engage.

CAUSES OF DECAY OF THE LEGION

The name of the legion remains indeed to this day in our armies, but its strength and substance are gone, since by the neglect of our predecessors, honours and preferments, which were formerly the recompenses of merit and long services, were to be attained only by interest and favour. Care is no longer taken to replace the soldiers, who after serving their full time, have received their discharges. The vacancies continually happening by sickness, discharges, desertion and various other casualties, if not supplied every year or even every month, must in time disable the most numerous army. Another cause of the weakness of our legions is that in them the soldiers find the duty hard, the arms heavy, the rewards distant and the discipline severe. To avoid these inconveniences, the young men enlist in the auxiliaries, where the service is less laborious and they have reason to expect more speedy recompenses.

Cato the Elder, who was often Consul and always victorious at the head of the armies, believed he should do his country more essential service by writing on military affairs, than by all his exploits in the field. For the consequences of brave actions are only temporary, while whatever is committed to writing for public good is of lasting benefit. Several others have followed his example, particularly Frontinus, whose elaborate works on this subject were so well received by the Emperor Trajan. These are the authors whose maxims and institutions I have undertaken to abridge in the most faithful and concise manner.

The expense of keeping up good or bad troops is the same; but it depends wholly on you, most August Emperor, to recover the excellent discipline of the ancients and to correct the abuses of later times. This is a reformation the advantages of which will be equally felt by ourselves and our posterity.

THE ORGANIZATION OF THE LEGION

All our writers agree that never more than two legions, besides auxiliaries, were sent under the command of each consul against the most numerous armies of the enemies. Such was the dependence on their discipline and resolution that this number was thought sufficient for any war they were engaged in. I shall therefore explain the organisation of the ancient legion according to the military constitution. But if the description appears obscure or imperfect, it is not to be imputed to me, but to the difficulty of the subject itself, which is therefore to be examined with the greater attention. A prince, skilled himself in military affairs, has it in his power to make himself invincible by keeping up whatever number of well disciplined forces he thinks proper.

The recruits having thus been carefully chosen with proper attention to their persons and dispositions, and having been daily exercised for the space of four months at least, the legion is formed by the command and under the auspices of the Emperor. The military mark, which is indelible, is first imprinted on the hands of the new levies, and as their names are inserted in the roll of the legions they take the usual oath, called the military oath. They swear by God, by Christ and by the Holy Ghost; and by the Majesty of the Emperor who, after God, should be the chief object of the love and veneration of mankind. For when he has once received the title of August, his subjects are bound to pay him the most sincere devotion and homage, as the representative of God on earth. And every man, whether in a private or military station, serves God in serving him faithfully who reigns by His authority. The soldiers, therefore, swear they will obey the Emperor willingly and implicitly in all his commands, that they will never desert and will always be ready to sacrifice their lives for the Roman Empire.

The legion should consist of ten cohorts, the first of which exceeds the others both in number and quality of its soldiers, who are selected to serve in it as men of some family and education. This cohort has the care of the eagle, the chief ensign in the Roman armies and the standard of the whole legion, as well as of the images of the emperors which are always considered as sacred. It consists of eleven hundred and five foot and one hundred and thirty-two horse cuirassiers, and is distinguished by the name of the Millarian Cohort. It is the head of the legion and is always first formed on the right of the first line when the legion draws up in order of battle.

The second cohort contains five hundred and fifty-five foot and sixty-six horse, and is called the Quingentarian Cohort. The third is composed of five hundred and fifty five foot and sixty-six horse, generally chosen men, on account of its situation in the centre of the first line. The fourth consists of the same number of five hundred and fifty-five foot and sixty-six horse. The fifth has likewise five hundred and fifty-five foot and sixty-six horse, which should be some of the best men, being posted on the left flank as the first cohort is on the right. These five cohorts compose the first line.

The sixth includes five hundred and fifty-five foot and sixty-six horse, which should be the flower of the young soldiers as it draws up in the rear of the eagle and the images of the emperors, and on the right of the second line. The seventh contains five hundred and fifty-five foot and sixty-six horse. The eighth is composed of five hundred and fifty-five foot and sixty-six horse, all selected troops, as it occupies the centre of the second line. The ninth has five hundred and fifty-five foot and sixty-six horse. The tenth consists of the same number of five hundred and fifty-five foot and sixty-six horse and requires good men, as it closes the left flank of the second line. These ten cohorts form the complete legions, consisting in the whole of six thousand one hundred foot and seven hundred and twenty-six horses. A legion should never be composed of a less number of men, but it is sometimes stronger by the addition of other Millarian Cohorts.

THE OFFICERS OF THE LEGION

Having shown the ancient establishment of the legion, we shall now explain the names of the principal soldiers or, to use the proper term, the officers, and their ranks according to the present rolls of the legions. The first tribune is appointed by the express commission and choice of the Emperor.

The second tribune rises to that rank by length of service. The tribunes are so called from their command over the soldiers, who were at first levied by Romulus out of the different tribes. The officers who in action commanded the orders or divisions are called Ordinarii. The Augustales were added by Augustus to the Ordinarii; and the Flaviales were appointed by Flavius Vespasian to double the number of the Augustales. The eagle-bearers and the image-bearers are those who carry the eagles and images of the Emperors. The Optiones are subaltern officers, so denominated from their being selected by the option of their superior officers, to do their duty as their substitutes or lieutenants in case of sickness or other accident. The ensign-bearers carry the ensigns and are called Draconarii. The Tesserarii deliver the parole and the orders of the general to the different messes of the soldiers. The Campignei or Antefignani are those whose duty it is to keep the proper exercises and discipline among the troops. The Metatores are ordered before the army to fix on the ground for its encampments. The Beneficiarii are so named from their owing their promotion to the benefit or interest of the Tribunes. The Librarii keep the legionary accounts. The Tubicines, Cornicines, and Buccinatores derive their appellations from blowing the trumpet, cornet, and buccina. Those who, expert in their exercises, receive a double allowance of provisions, are called Armaturae Duplares, and those who have but a single portion, Simplares. The Mensores mark out the ground by measure for the tents in an encampment, and assign the troops their respective quarters in garrison. The Torquati, so denominated from the gold collars given them in reward for their bravery, had besides this honour different allowances. Those who received double were called Torquati Duplares, and those who had only single, Simplares. There were, for the same reason, Candidatii Duplares, and Candidatii Simplares. These are the principal soldiers or officers distinguished by their rank and privileges thereto annexed. The rest are called Munifices, or working soldiers, from their being obliged to every kind of military work without exception. Formerly it was the rule that the first Princeps of the legion should be promoted regularly to the rank of Centurion of the Primiple. He not only was entrusted with the eagle but commanded four centuries, that is, four hundred men in the first line. As head of the legion he had appointments of great honour and profit. The first Hastatus had the command of two centuries or two hundred men in the second line, and is now called Ducenarius. The Princeps of the first cohort commanded a century and a half, that is, one hundred and fifty men, and kept in a great measure the general detail of the legion. The second Hastatus had likewise a century and a half, or one hundred and fifty men. The first Triarius had the command of one hundred men. Thus the ten centuries of the first cohort were commanded by five Ordinarii, who by the ancient establishment enjoyed great honours and emoluments that were annexed to this rank in order to inspire the soldiers of the legions with emulation to attain such ample and considerable rewards. They had also Centurions appointed to each century, now called Centenarii and Decani, who commanded ten men, now called heads of messes. The second cohort had five Centurions; and all the rest to the tenth inclusively the same number. In the whole legion there were fifty five.

Lieutenants of consular dignity were formerly sent to command in the armies under the general, and their authority extended over both the legions and auxiliaries in peace and war. Instead of these officers, persons of high rank are now substituted with the title of Masters of the Forces. They are not limited to the command of two legions only, but have often a greater number. But the peculiar officer of the legion was the Praefect, who was always a count of the first order. On him the chief command devolved in the absence of the lieutenant. The Tribunes, Centurions, and all the soldiers in general were under his orders: He gave out the parole and order for the march and for the guards. And if a soldier committed a crime, by his authority the Tribune adjudged him to punishment. He had charge of the arms, horses, clothing and provisions. It was also his duty to keep both the legionary horse and foot in daily exercise and to maintain the strictest discipline. He ought to be a careful and diligent officer, as the sole charge of forming the legion to regularity and obedience depended on him and the excellence of the soldiers redounded entirely to his own honour and credit.

The Praefect of the camp, though inferior in rank to the former, had a post of no small importance. The position of the camp, the direction of the entrenchments, the inspection of the tents or huts of the soldiers and the baggage were comprehended in his province. His authority extended over the sick, and the physicians who had the care of them; and he regulated the expenses relative thereto. He had the charge of providing carriages, bathorses and the proper tools for sawing and cutting wood, digging trenches, raising parapets, sinking wells and bringing water into the camp. He likewise had the care of furnishing the troops with wood and straw, as well as the rams, *onagri, balistae* and all the other engines of war under his direction. This post was always conferred on an officer of great skill, experience and long service, and who consequently was capable of instructing others in those branches of the profession in which he had distinguished himself.

THE PRAEFECT OF THE WORKMEN

The legion had a train of joiners, masons, carpenters, smiths, painters, and workmen of every kind for the construction of barracks in the winter-camps and for making or repairing the wooden towers, arms, carriages and the various sorts of machines and engines for the attack or defence of places. They had also traveling workshops in which they made shields, cuirasses, helmets, bows, arrows, javelins and offensive and defensive arms of all kinds. The ancients made it their chief care to have every thing for the service of the army within the camp. They even had a body of miners who, by working under ground and piercing the foundations of walls, according to the practice of the Beffi, penetrated into the body of a place. All these were under the direction of the officer called the praefect of the workmen.

THE TRIBUNE OF THE SOLDIERS

We have observed that the legions had ten cohorts, the first of which, called the Millarian Cohort, was composed of men selected on account of their circumstances, birth, education, person and bravery. The tribune who commanded them was likewise distinguished for his skill in his exercises, for the advantages of his person and the integrity of his manners. The other cohorts were commanded, according to the Emperor's pleasure, either by tribunes or other officers commissioned for that purpose. In former times the discipline was so strict that the tribunes or officers abovementioned not only caused the troops under their command to be exercised daily in their presence, but were themselves so perfect in their military exercises as to set them the example. Nothing does so much honour to the abilities or application of the tribune as the appearance and discipline of the soldiers, when their apparel is neat and clean, their arms bright and in good order and when they perform their exercises and evolutions with dexterity.

CENTURIES AND ENSIGNS OF THE FOOT

The chief ensign of the whole legion is the eagle and is carried by the eagle-bearer. Each cohort has also its own peculiar ensign, the Dragon, carried by the Draconarius. The ancients, knowing the ranks were easily disordered in the confusion of action, divided the cohorts into centuries and gave each century an ensign inscribed with the number both of the cohort and century so that the men keeping it in sight might be prevented from separating from their comrades in the greatest tumults. Besides the centurions, now called *centenarii*, were distinguished by different crests on their helmets, to be more easily known by the soldiers of their respective centuries. These precautions prevented any mistake, as every century was guided not only by its own ensign but likewise by the peculiar form of the helmet of its commanding officers. The centuries were also subdivided into messes of ten men each who lay in the same tent and were under orders and inspection of a *Decanus* or head of the mess. These messes were also called Maniples from their constant custom of fighting together in the same company or division.

LEGIONARY TROOPS OF HORSE

As the divisions of the infantry are called centuries, so those of the cavalry are called troops. A troop consists of thirty-two men and is commanded by a Decurion. Every century has its ensign and every troop its Standard. The centurion in the infantry is chosen for his size, strength and dexterity in throwing his missile weapons and for his skill in the use of his sword and shield; in short for his expertness in all the exercises. He is to be vigilant, temperate, active and readier to execute the orders he receives than to talk; Strict in exercising and keeping up proper discipline among his soldiers, in obliging them to appear clean and well-dressed and to have their arms constantly rubbed and bright. In like manner the Decurion is to be preferred to the command of a troop for his activity and address in mounting his horse completely armed; for his skill in riding and in the use of the lance and bow; for his attention in forming his men to all the evolutions of the cavalry; and for his care in obliging them to keep their cuirasses, lances and helmets always bright and in good order. The splendor of the arms has no inconsiderable effect in striking terror into an enemy. Can that man be reckoned a good soldier who through negligence suffers his arms to be spoiled by dirt and rust? In short, it is the duty of the Decurion to be attentive to whatever concerns the health or discipline of the men or horses in his troop.

DRAWING UP A LEGION IN ORDER OF BATTLE

We shall exemplify the manner of drawing up an army in order of battle in the instance of one legion, which may serve for any number. The cavalry are posted on the wings. The infantry begin to form on a line with the first cohort on the right. The second cohort draws up on the left of the first; the third occupies the centre; the fourth is posted next; and the fifth closes the left flank. The *ordinarii,* the other officers and the soldiers of the first line, ranged before and round the ensigns, were called the *principes*. They were all heavy armed troops and had helmets, cuirasses, greaves, and shields. Their offensive weapons were large swords, called *spathae*, and smaller ones called *semispathae* together with five loaded javelins in the concavity of the shield, which they threw at the first charge. They had likewise two other javelins, the largest of which was composed of a staff five feet and a half long and a triangular head of iron nine inches long. This was formerly called the *pilum*, but now it is known by the name of *spiculum*. The soldiers were particularly exercised in the use of this weapon, because when thrown with force and skill it often penetrated the shields of the foot and the cuirasses of the horse. The other javelin was of smaller size; its triangular point was only five inches long and the staff three feet and one half. It was anciently called *verriculum* but now *verutum*.

The first line, as I said before, was composed of the *principes*; the *hastati* formed the second and were armed in the same manner. In the second line the sixth cohort was posted on the right flank, with the seventh on its left; the eighth drew up in the centre; the ninth was the next; and the tenth always closed the left flank. In the rear of these two lines were the *ferentarii,* light infantry and the troops armed with shields, loaded javelins, swords and common missile weapons, much in the same manner as our modern soldiers. This was also the post of the archers who had helmets, cuirasses, swords, bows and arrows; of the slingers who threw stones with the common sling or with the *fustibalus*; and of the *tragularii* who annoyed the enemy with arrows from the *manubalistae* or *arcubalistae*.

In the rear of all the lines, the *triarii*, completely armed, were drawn up. They had shields, cuirasses, helmets, greaves, swords, daggers, loaded javelins, and two of the common missile weapons. They rested during the action on one knee, so that if the first lines were obliged to give way, they might be fresh when brought up to the charge, and thereby retrieve what was lost and recover the victory. All the ensigns though, of the infantry, wore cuirasses of a smaller sort and covered their helmets with the shaggy skins of beasts to make themselves appear more terrible to the enemy. But the centurions had complete cuirasses, shields, and helmets of iron, the crest of which, placed transversely thereon, were ornamented with silver that they might be more easily distinguished by their respective soldiers.

The following disposition deserves the greatest attention. In the beginning of an engagement, the first and second lines remained immovable on their ground, and the *trairii* in their usual positions. The light-armed troops, composed as above mentioned, advanced in the front of the line, and attacked the enemy. If they could make them give way, they pursued them; but if they were repulsed by superior bravery or numbers, they retired behind their own heavy armed infantry, which appeared like a wall of iron and renewed the action, at first with their missile weapons, then sword in hand. If they broke the enemy they never pursued them, least they should break their ranks or throw the line into confusion, and lest the enemy, taking advantage of their disorder, should return to the attack and destroy them without difficulty. The pursuit therefore was entirely left to the light-armed troops and the cavalry. By these precautions and dispositions the legion was victorious without danger, or if the contrary happened, was preserved without any considerable loss, for as it is not calculated for pursuit, it is likewise not easily thrown into disorder.

NAMES OF SOLDIERS INSCRIBED ON THEIR SHIELDS

Lest the soldiers in the confusion of battle should be separated from their comrades, every cohort had its shields painted in a manner peculiar to itself. The name of each soldier was also written on his shield, together with the number of the cohort and century to which he belonged. From this description we may compare the legion, when in proper order, to a well fortified city as containing within itself every thing requisite in war, wherever it moved. It was secure from any sudden attempt or surprise of an enemy by its expeditious method of entrenching its camp even in the open plains and it was always provided with troops and arms of every kind. To be victorious, therefore, over our enemies in the field, we must unanimously supplicate heaven to dispose the Emperor to reform the abuses in raising our levies and to recruit our legions after the method of the ancients. The same care in choosing and instructing our young soldiers in all military exercises and drills will soon make them equal to the old Roman troops who subdued the whole world. Nor let this alteration and loss of ancient discipline in any way affect Your Majesty, since it is a happiness reserved for You alone both to restore the ancient ordinances and establish new ones for the public welfare. Every work before the attempt carries in it an appearance of difficulty; but in this case, if the levies are made by careful and experienced officers, an army may be raised, disciplined and rendered fit for service in a very short time; for the necessary expenses once provided, diligence soon effects whatever it undertakes.

RECORDS AND ACCOUNTS

Several posts in the legion requiring men of some education, the superintendents of the levies should select some recruits for their skill in writing and accounts, besides the qualification to be attended to in general, such as size, strength and proper disposition for the service. For the whole detail of the legion, including the lists of the soldiers exempted from duty on private accounts, the rosters for their tour of military duties and their pay lists, is daily entered in the legionary books and kept we may almost say, with greater exactness than the regulations of provisions or other civil matters in the registers of the police. The daily guards in time of peace, the advanced guards and outposts in time of war, which are mounted regularly by the centuries and messes in their turns, are likewise punctually kept in rolls for that purpose, with the name of each soldier whose tour is past, that no one may have injustice done him or be excused from his duty by favour.

They are also exact in entering the time and limitation of furloughs, which formerly were never granted without difficulty and only on real and urgent business. They then never suffered the soldiers to attend on any private person or to concern themselves in private occupations, thinking it absurd and improper that the Emperor's soldiers, clothed and subsisted at the public expense, should follow any other profession. Some soldiers, however, were allowed for the service of the praefects, tribunes and even of the other officers, our of the number of the *accensi* or such as were raised after the legion was complete. These latter are now called supernumeraries. The regular troops were obliged to carry their wood, hay, water and straw into the camp themselves. From such kind of services they were called munifices.

SOLDIER'S DEPOSITS

The institution of the ancients which obliged the soldiers to deposit half of every donation they received at the colours was wise and judicious; the intent was to preserve it for their use so that they might not squander it in extravagance or idle expense. For most men, particularly the poorer sort, soon spend whatever they can get. A reserve of this kind therefore is evidently of the greatest service to the soldiers themselves; since they are maintained at the public expense, their military stock by this method is continually increasing. The soldier, who knows all his fortune is deposited at his colours, entertains no thoughts of desertion, conceives a greater affection for them and fights with greater intrepidity in their defence. He is also prompted thereto by interest, the most prevailing consideration among men. This money was contained in ten bags, one for each cohort. There was an eleventh bag also for a small contribution from the whole legion, as a common fund to defray the expense of burial of any of their deceased comrades. These collections were kept in baskets in the custody of the ensigns, chosen for their integrity and capacity, and answerable for the trust and obliged to account with every man for his own proportion.

PROMOTION IN THE LEGION

Heaven certainly inspired the Romans with the organisation of the legion, so superior does it seem to human invention. Such is the arrangement and disposition of the ten cohorts that compose it, as to appear one perfect body and form one complete whole. A soldier, as he advances in rank, proceeds as it were by rotation through the different degrees of the several cohorts in such a manner that one who is promoted passes from the first cohort to the tenth, and returns again regularly through all the others with a continual increase of rank and pay to the first. Thus the centurion of the *primiple*, after having commanded in the different ranks of every cohort, attains that great dignity in the first with infinite advantages from the whole legion. The chief praefect of the Praetorian Guards rises by the same method of rotation to that lucrative and honourable rank. Thus the legionary horse contract an affection for the foot of their own cohorts, notwithstanding the natural antipathy existing between the two corps. And this connection establishes a reciprocal attachment and union between all the cohorts and the cavalry and infantry of the legion.

LEGIONARY MUSIC

The music of the legion consists of trumpets, cornets and *buccinae*. The trumpet sounds the charge and the retreat. The cornets are used only to regulate the motions of the colours; the trumpets serve when the soldiers are ordered out to any work without the colours; but in time of action, the trumpets and cornets sound together. The *classicum,* which is a particular sound of the *buccina* or horn, is appropriated to the commander-in-chief and is used in the presence of the general, or at the execution of a soldier, as a mark of its being done by his authority. The ordinary guards and outposts are always mounted and relieved by the sound of trumpet, which also directs the motions of the soldiers on working parties and on field days. The cornets sound whenever the colours are to be struck or planted. These rules must be punctually observed in all exercises and reviews so that the soldiers may be ready to obey them in action without hesitation according to the general's orders either to charge or halt, to pursue the enemy or to retire. F or reason will convince us that what is necessary to be performed in the heat of action should constantly be practiced in the leisure of peace.

THE DRILLING OF THE TROOPS

The organisation of the legion being thus explained, let us return to the drills. The younger soldiers and recruits went through their drills of every kind every morning and afternoon and the veterans and most expert regularly once a day. Length of service or age alone will never form a military man, for after serving many years an undisciplined soldier is still a novice in his profession. Not only those under the masters at arms, but all the soldiers in general, were formerly trained incessantly in those drills which now are only exhibited as shows in the circus for particular solemnities. By practice only can be acquired agility of body and the skill requisite to engage an enemy with advantage, especially in close fight. But the most essential point of all is to teach soldiers to keep their ranks and never abandon their colours in the most difficult evolutions. Men thus trained are never at a loss amidst the greatest confusion of numbers.

The recruits likewise are to be exercised with wooden swords at the post, to be taught to attack this imaginary antagonist on all sides and to aim at the sides, feet or head, both with the point and edge of the sword. They must be instructed how to spring forward to give the blow, to rise with a bound above the shield and then to sink down and shelter themselves under cover of it, and how to advance and retire. They must also throw their javelins at the post from a considerable distance in order to acquire a good aim and strengthen the arm.

The archers and slingers set up bundles of twigs or straw for marks, and generally strike them with arrows and with stones from the *fustiablus* at the distance of six hundred feet. They acquired coolness and exactness in action from familiar custom and exercise in the field. The slingers should be taught to whirl the sling but once about the head before they cast the stone. Formerly all soldiers were trained to the practice of throwing stones of a pound weight with the hand, as this was thought a readier method since it did not require a sling. The use of the common missile weapons and loaded javelins was another part of the drill strictly attended to.

To continue this drill without interruption during the winter, they erected for the cavalry porticos or riding halls covered with tiles or shingles, and if they were not to be procured, with reeds, rushes or thatch. Large open halls were likewise constructed in the same manner for the use of the infantry. By these means the troops were provided with places of drill sheltered from bad weather. But even in winter, if it did not rain or snow, they were obliged to perform their drills in the field, lest an intermission of discipline should affect both the courage and constitution of the soldier. In short, both legionary and auxiliary troops should continually be drilled in cutting wood, carrying burdens, passing ditches, swimming in the sea or in rivers, marching in the full step and even running with their arms and baggage, so that, inured to labour in peace, they may find no difficulty in war. For, as the well trained soldier is eager for action, so does the untaught fear it. In war discipline is superior to strength; but if that discipline is neglected, there is no longer any difference between the soldier and the peasant. The old maxim is certain that the very essence of an art consists in constant practice.

MACHINES AND TOOLS OF THE LEGION

The legion owes its success to its arms and machines, as well as to the number and bravery of its soldiers. In the first place every century has a *balista* mounted on a carriage drawn by mules and served by a mess, that is by ten men from the century to which it belongs. The larger these engines are, the greater distance they carry and with the greater force. They are used not only to defend the entrenchments of camps, but are also placed in the field in the rear of the heavy armed infantry. And such is the violence with which they throw the darts that neither the cuirasses of the horse nor shields of the foot can resist them. The number of these engines in a legion is fifty five. Besides these are ten *onagri*, one for each cohort; they are drawn ready armed on carriages by oxen; in case of an attack, they defend the works of the camp by throwing stones as the *balistae* do darts.

The legion carries with it a number of small boats, each hollowed out of a single piece of timber, with long cables and sometimes iron chains to fasten them together. These boats, joined and covered with planks, serve as bridges over unfordable rivers, on which both cavalry and infantry pass without danger. The legion is provided with iron hooks, called wolves, and iron scythes fixed to the ends of long poles; and with forks, spades, shovels, pickaxes, wheelbarrows and baskets for digging and transporting earth; together with hatchets, axes and saws for cutting wood. Besides which, a train of workmen attend on it furnished with all instruments necessary for the construction of tortoises, *musculi*, rams, vines, moving towers and other machines for the attack of places. As the enumeration of all the particulars of this sort would be too tedious, I shall only observe that the legion should carry with it wherever it moves, whatever is necessary for every kind of service so that the encampments may have all the strength and conveniences of a fortified city.

PREFACE TO BOOK III

TO THE EMPEROR VALENTINIAN

The Athenians and Lacedaemonians were masters of Greece before the Macedonians, as history informs us. The Athenians excelled not only in war but in other arts and sciences. The Lacedaemonians made war their chief study. They are affirmed to be the first who reasoned on the events of battles and committed their observations thereon to writing with such success as to reduce the military art, before considered as totally dependent on courage or fortune, to certain rules and fixed principles. As a consequence they established schools of tactics for the instruction of youth in all the manoeuvres of war. How worthy of admiration are these people for particularly applying themselves to the study of an art, without which no other art can possibly exist. The Romans followed their example, and both practiced their institutions in their armies and preserved them in their writings. These are the maxims and instructions dispersed through the works of different authors, which Your Majesty has ordered me to abridge, since the perusal of the whole would be too tedious, and the authority of only a part unsatisfactory. The effect of the Lacedaemonian skill in dispositions for general actions appears evidently in the single instance of Xantippus, who assisted the Carthaginians after the repeated ruin of their armies. And merely superior skill and conduct defeated Attilius Regulus at the head of a Roman army, till that time always victorious. Xantippus took him prisoner and thus terminated the war by a single action. Hannibal, also, before he set out on his expedition into Italy, chose a Lacedaemonian for his counsellor in military operations; and by his advice, though inferior to the Romans both in number and strength, overthrew so many consuls and such mighty legions. He, therefore, who desires peace, should prepare for war. He who aspires to victory, should spare no pains to form his soldiers. And he who hopes for success, should fight on principle, not chance. No one dares to offend or insult a power of known superiority in action.

BOOK III: DISPOSITIONS FOR ACTION

THE NUMBER WHICH SHOULD COMPOSE AN ARMY

The first book treats of the choice and exercises of new levies; the second explains the establishment of the legion and the method of discipline; and the third contains the dispositions for action. By this methodical progression, the following instructions on general actions and means of victory will be better understood and of greater use. By an army is meant a number of troops, legions and auxiliaries, cavalry and infantry, assembled to make war. This number is limited by judges of the profession. The defeats of Xerxes, Darius, Mithridates and other monarchs who brought innumerable multitudes into the field, plainly show that the destruction of such prodigious armies is owing more to their own numbers than to the bravery of their enemies. An army too numerous is subject to many dangers and inconveniences. Its bulk makes it slow and unwieldy in its motions; and as it is obliged to march in columns of great length, it is exposed to the risk of being continually harassed and insulted by inconsiderable parties of the enemy. The encumbrance of the baggage is often an occasion of its being surprised in its passage through difficult places or over rivers. The difficulty of providing forage for such numbers of horses and other beasts of burden is very great. Besides, scarcity of provisions, which is to be carefully guarded against in all expeditions, soon ruins such large armies where the consumption is so prodigious, that notwithstanding the greatest care in filling the magazines they must begin to fail in a short time. And sometimes they unavoidably will be distressed for want of water. But, if unfortunately this immense army should be defeated, the numbers lost must necessarily be very great, and the remainder, who save themselves by flight, too much dispirited to be brought again to action.

The ancients, taught by experience, preferred discipline to numbers. In wars of lesser importance they thought one legion with auxiliaries, that is, ten thousand foot and two thousand horse, sufficient. And they often gave the command to a *praeter* as to a general of the second rank. When the preparations of the enemy were formidable, they sent a general of consular dignity with twenty thousand foot and four thousand horse. In our times this command was given to a count of the first order. But when there happened any dangerous insurrection supported by infinite multitudes of fierce and barbarous nations, on such emergencies they took the field with two armies under two consuls, who were charged, both singly and jointly, to take care to preserve the Republic from danger. In short, by this management, the

Romans, almost continually engaged in war with different nations in different parts of the world, found themselves able to oppose them in every quarter. The excellence of their discipline made their small armies sufficient to encounter all their enemies with success. But it was an invariable rule in their armies that the number of allies or auxiliaries should never exceed that of the Roman citizens.

MEANS OF PRESERVING IT IN HEALTH

The next article is of the greatest importance: the means of preserving the health of the troops. This depends on the choice of situation and water, on the season of the year, medicine, and exercise. As to the situation, the army should never continue in the neighbourhood of unwholesome marshes any length of time, or on dry plains or eminences without some sort of shade or shelter. In the summer, the troops should never encamp without tents. And their marches, in that season of the year when the heat is excessive, should begin by break of day so that they may arrive at the place of destination in good time. Otherwise they will contract diseases from the heat of the weather and the fatigue of the march. In severe winter they should never march in the night in frost and snow, or be exposed to want of wood or clothes. A soldier, starved with cold, can neither be healthy nor fit for service. The water must be wholesome and not marshy. Bad water is a kind of poison and the cause of epidemic distempers.

It is the duty of the officers of the legion, of the tribunes, and even of the commander-in-chief himself, to take care that the sick soldiers are supplied with proper diet and diligently attended by the physicians. Little can be expected from men who have both the enemy and diseases to struggle with. However, the best judges of the service have always been of the opinion that daily practice of the military exercises is much more efficacious towards the health of an army than all the art of medicine. For this reason they exercised their infantry without intermission. If it rained or snowed, they performed under cover; and in fine weather, in the field. They also were assiduous in exercising their cavalry, not only in plains, but also on uneven ground, broken and cut with ditches. The horses as well as the men were thus trained, both on the above mentioned account and to prepare them for action. Hence we may perceive the importance and necessity of a strict observance of the military exercises in an army, since health in the camp and victory in the field depend on them. If a numerous army continues long in one place in the summer or in the autumn, the waters become corrupt and the air infected. Malignant and fatal distempers proceed from this and can be avoided only by frequent changes of encampments.

CARE TO PROVIDE FORAGE AND PROVISIONS

Famine makes greater havoc in an army than the enemy, and is more terrible than the sword. Time and opportunity may help to retrieve other misfortunes, but where forage and provisions have not been carefully provided, the evil is without remedy. The main and principal point in war is to secure plenty of provisions and to destroy the enemy by famine. An exact calculation must therefore be made before the commencement of the war as to the number of troops and the expenses incident thereto, so that the provinces may in plenty of time furnish the forage, corn, and all other kinds of provisions demanded of them to be transported. They must be in more than sufficient quantity, and gathered into the strongest and most convenient cities before the opening of the campaign. If the provinces cannot raise their quotas in kind, they must commute for them in money to be employed in procuring all things requisite for the service. For the possessions of the subjects cannot be kept secure otherwise than by the defence of arms.

These precautions often become doubly necessary as a siege is sometimes protracted beyond expectation, the besiegers resolving to suffer themselves all the inconveniences of want sooner than raise the siege, if they have any hopes of reducing the place by famine. Edicts should be issued out requiring the country people to convey their cattle, grain, wine and all kinds of provisions that may be of service to the enemy, into garrisoned fortresses or into the safest cities. And if they do not comply with the order, proper officers are to appointed to compel them to do it. The inhabitants of the province must likewise be obliged to retire with their effects into some fortified place before the irruption of the enemy. The fortifications and all the machines of different kinds must also be examined and repaired in time. For if you are once surprised by the enemy before you are in a proper posture of defence, you are thrown into irrecoverable confusion, and you can no longer draw any assistance from the neighbouring places, all communication with them being cut off. But a faithful management of the magazines and a frugal distribution of the provisions, with proper precautions taken at first, will insure sufficient plenty. When provisions once begin to fail, parsimony is ill-timed and comes too late.

On difficult expeditions the ancients distributed the provisions at a fixed allowance to each man without distinction of rank; and when the emergency was past, the government accounted for the full proportions. The troops should never want wood and forage in winter or water in summer. They should have corn, wine, vinegar, and even salt, in plenty at all times. Cities and fortresses are garrisoned by such men as are least fit for the service of the field. They arc provided with all sorts of arms, arrows, *fustibali*, slings, stones, *onagri* and *balistae* for their defence. Great caution is requisite that the unsuspecting simplicity of the inhabitants be not imposed on by the treachery or perjury of the enemy, for pretended conferences and deceitful appearance of truces have often been more fatal than force. By observing the foregoing precautions, the besieged may have it in their power to ruin the enemy by famine, if he keeps his troops together, and if he divides them, by frequent sallies and surprises.

METHODS TO PREVENT MUTINY IN AN ARMY

An army drawn together from different parts sometimes is disposed to mutiny. And the troops, though not inclined to fight, pretend to be angry at not being led against the enemy. Such seditious dispositions principally show themselves in those who have lived in their quarters in idleness and effeminacy. These men, unaccustomed to the necessary fatigue of the field, are disgusted at its severity. Their ignorance of discipline makes them afraid of action and inspires them with insolence.

There are several remedies for this evil. While the troops are yet separated and each corps continues in its respective quarters, let the tribunes, their lieutenants and the officers in general make it their business to keep up so strict a discipline as to leave them no room to harbour any thoughts but of submission and obedience. Let them be constantly employed either in field days or in the inspection of their arms. They should not be allowed to be absent on furlough. They should be frequently called by roll and trained to be exact in the observance of every signal. Let them be exercised in the use of the bow, in throwing missile weapons and stones, both with the hand and sling, and with the wooden sword at the post; let all this be continually repeated and let them be often kept under arms till they are tired. Let them be exercised in running and leaping to facilitate the passing of ditches. And if their quarters are near the sea or a river, let them all, without exception, be obliged in the summer to have the frequent practice of swimming. Let them be accustomed to march through thickets, enclosures and broken grounds, to fell trees and cut out timber, to break ground and to defend a post against their comrades who are to endeavour to dispossess them; and in the encounter each party should use their shields to dislodge and bear down their antagonists. All the different kinds of troops thus trained and exercised in their quarters will find themselves inspired with emulation for glory and eagerness for action when they come to take the field. In short, a soldier who has proper confidence in his own skill and strength entertains no thought of mutiny.

A general should be attentive to discover the turbulent and seditious soldiers in the army, legions or auxiliaries, cavalry or infantry. He should endeavour to procure his intelligence not from informers, but from the tribunes, their lieutenants and other officers of undoubted veracity. It would then be prudent in him to separate them from the rest under pretence of some service agreeable to them, or detach them to garrison cities or castles, but with such address that though he wants to get rid of them, they may think themselves employed by preference and favour. A multitude never broke out into open sedition at once and with unanimous consent. They are prepared and excited by some few mutineers, who hope to secure impunity for their crimes by the number of their associates. But if the height of the mutiny requires violent remedies, it will be most advisable, after the manner of the ancients, to punish the ring-leaders only in order that, though few suffer, all may be terrified by the example. But it is much more to the credit of a general to form his troops to submission and obedience by habit and discipline than to be obliged to force them to their duty by the terror of punishment.

MARCHES IN THE NEIGHBOURHOOD OF THE ENEMY

It is asserted by those who have made the profession their study that an army is exposed to more danger on marches than in battles. In an engagement the men are properly armed, they see their enemies before them and come prepared to fight. But on a march the soldier is less on his guard, has not his arms always ready and is thrown into disorder by a sudden attack or ambuscade. A general, therefore, cannot be too careful and diligent in taking necessary precautions to prevent a surprise on the march and in making proper dispositions to repulse the enemy, in case of such accident, without loss.

In the first place, he should have an exact description of the country that is, the seat of war, in which the distances of places specified by the number of miles, the nature of the roads, the shortest routes, by-roads, mountains and rivers, should be correctly inserted. We are told that the greatest generals have carried their precautions on this head so far that, not satisfied with the simple description of the country wherein they were engaged, they caused plans to be taken of it on the spot, that they might regulate their marches by the eye with greater safety. A general should also inform himself of all these particulars from persons of sense and reputation well acquainted with the country by examining them separately at first, and then comparing their accounts in order to come at the truth with certainty.

If any difficulty arises about the choice of roads, he should procure proper and skilful guides. He should put them under a guard and spare neither promises nor threat to induce them to be faithful. They will acquit themselves well when they know it is impossible to escape and are certain of being rewarded for their fidelity or punished for their perfidy. He must be sure of their capacity and experience, that the whole army be not brought into danger by the errors of two or three persons. For sometimes the common sort of people imagine they know what they really do not, and through ignorance promise more than they can perform.

But of all precautions the most important is to keep entirely secret which way or by what route the army is to march. For the security of an expedition depends on the concealment of all motions from the enemy. The figure of the Minotaur was anciently among the legionary ensigns, signifying that this monster, according to the fable, was concealed in the most secret recesses and windings of the labyrinth, just as the designs of a general should always be impenetrable. When the enemy has no intimation of a march, it is made with security; but as sometimes the scouts either suspect or discover the decampment, or traitors or deserters give intelligence thereof, it will be proper to mention the method of acting in case of an attack on the march.

The general, before he puts his troops in motion, should send out detachments of trusty and experienced soldiers well mounted, to reconnoiter the places through which he is to march, in front, in rear, and on the right and left, lest he should fall into ambuscades. The night is safer and more advantageous for your spies to do their business in than day, for if they are taken prisoners, you have, as it were, betrayed yourself. After this, the cavalry should march off first, then the infantry; the baggage, bat horses, servants and carriages follow in the centre; and part of the best cavalry and infantry come in the rear, since it is oftener attacked on a march than the front. The flanks of the baggage, exposed to frequent ambuscades, must also be covered with a sufficient guard to secure them. But above all, the part where the enemy is most expected must be reinforced with some of the best cavalry, light infantry and foot archers.

If surrounded on all sides by the enemy, you must make dispositions to receive them wherever they come, and the soldiers should be cautioned beforehand to keep their arms in their hands, and to be ready in order to prevent the bad effects of a sudden attack. Men are frightened and thrown into disorder by sudden accidents and surprises of no consequence when foreseen. The ancients were very careful that the servants or followers of the army, if wounded or frightened by the noise of the action, might not disorder the troops while engaged, and also to prevent their either straggling or crowding one another too much, which might incommode their own men and give advantage to the enemy. They ranged the baggage, therefore, in the same manner as the regular troops under particular ensigns. They selected from among the servants the most proper and experienced and gave them the command of a number of servants and boys, not exceeding two hundred, and their ensigns directed them where to assemble the baggage. Proper intervals should always be kept between the baggage and the troops, that the latter may not be embarrassed for want of room in case of an attack during the march. The manner and disposition of defence must be varied according to the difference of ground. In an open country you are more liable to be attacked by horse than foot. But in a woody, mountainous or marshy situation, the danger to be apprehended is from foot. Some of the divisions being apt through negligence to move too fast, and others too slow, great care is to be taken to prevent the army from being broken or from running into too great a length, as the enemy would instantly take advantage of the neglect and penetrate without difficulty.

The tribunes, their lieutenants or the masters at arms of most experience, must therefore be posted at proper distances, in order to halt those who advance too fast and quicken such as move too slow. The men at too great a distance in the front, on the appearance of an enemy, are more disposed to fly than to join their comrades. And those too far behind, destitute of assistance, fall a sacrifice to the enemy and their own despair. The enemy, it may be concluded, will either plant ambuscades or make his attack by open force, according to the advantage of the ground. Circumspection in examining every place will be a security against concealed danger; and an ambuscade, if discovered and promptly surrounded, will return the intended mischief with interest.

If the enemy prepare to fall upon you by open force in a mountainous country, detachments must be sent forward to occupy the highest eminences, so that on their arrival they may not dare to attack you under such a disadvantage of ground, your troops being posted so much above theirs and presenting a front ready for their reception. It is better to send men forward with hatchets and other tools in order to open ways that are narrow but safe, without regard to the labour, rather than to run any risk in the finest roads.

It is necessary to be well acquainted whether the enemy usually makes their attempts in the night, at break of day or in the hours of refreshment or rest; and by knowledge of their customs to guard against what we find their general practice. We must also inform ourselves whether they are strongest in infantry or cavalry; whether their cavalry is chiefly armed with lances or with bows; and whether their principal strength consists in their numbers or the excellence of their arms. All of this will enable us to take the most proper measures to distress them and for our advantage. When we have a design in view, we must consider whether it will be most advisable to begin the march by day or by night; we must calculate the distance of the places we want to reach; and take such precautions that in summer the troops may not suffer for want of water on their march, nor be obstructed in winter by impassable morasses or torrents, as these would expose the army to great danger before it could arrive at the place of its destination. As it highly concerns us to guard against these inconveniences with prudence, so it would be inexcusable not to take advantage of an enemy that fell into them through ignorance or negligence. Our spies should be constantly abroad; we should spare no pains in tampering with their men, and give all manner of encouragement to deserters. By these means we may get intelligence of their present or future designs. And we should constantly keep in readiness some detachments of cavalry and light infantry, to fall upon them when they least expect it, either on the march, or when foraging or marauding.

PASSAGES OF RIVERS

The passages of rivers are very dangerous without great precaution. In crossing broad or rapid streams, the baggage, servants, and sometimes the most indolent soldiers are in danger of being lost. Having first sounded the ford, two lines of the best mounted cavalry are ranged at a convenient distance entirely across the river, so that the infantry and baggage may pass between them. The line above the ford breaks the violence of the stream, and the line below recovers and transports the men carried away by the current. When the river is too deep to be forded either by the cavalry or infantry, the water is drawn off, if it runs in a plain, by cutting a great number of trenches, and thus it is passed with ease.

Navigable rivers are passed by means of piles driven into the bottom and floored with planks; or in a sudden emergency by fastening together a number of empty casks and covering them with boards. The cavalry, throwing off their accoutrements, make small floats of dry reeds or rushes on which they lay their rams and cuirasses to preserve them from being wet. They themselves swim their horses across the river and draw the floats after them by a leather thong.

But the most commodious invention is that of the small boats hollowed out of one piece of timber and very light both by their make and the quality of the wood. The army always has a number of these boats upon carriages, together with a sufficient quantity of planks and iron nails. Thus with the help of cables to lash the boats together, a bridge is instantly constructed, which for the time has the solidity of a bridge of stone.

As the enemy generally endeavour to fall upon an army at the passage of a river either by surprise or ambuscade, it is necessary to secure both sides thereof by strong detachments so that the troops may not be attacked and defeated while separated by the channel of the river. But it is still safer to palisade both the posts, since this will enable you to sustain any attempt without much loss. If the bridge is wanted, not only for the present transportation of the troops but also for their return and for convoys, it will be proper to throw up works with large ditches to cover each head of the bridge, with a sufficient number of men to defend them as long as the circumstances of affairs require.

RULES FOR ENCAMPING AN ARMY

An army on the march cannot expect always to find walled cities for quarters, and it is very imprudent and dangerous to encamp in a straggling manner without some sort of entrenchment. It is an easy matter to surprise troops while refreshing themselves or dispersed in the different occupations of the service. The darkness of night, the necessity of sleep and the dispersion of the horses at pasture afford opportunities of surprise. A good situation for a camp is not sufficient; we must choose the very best that can be found lest, having failed to occupy a more advantageous post the enemy should get possession of it to our great detriment.

An army should not encamp in summer near bad waters or far from good ones, nor in winter in a situation without plenty of forage and wood. The camp should not be liable to sudden inundations. The avenues should not be too steep and narrow lest, if invested, the troops should find it difficult to make their retreat; nor should it be commanded by any eminences from which it may be annoyed by the enemy's weapons. After these precautions, the camp is formed square, round, triangular or oblong, according to the nature of the ground. For the form of a camp does not constitute its goodness. Those camps, however, are thought best where the length is one third more than the depth. The dimensions must be exactly computed by the engineers, so that the size of the camp may be proportioned to the number of troops. A camp which is too confined will not permit the troops to perform their movements with freedom, and one which is too extensive divides them too much. There are three methods of entrenching a camp. The first is for the case when the army is on the march and will continue in the camp for only one night. They then throw up a slight parapet of turf and plant it with a row of palisades or caltrops of wood. The sods are cut with iron instruments. If the earth is held strongly together by the roots of the grass, they are cut in the form of a brick a foot and one half high, a foot broad and a foot and one half long. If the earth is so loose that the turf cannot be cut in this form, they run a slight trench round the camp, five feet broad and three feet deep. The earth taken from the trench forms a parapet on the inside and this secures the army from danger. This is the second method.

But permanent camps, either for summer or winter, in the neighbourhood of an enemy, are fortified with greater care and regularity. After the ground is marked out by the proper officers, each century receives a certain number of feet to entrench. They then range their shields and baggage in a circle about their own colours and, without other arms than their swords, open a trench nine, eleven or thirteen feet broad. Or, if they are under great apprehensions of the enemy, they enlarge it to seventeen feet (it being a general rule to observe odd numbers). Within this they construct a rampart with fascines or branches of trees well fastened together with pickets, so that the earth may be better supported. Upon this rampart they raise a parapet with battlements as in the fortifications of a city. The centurions measure the work with rods ten feet long and examine whether every one has properly completed the proportion assigned to him. The tribunes likewise inspect the work and should not leave the place till the whole is finished. And that the workmen may not be suddenly interrupted by the enemy, all the cavalry and that part of the infantry exempted by the privilege of their rank from working, remain in order of battle before the entrenchment to be ready to repel any assault.

The first thing to be done after entrenching the camp, is to plant the ensigns, held by the soldiers in the highest veneration and respect, in their proper places. After this the *praetorium* is prepared for the general and his lieutenants, and the tents pitched for the tribunes, who have soldiers particularly appointed for that service and to fetch their water, wood, and forage. Then the legions and auxiliaries, cavalry and infantry, have the ground distributed to them to pitch their tents according to the rank of the several corps. Four foot-soldiers of each century and four troopers of each troop are on guard every night. As it seemed impossible for a sentinel to remain a whole night on his post, the watches were divided by the hourglass into four parts, that each man might stand only three hours. All guards are mounted by the sound of trumpet and relieved by the sound of cornet. The tribunes choose proper and trusty men to visit the different posts and report to them whatever they find amiss. This is now a military office and the persons appointed to it are called officers of the rounds.

The cavalry furnish the grand guards at night and the outposts by day. They are relieved every morning and afternoon because of the fatigue of the men and horses. It is particularly incumbent upon the general to provide for the protection of the pastures and of the convoys of grain and other provisions both in camp or garrison, and to secure wood, water and forage against the incursions of the enemy. This can only be effected by posting detachments advantageously in the cines or walled castles on the roads along which the convoys advance. And if no ancient fortifications are to be met with, small forts must be built in proper situations, surrounded with large ditches, for the reception of detachments of horse and foot, so that the convoys will be effectually protected. For an enemy will hardly venture far into a country where he knows his adversary's troops are so disposed as to be ready to encompass him on all sides.

MOTIVES FOR THE PLAN OF OPERATIONS OF A CAMPAIGN

Readers of this military abridgement will perhaps be impatient for instructions relative to general engagements. But they should consider that a battle is commonly decided in two or three hours, after which no further hopes are left for the worsted army. Every plan, therefore, is to be considered, every expedient tried and every method taken before matters are brought to this last extremity. Good officers decline general engagements where the danger is common, and prefer the employment of stratagem and finesse to destroy the enemy as much as possible in detail and intimidate them without exposing our own forces.

I shall insert some necessary instructions on this head collected from the ancients. It is the duty and interest of the general frequently to assemble the most prudent and experienced officers of the different corps of the army and consult with them on the state both of his own and the enemy's forces. All overconfidence, as most pernicious in its consequences, must be banished from the deliberations. He must examine which has the superiority in numbers, whether his or the adversary's troops are best armed, which are in the best condition, best disciplined and most resolute in emergencies. The state of the cavalry of both armies must be inquired into, but more especially that of the infantry, for the main strength of an army consists of the latter. With respect to the cavalry, he must endeavour to find out in which are the greatest numbers of archers or of troopers armed with lances, which has the most cuirassiers and which the best horses. Lastly he must consider the field of battle and to judge whether the ground is more advantageous for him or his enemy. If strongest in cavalry, we should prefer plains and open ground; if superior in infantry, we should choose a situation full of enclosures, ditches, morasses and woods, and sometimes mountainous. Plenty or scarcity in either army are considerations of no small importance, for famine, according to the common proverb, is an internal enemy that makes more havoc than the sword. But the most material article is to determine whether it is most proper to temporize or to bring the affair to a speedy decision by action. The enemy sometimes expect an expedition will soon be over; and if it is protracted to any length, his troops are either consumed by want, induced to return home by the desire of seeing their families or, having done nothing considerable in the field, disperse themselves from despair of success. Thus numbers, tired out with fatigue and disgusted with the service, desert, others betray them and many surrender themselves. Fidelity is seldom found in troops disheartened by misfortunes. And in such case an army which was numerous on taking the field insensibly dwindles away to nothing.

It is essential to know the character of the enemy and of their principal officers-whether they be rash or cautious, enterprising or timid, whether they fight on principle or from chance and whether the nations they have been engaged with were brave or cowardly.

We must know how far to depend upon the fidelity and strength of auxiliaries, how the enemy's troops and our own are affected and which appear most confident of success, a consideration of great effect in raising or depressing the courage of an army. A harangue from the general, especially if he seems under no apprehension himself, may reanimate the soldiers if dejected. Their spirits revive if any considerable advantage is gained either by stratagem or otherwise, if the fortune of the enemy begins to change or if you can contrive to beat some of their weak or poorly-armed detachments.

But you must by no means venture to lead an irresolute or diffident army to a general engagement. The difference is great whether your troops are raw or veterans, whether inured to war by recent service or for some years unemployed. For soldiers unused to fighting for a length of time must be considered in the same light as recruits. As soon as the legions, auxiliaries and cavalry are assembled from their several quarters, it is the duty of a good general to have every corps instructed separately in every part of the drill by tribunes of known capacity chosen for that purpose. He should afterwards form them into one body and train them in all the manoeuvres of the line as for a general action. He must frequently drill them himself to try their skill and strength, and to see whether they perform their evolutions with proper regularity and are sufficiently attentive to the sound of the trumpets, the motions of the colours and to his own orders and signals. If deficient in any of these particulars, they must be instructed and exercised till perfect.

But though thoroughly disciplined and complete in their field exercises, in the use of the bow and javelin, and in the evolutions of the line, it is not advisable to lead them rashly or immediately to battle. A favourable opportunity must be watched for, and they must first be prepared by frequent skirmishes and slight encounters. Thus a vigilant and prudent general will carefully weigh in his council the state of his own forces and of those of the enemy, just as a civil magistrate judging between two contending parties. If he finds himself in many respects superior to his adversary, he must by no means defer bringing on an engagement. But if he knows himself inferior, he must avoid general actions and endeavour to succeed by surprises, ambuscades and stratagems. These, when skilfully managed by good generals, have often given them the victory over enemies superior both in numbers and strength.

HOW TO MANAGE RAW AND UNDISCIPLINED TROOPS

All arts and trades whatever are brought to perfection by continual practice. How much more should this maxim, true in inconsiderable matters, be observed in affairs of importance! And how much superior to all others is the art of war, by which our liberties are preserved, our dignities perpetuated and the provinces and the whole Empire itself exist. The Lacedaemonians, and after them the Romans, were so aware of this truth that to this science they sacrificed all others. And the barbarous nations even at this day think only this art worth attention, believing it includes or confers everything else. In short, it is indispensably necessary for those engaged in war not only to instruct them in the means of preserving their own lives, but how to gain the victory over their enemies.

A commander-in-chief therefore, whose power and dignity are so great and to whose fidelity and bravery the fortunes of his countrymen, the defence of their cities, the lives of the soldiers, and the glory of the state, are entrusted, should not only consult the good of the army in general, but extend his care to every private soldier in it. For when any misfortunes happen to those under his command, they are considered as public losses and imputed entirely to his misconduct. If therefore he finds his army composed of raw troops or if they have long been unaccustomed to fighting, he must carefully study the strength, the spirit, the manners of each particular legion, and of each body of auxiliaries, cavalry and infantry. He must know, if possible, the name and capacity of every count, tribune, subaltern and soldier. He must assume the most respectable authority and maintain it by severity. He must punish all military crimes with the greatest rigor of the laws. He must have the character of being inexorable towards offenders and endeavour to give public examples thereof in different places and on different occasions.

Having once firmly established these regulations, he must watch the opportunity when the enemy, dispersed in search of plunder, think themselves in security, and attack them with detachments of tried cavalry or infantry, intermingled with young soldiers, or such as are under the military age. The veterans will acquire fresh experience and the others will be inspired with courage by the advantages such opportunities will give him. He should form ambuscades with the greatest secrecy to surprise the enemy at the passages of rivers, in the rugged passes of mountains, in defiles in woods and when embarrassed by morasses or difficult roads. He should regulate his march so as to fall upon them while taking their refreshments or sleeping, or at a time when they suspect no dangers and are dispersed, unarmed and their horses unsaddled. He should continue these kinds of encounters till his soldiers have imbibed a proper confidence in themselves. For troops that have never been in action or have not for some time been used to such spectacles, are greatly shocked at the sight of the wounded and dying; and the impressions of fear they receive dispose them rather to fly than fight.

If the enemy makes excursions or expeditions, the general should attack him after the fatigue of a long march, fall upon him unexpectedly, or harass his rear. He should detach parties to endeavour to carry off by surprise any quarters established at a distance from the hostile army for the convenience of forage or provisions. For such measures should be pursued at first as can produce no very bad effects if they should happen to miscarry, but would be of great advantage if attended with success. A prudent general will also try to sow dissention among his adversaries, for no nation, though ever so weak in itself can be completely ruined by its enemies unless its fall be facilitated by its own distraction. In civil dissensions men are so intent on the destruction of their private enemies that they are entirely regardless of the public safety.

One maxim must be remembered throughout this work: that no one should ever despair of effecting what has been already performed. It may be said that our troops for many years past have not even fortified their permanent camps with ditches, ramparts or palisades. The answer is plain. If those precautions had been taken, our armies would never have suffered by surprises of the enemy both by day and night. The Persians, after the example of the old Romans, surround their camps with ditches and, as the ground in their country is generally sandy, they always carry with them empty bags to fill with the sand taken out of the trenches and raise a parapet by piling them one on the other. All the barbarous nations range their carriages round them in a circle, a method which bears some resemblance to a fortified camp. They thus pass their nights secure from surprise.

Are we afraid of not being able to learn from others what they before have learned from us? At present all this is to be found in books only, although formerly constantly practiced. Inquiries are now no longer made about customs that have been so long neglected, because in the midst of peace, war is looked upon as an object too distant to merit consideration. But former instances will convince us that the reestablishment of ancient discipline is by no means impossible, although now so totally lost.

In former ages the art of war, often neglected and forgotten, was as often recovered from books and reestablished by the authority and attention of our generals. Our armies in Spain, when Scipio Africanus took the command, were in bad order and had often been beaten under preceding generals. He soon reformed them by severe discipline and obliged them to undergo the greatest fatigue in the different military works, reproaching them that since they would not wet their hands with the blood of their enemies, they should soil them with the mud of the trenches. In short, with these very troops he afterwards took the city of Numantia and burned it to the ground with such destruction of its inhabitants that not one escaped. In Africa an army, which under the command of Albinus had been forced to pass under the yoke, was by Metellus brought into such order and discipline, by forming it on the ancient model, that they afterwards vanquished those very enemies who had subjected them to that ignominious treatment. The Cimbri defeated the legions of Caepio, Manilus and Silanus in Gaul, but Marius collected their shattered remnants and disciplined them so effectually that he destroyed an innumerable multitude of the Cimbri, Teutones and Ambrones in one general engagement. Nevertheless it is easier to form young soldiers and inspire them with proper notions of honour than to reanimate troops who have been once disheartened.

PREPARATIONS FOR A GENERAL ENGAGEMENT

Having explained the less considerable branches of the art of war, the order of military affairs naturally leads us to the general engagement. This is a conjuncture full of uncertainty and fatal to kingdoms and nations, for in the decision of a pitched battle consists the fullness of victory. This eventuality above all others requires the exertion of all the abilities of a general, as his good conduct on such an occasion gains him greater glory, or his dangers expose him to greater danger and disgrace. This is the moment in which his talents, skill and experience show themselves in their fullest extent.

Formerly to enable the soldiers to charge with greater vigour, it was customary to order them a moderate refreshment of food before an engagement, so that their strength might be the better supported during a long conflict. When the army is to march out of a camp or city in the presence of their enemies drawn up and ready for action, great precaution must be observed lest they should be attacked as they defile from the gates and be cut to pieces in detail. Proper measures must therefore be taken so that the whole army may be clear of the gates and form in order of battle before the enemy's approach. If they are ready before you can have quitted the place, your design of marching out must either be deferred till another opportunity or at least dissembled, so that when they begin to insult you on the supposition that you dare not appear, or think of nothing but plundering or returning and no longer keep their ranks, you may sally out and fall upon them while in confusion and surprise. Troops must never be engaged in a general action immediately after a long march, when the men are fatigued and the horses tired. The strength required for action is spent in the toil of the march. What can a soldier do who charges when out of breath? The ancients carefully avoided this inconvenience, but in later times some of our Roman generals, to say nothing more, have lost their armies by unskillfully neglecting this precaution. Two armies, one tired and spent, the other fresh and in full vigour, are by no means an equal match.

THE SENTIMENTS OF THE TROOPS SHOULD BE DETERMINED BEFORE BATTLE

It is necessary to know the sentiments of the soldiers on the day of an engagement. Their confidence or apprehensions are easily discovered by their looks, their words, their actions and their motions. No great dependence is to be placed on the eagerness of young soldiers for action, for fighting has something agreeable in the idea to those who are strangers to it. On the other hand, it would be wrong to hazard an engagement, if the old experienced soldiers testify to a disinclination to fight. A general, however, may encourage and animate his troops by proper exhortations and harangues, especially if by his account of the approaching action he can persuade them into the belief of an easy victory. With this view, he should lay before them the cowardice or lack of skill of their enemies and remind them of any former advantages they may have gained over them. He should employ every argument capable of exciting rage, hatred and indignation against the adversaries in the minds of his soldiers.

It is natural for men in general to be affected with some sensations of fear at the beginning of an engagement, but there are without doubt some of a more timorous disposition who are disordered by the very sight of the enemy. To diminish these apprehensions before you venture on action, draw up your army frequently in order of battle in some safe situation, so that your men may be accustomed to the sight and appearance of the enemy. When opportunity offers, they should be sent to fall upon them and endeavour to put them to flight or kill some of their men. Thus they will become acquainted with their customs, arms and horses. And the objects with which we are once familiarized are no longer capable of inspiring us with terror.

CHOICE OF THE FIELD OF BATTLE

Good generals are acutely aware that victory depends much on the nature of the field of battle. When you intend therefore to engage, endeavour to draw the chief advantage from your situation. The highest ground is reckoned the best. Weapons thrown from a height strike with greater force; and the party above their antagonists can repulse and bear them down with greater impetuosity, while they who struggle with the ascent have both the ground and the enemy to contend with. There is, however, this difference with regard to place: if you depend on your foot against the enemy's horse, you must choose a rough, unequal and mountainous situation. But if, on the contrary, you expect your cavalry to act with advantage against the enemy's infantry, your ground must indeed be higher, but plain and open, without any obstructions of woods or morasses.

ORDER OF BATTLE

In drawing up an army in order of battle, three things are to be considered: the sun, the dust and the wind. The sun in your face dazzles the sight: if the wind is against you, it turns aside and blunts the force of your weapons, while it assists those of your adversary; and the dust driving in your front fills the eyes of your men and blinds them. Even the most unskilful endeavour to avoid these inconveniences in the moment of making their dispositions; but a prudent general should extend his views beyond the present; he should take such measures as not to be incommoded in the course of the day by different aspects of the sun or by contrary winds which often rise at a certain hour and might be detrimental during action. Our troops should be so disposed as to have these inconveniences behind them, while they are directly in the enemy's front.

PROPER DISTANCES AND INTERVALS

Having explained the general disposition of the lines, we now come to the distances and dimensions. One thousand paces contain a single rank of one thousand six hundred and fifty-six foot soldiers, each man being allowed three feet. Six ranks drawn up on the same extent of ground will require nine thousand nine hundred and ninety-six men. To form only three ranks of the same number will take up two thousand paces, but it is much better to increase the number of ranks than to make your front too extensive. We have before observed the distance between each rank should be six feet, one foot of which is taken up by the men. Thus if you form a body of ten thousand men into six ranks they will occupy thirty-six feet in depth and a thousand paces in front. By this calculation it is easy to compute the extent of ground required for twenty or thirty thousand men to form upon. Nor can a general be mistaken when thus he knows the proportion of ground for any fixed number of men.

But if the field of battle is not spacious enough or your troops are very numerous, you may form them into nine ranks or even more, for it is more advantageous to engage in close order that to extend your line too much. An army that takes up too much ground in front and too little in depth, is quickly penetrated by the enemy's first onset. After this there is no remedy. As to the post of the different corps in the right or left wing or in the centre, it is the general rule to draw them up according to their respective ranks or to distribute them as circumstances or the dispositions of the enemy may require.

DISPOSITION OF THE CAVALRY

The line of infantry being formed, the cavalry are drawn up in the wings. The heavy horse, that is, the cuirassiers and troopers armed with lances, should join the infantry. The light cavalry, consisting of the archers and those who have no cuirasses, should be placed at a greater distance. The best and heaviest horses are to cover the flanks of the foot, and the light horses are posted as abovementioned to surround and disorder the enemy's wings. A general should know what part of his own cavalry is most proper to oppose any particular squadrons or troops of the enemy. For from some causes not to be accounted for some particular corps fight better against others, and those who have defeated superior enemies are often overcome by an inferior force.

If your cavalry is not equal to the enemy's it is proper, after the ancient custom, to intermingle it with light infantry armed with small shields and trained to this kind of service. By observing this method, even though the flower of the enemy's cavalry should attack you, they will never be able to cope with this mixed disposition. This was the only resource of the old generals to supply the defects of their cavalry, and they intermingled the men, used to running and armed for this purpose with light shields, swords and darts, among the horse, placing one of them between two troopers.

RESERVES

The method of having bodies of reserves in rear of the army, composed of choice infantry and cavalry, commanded by the supernumerary lieutenant generals, counts and tribunes, is very judicious and of great consequence towards the gaining of a battle. Some should be posted in rear of the wings and some near the centre, to be ready to fly immediately to the assistance of any part of the line which is hard pressed, to prevent its being pierced, to supply the vacancies made therein during the action and thereby to keep up the courage of their fellow soldiers and check the impetuosity of the enemy. This was an invention of the Lacedaemonians, in which they were imitated by the Carthaginians. The Romans have since observed it, and indeed no better disposition can be found.

The line is solely designed to repulse, or if possible, break the enemy. If it is necessary to form the wedge or the pincers, it must be done by the supernumerary troops stationed in the rear for that purpose. If the saw is to be formed, it must also be done from the reserves, for if once you begin to draw off men from the line you throw all into confusion. If any flying platoon of the enemy should fall upon your wing or any other part of your army, and you have no supernumerary troops to oppose it or if you pretend to detach either horse or foot from your line for that service by endeavouring to protect one part, you will expose the other to greater danger. In armies not very numerous, it is much better to contract the front, and to have strong reserves. In short, you must have a reserve of good and well-armed infantry near the centre to form the wedge and thereby pierce the enemy's line; and also bodies of cavalry armed with lances and cuirasses, with light infantry, near the wings, to surround the flanks of the enemy.

THE POST OF THE GENERAL AND OF THE SECOND AND THIRD IN COMMAND

The post of the commander-in-chief is generally on the right between the cavalry and infantry. For from this place he can best direct the motions of the whole army and move elements with the greatest ease wherever he finds it necessary. It is also the most convenient spot to give his orders to both horse and foot and to animate them equally by his presence. It is his duty to surround the enemy's left wing opposed to him with his reserve of horse and light infantry, and attack it in the flank and rear. The second in command is posted in the centre of the infantry to encourage and support them. A reserve of good and well-armed infantry is near him and under his orders. With this reserve he either forms the wedge to pierce the enemy's line or, if they form the wedge first, prepares the pincers for its reception. The post of the third in command is on the left. He should be a careful and intrepid officer, this part of the army being difficult to manage and defective, as it were, from its situation in the line. He should therefore have a reserve of good cavalry and active infantry to enable him always to extend his left in such a manner as to prevent its being surrounded.

The war shout should not be begun till both armies have joined, for it is a mark of ignorance or cowardice to give it at a distance. The effect is much greater on the enemy when they find themselves struck at the same instant with the horror of the noise and the points of the weapons.

You must always endeavour to get the start of your enemy in drawing up in order of battle, as you will then have it in your power to make your proper dispositions without obstruction. This will increase the courage of your own troops and intimidate your adversaries. For a superiority of courage seems to be implied on the side of an army that offers battle, whereas troops begin to be fearful who see their enemies ready to attack them. You will also secure another great advantage, that of marching up in order and falling upon them while forming and still in confusion. For part of the victory consists in throwing the enemy into disorder before you engage them.

MANEOUVRES IN ACTION

An able general never loses a favourable opportunity of surprising the enemy either when tired on the march, divided in the passage of a river, embarrassed in morasses, struggling with the declivities of mountains, when dispersed over the country they think themselves in security or are sleeping in their quarters. In all these cases the adversaries are surprised and destroyed before they have time to put themselves on their guard. But if they are too cautious to give you an opportunity of surprising or ensnaring them, you are then obliged to engage openly and on equal terms. This at present is foreign to the subject. However military skill is no less necessary in general actions than in carrying on war by subtlety and stratagem.

Your first care is to secure your left wing from being surrounded by the enemy's numbers or attacked in flank or rear by flying platoons, a misfortune that often happens. Nor is your right to be neglected, though less frequently in danger. There is only one remedy for this: to wheel back your wing and throw it into a circular position. By this evolution your soldiers meet the enemy on the quarter attacked and defend the rear of their comrades. But your best men should be posted on the angles of the flanks, since it is against them the enemy make their principal efforts.

There is also a method of resisting the wedge when formed by the enemy. The wedge is a disposition of a body of infantry widening gradually towards the base and terminating in a point towards the front. It pierces the enemy's line by a multitude of darts directed to one particular place. The soldiers call it the swine's head. To oppose this disposition, they make use of another called the pincers, resembling the letter V, composed of a body of men in close order. It receives the wedge, inclosing it on both sides, and thereby prevents it from penetrating the line.

The saw is another disposition formed of resolute soldiers drawn up in a straight line advanced into the front against the enemy, to repair any disorder. The platoon is a body of men separated from the line, to hover on every side and attack the enemy wherever they find opportunity. And against this is to be detached a stronger and more numerous platoon.

Above all, a general must never attempt to alter his dispositions or break his order of battle during the time of action, for such an alteration would immediately Occasion disorder and confusion which the enemy would not fail to improve to their advantage.

VARIOUS FORMATIONS FOR BATTLE

An army may be drawn up for a general engagement in seven different formations. The first formation is an oblong square of a large front, of common use both in ancient and modern times, although not thought the best by various judges of the service, because an even and level plain of an extent sufficient to contain its front cannot always be found, and if there should be any irregularity or hollow in the line, it is often pierced in that part. Besides, an enemy superior in number may surround either your right or left wing, the consequence of which will be dangerous, unless you have a reserve ready to advance and sustain his attack. A general should make use of this disposition only when his forces are better and more numerous than the enemy's, it being thereby in his power to attack both the flanks and surround them on every side.

The second and best disposition is the oblique. For although your army consists of few troops, yet good and advantageously posted, it will greatly contribute to your obtaining the victory, notwithstanding the numbers and bravery of the enemy. It is as follows: as the armies are marching up to the attack, your left wing must be kept back at such a distance from the enemy's right as to be out of reach of their darts and arrows. Your right wing must advance obliquely upon the enemy's left, and begin the engagement. And you must endeavour with your best cavalry and infantry to surround the wing with which you are engaged, make it give way and fall upon the enemy in the rear. If they once give ground and the attack is properly seconded, you will undoubtedly gain the victory, while your left wing, which continued at a distance, will remain untouched. An army drawn up in this manner bears some resemblance to the letter A or a mason's level. If the enemy should be beforehand with you in this evolution, recourse must be had to the supernumerary horse and foot posted as a reserve in the rear, as I mentioned before. They must be ordered to support your left wing. This will enable you to make a vigorous resistance against the artifice of the enemy.

The third formation is like the second, but not so good, as it obliges you to begin the attack with your left wing on the enemy's right. The efforts of soldiers on the left are weak and imperfect from their exposed and defective situation in the line. I will explain this formation more clearly. Although your left wing should be much better than your right, yet it must be reinforced with some of the best horse and foot and ordered to commence the action with the enemy's right in order to disorder and surround it as expeditiously as possible. And the other part of your army, composed of the worst troops, should remain at such a distance from the enemy's left as not to be annoyed by their darts or in danger of being attacked sword in hand. In this oblique formation care must be taken to prevent the line being penetrated by the wedges of the enemy, and it is to be employed only when the enemy's right wing is weak and your greatest strength is on your left.

The fourth formation is this: as your army is marching to the attack in order of battle and you come within four or five hundred paces of the enemy, both your wings must be ordered unexpectedly to quicken their pace and advance with celerity upon them. When they find themselves attacked on both wings at the same time, the sudden surprise may so disconcert them as to give you an easy victory. But although this method, if your troops are very resolute and expert, may ruin the enemy at once, yet it is hazardous. The general who attempts it is obliged to abandon and expose his centre and to divide his army into three parts. If the enemy is not routed at the first charge, they have a fair opportunity of attacking the wings which are separated from each other and the centre which is destitute of assistance.

The fifth formation resembles the fourth but with this addition: the light infantry and the archers are formed before the centre to cover it from the attempts of the enemy. With this precaution the general may safely follow the above mentioned method and attack the enemy's left wing with his right, and their right with his left. If he puts them to flight, he gains an immediate victory, and if he fails of success his centre is in no danger, being protected by the light infantry and archers.

The sixth formation is very good and almost like the second. It is used when the general cannot depend either on the number or courage of his troops. If made with judgment, notwithstanding his inferiority, he has often a good chance for victory. As your line approaches the enemy, advance your right wing against their left and begin the attack with your best cavalry and infantry. At the same time keep the rest of the army at a great distance from the enemy's right, extended in a direct line like a javelin. Thus if you can surround their left and attack it in flank and rear, you must inevitably defeat them. It is impossible for the enemy to draw off reinforcements from their right or from their centre to sustain their left in this emergency, since the remaining part of your army is extended and at a great distance from them in the form of the letter L. It is a formation often used in an action on a march.

The seventh formation owes its advantages to the nature of the ground and will enable you to oppose an enemy with an army inferior both in numbers and goodness, provided one of your flanks can be covered either with an eminence, the sea, a river, a lake, a city, a morass or broken ground inaccessible to the enemy. The rest of the army must be formed, as usual, in a straight line and the unsecured flank must be protected by your light troops and all your cavalry. Sufficiently defended on one side by the nature of the ground and on the other by a double support of cavalry, you may then safely venture on action.

One excellent and general rule must be observed. If you intend to engage with your right wing only, it must be composed of your best troops. And the same method must be taken with respect to the left. Or if you intend to penetrate the enemy's line, the wedges which you form for that purpose before your centre, must consist of the best disciplined soldiers. Victory in general is gained by a small number of men. Therefore the wisdom of a general appears in nothing more than in such choice of disposition of his men as is most consonant with reason and service.

THE FLIGHT OF AN ENEMY SHOULD NOT BE PREVENTED, BUT FACILITATED

Generals unskilled in war think a victory incomplete unless the enemy are so straightened in their ground or so entirely surrounded by numbers as to have no possibility of escape. But in such situation, where no hopes remain, fear itself will arm an enemy and despair inspires courage. When men find they must inevitably perish, they willingly resolve to die with their comrades and with their arms in their hands. The maxim of Scipio, that a golden bridge should be made for a flying enemy, has much been commended. For when they have free room to escape they think of nothing but how to save themselves by flight, and the confusion becoming general, great numbers are cut to pieces. The pursuers can be in no danger when the vanquished have thrown away their arms for greater haste. In this case the greater the number of the flying army, the greater the slaughter. Numbers are of no signification where troops once thrown into consternation are equally terrified at the sight of the enemy as at their weapons. But on the contrary, men when shut up, although weak and few in number, become a match for the enemy from this very reflection, that they have no resource but in despair.

"The conquered's safety is, to hope for none."

MANNER OF CONDUCTING A RETREAT

Having gone through the various particulars relative to general actions, it remains at present to explain the manner of retreating in presence of the enemy. This is an operation, which, in the judgment of men of greatest skill and experience, is attended with the utmost hazard. A general certainly discourages his own troops and animates his enemies by retiring out of the field without fighting. Yet as this must sometimes necessarily happen, it will be proper to consider how to perform it with safety.

In the first place your men must not imagine that you retire to decline an action, but believe your retreat an artifice to draw the enemy into an ambuscade or more advantageous position where you may easier defeat them in case they follow you. For troops who perceive their general despairs of success are prone to flight. You must be cautious lest the enemy should discover your retreat and immediately fall upon you. To avoid this danger the cavalry are generally posted in the front of the infantry to conceal their motions and retreat from the enemy. The first divisions are drawn off first, the others following in their turns. The last maintain their ground till the rest have marched off, and then file off themselves and join them in a leisurely and regular succession. Some generals have judged it best to make their retreat in the night after reconnoitering their routes, and thus gain so much ground that the enemy, not discovering their departure till daybreak, were not able to come up with them. The light infantry was also sent forward to possess the eminences under which the army might instantly retire with safety; and the enemy, in case they pursued, be exposed to the light infantry, masters of the heights, seconded by the cavalry.

A rash and inconsiderate pursuit exposes an army to the greatest danger possible, that of falling into ambuscades and the hands of troops ready for their reception. As the temerity of an army is increased and their caution lessened by the pursuit of a flying enemy, this is the most favourable opportunity for such snares. The greater the security, the greater the danger. Troops, when unprepared, at their meals, fatigued after a march, when their horses are feeding, and in short, when they believe themselves most secure, are generally most liable to a surprise. All risks of this sort are to be carefully avoided and all opportunities taken of distressing the enemy by such methods. Neither numbers nor courage avail in misfortunes of this nature.

A general who has been defeated in a pitched battle, although skill and conduct have the greatest share in the decision, may in his defence throw the blame on fortune. But if he has suffered himself to be surprised or drawn into the snares of his enemy, he has no excuse for his fault, because he might have avoided such a misfortune by taking proper precautions and employing spies on whose intelligence he could depend.

When the enemy pursue a retreating foe, the following snare is usually laid. A small body of cavalry is ordered to pursue them on the direct road.

At the same time a strong detachment is secretly sent another way to conceal itself on their route. When the cavalry have overtaken the enemy, they make some feint attacks and retire. The enemy, imagining the danger past, and that they have escaped the snare, neglect their order and march without regularity. Then the detachment sent to intercept them, seizing the opportunity, falls upon them unexpectedly and destroys them with ease.

Many generals when obliged to retreat through woods send forward parties to seize the defiles and difficult passes, to avoid ambuscades and block the roads with barricades of felled trees to secure themselves from being pursued and attacked in the rear. In short both sides have equal opportunities of surprising or laying ambuscades on the march. The army which retreats leaves troops behind for that purpose posted in convenient valleys or mountains covered with woods, and if the enemy falls into the snare, it returns immediately to their assistance. The army that pursues detaches different parties of light troops to march ahead through by-roads and intercepts the enemy, who are thus surrounded and attacked at once in front and rear. The flying army may return and fall on the enemy while asleep in the night. And the pursuing army may, even though the distance is great, surprise the adversary by forced marches. The former endeavour may be at the crossing of a river in order to destroy such part of the enemy's army as has already crossed. The pursuers hasten their march to fall upon those bodies of the enemy that have not yet crossed.

ARMED CHARIOTS AND ELEPHANTS

The armed chariots used in war by Antiochus and Mithridates at first terrified the Romans, but they afterwards made a jest of them. As a chariot of this sort does not always meet with plain and level ground, the least obstruction stops it. And if one of the horses be either killed or wounded, it falls into the enemy's hands. The Roman soldiers rendered them useless chiefly by the following contrivance: at the instant the engagement began, they strewed the field of battle with caltrops, and the horses that drew the chariots, running full speed on them, were infallibly destroyed. A caltrop is a machine composed of four spikes or points arranged so that in whatever manner it is thrown on the ground, it rests on three and presents the fourth upright.

Elephants by their vast size, horrible noise and the novelty of their form are at first very terrible both to men and horses. Pyrrhus first used them against the Romans in Lucania. And afterwards Hannibal brought them into the field in Africa. Antiochus in the east and Jugurtha in Numidia had great numbers. Many expedients have been used against them. In Lucania a centurion cut off the trunk of one with his sword. Two soldiers armed from head to foot in a chariot drawn by two horses, also covered with armour, attacked these beasts with lances of great length. They were secured by their armour from the archers on the elephants and avoided the fury of the animals by the swiftness of their horses. Foot soldiers completely armoured, with the addition of long iron spikes fixed on their arms, shoulders and helmets, to prevent the elephant from seizing them with his trunk, were also employed against them.

But among the ancients, the *velites* usually engaged them. They were young soldiers, lightly armed, active and very expert in throwing their missile weapons on horseback. These troops kept hovering round the elephants continually and killed them with large lances and javelins. Afterwards, the soldiers, as their apprehensions decreased, attacked them in a body and, throwing their javelins together, destroyed them by the multitude of wounds. Slingers with round stones from the *fustibalus* and sling killed both the men who guided the elephants and the soldiers who fought in the towers on their backs. This was found by experience to be the best and safest expedient. At other times on the approach of these beasts, the soldiers opened their ranks and let them pass through. When they got into the midst of the troops, who surrounded them on all sides, they were captured with their guards unhurt.

Large *balistae*, drawn on carriages by two horses or mules, should be placed in the rear of the line, so that when the elephants come within reach they may be transfixed with the darts. The *balistae* should be larger and the heads of the darts stronger and broader than usual, so that the darts may be thrown farther, with greater force and the wounds be proportioned to the bodies of the beasts. It was proper to describe these several methods and contrivances employed against elephants, so that it may be known on occasion in what manner to oppose those prodigious animals.

RESOURCES IN CASE OF DEFEAT

If while one part of your army is victorious the other should be defeated, you are by no means to despair, since even in this extremity the constancy and resolution of a general may recover a complete victory. There are innumerable instances where the party that gave least way to despair was esteemed the conqueror. For where losses and advantages seem nearly equal, he is reputed to have the superiority who bears up against his misfortunes with greatest resolution. He is therefore to be first, if possible, to seize the spoils of the slain and to make rejoicings for the victory. Such marks of confidence dispirit the enemy and redouble your own courage.

Yet notwithstanding an entire defeat, all possible remedies must be attempted, since many generals have been fortunate enough to repair such a loss. A prudent officer will never risk a general action without taking such precautions as will secure him from any considerable loss in case of a defeat, for the uncertainty of war and the nature of things may render such a misfortune unavoidable. The neighbourhood of a mountain, a fortified post in the rear or a resolute stand made by a good body of troops to cover the retreat, may be the means of saving the army.

An army after a defeat has sometimes rallied, returned on the enemy, dispersed him by pursuing in order and destroyed him without difficulty. Nor can men be in a more dangerous situation than, when in the midst of joy after victory, their exultation is suddenly converted into terror. Whatever be the event, the remains of the army must be immediately assembled, reanimated by suitable exhortations and furnished with fresh supplies of arms. New levies should immediately be made and new reinforcements provided. And it is of much the greatest consequence that proper opportunities should be taken to surprise the victorious enemies, to draw them into snares and ambuscades and by this means to recover the drooping spirits of your men. Nor will it be difficult to meet with such opportunities, as the nature of the human mind is apt to be too much elated and to act with too little caution in prosperity. If anyone should imagine no resource is left after the loss of a battle, let him reflect on what has happened in similar cases and he will find that they who were victorious in the end were often unsuccessful in the beginning.

GENERAL MAXIMS

- It is the nature of war that what is beneficial to you is detrimental to the enemy and what is of service to him always hurts you. It is therefore a maxim never to do, or to omit doing, anything as a consequence of his actions, but to consult invariably your own interest only. And you depart from this interest whenever you imitate such measures as he pursues for his benefit. For the same reason it would be wrong for him to follow such steps as you take for your advantage.
- The more your troops have been accustomed to camp duties on frontier stations and the more carefully they have been disciplined, the less danger they will be exposed to in the field. Men must be sufficiently tried before they are led against the enemy.

- It is much better to overcome the enemy by famine, surprise or terror than by general actions, for in the latter instance fortune has often a greater share than valour. Those designs are best which the enemy are entirely ignorant of till the moment of execution. Opportunity in war is often more to be depended on than courage.
- To debauch the enemy's soldiers and encourage them when sincere in surrendering themselves, is of especial service, for an adversary is more hurt by desertion than by slaughter.
- It is better to have several bodies of reserves than to extend your front too much.
- A general is not easily overcome who can form a true judgment of his own and the enemy's forces.
- Valour is superior to numbers.
- The nature of the ground is often of more consequence than courage.
- Few men are born brave; many become so through care and force of discipline.
- An army is strengthened by labour and enervated by idleness.
- Troops are not to be led to battle unless confident of success.
- Novelty and surprise throw an enemy into consternation; but common incidents have no effect.
- He who rashly pursues a flying enemy with troops in disorder, seems inclined to resign that victory which he had before obtained.
- An army unsupplied with grain and other necessary provisions will be vanquished without striking a blow.
- A general whose troops are superior both in number and bravery should engage in the oblong square, which is the first formation.
- He who judges himself inferior should advance his right wing obliquely against the enemy's left. This is the second formation.
- If your left wing is strongest, you must attack the enemy's right according to the third formation.
- The general who can depend on the discipline of his men should begin the engagement by attacking both the enemy's wings at once, the fourth formation.
- He whose light infantry is good should cover his centre by forming them in its front and charge both the enemy's wings at once. This is the fifth formation.
- He who cannot depend either on the number or courage of his troops, if obliged to engage, should begin the action with his right and

endeavour to break the enemy's left, the rest of his army remaining formed in a line perpendicular to the front and extended to the rear like a javelin. This is the sixth formation.

- If your forces are few and weak in comparison to the enemy, you must make use of the seventh formation and cover one of your flanks either with an eminence, a city, the sea, a river or some protection of that kind.
- A general who trusts to his cavalry should choose the proper ground for them and employ them principally in the action.
- He who depends on his infantry should choose a situation most proper for them and make most use of their service.
- When an enemy's spy lurks in the camp, order all your soldiers in the day time to their tents, and he will instantly be apprehended.
- On finding the enemy has notice of your designs, you must immediately alter your plan of operations.
- Consult with many on proper measures to be taken, but communicate the plans you intend to put in execution to few, and those only of the most assured fidelity; or rather trust no one but yourself.
- Punishment, and fear thereof, are necessary to keep soldiers in order in quarters; but in the field they are more influenced by hope and rewards.
- Good officers never engage in general actions unless induced by opportunity or obliged by necessity.
- To distress the enemy more by famine than the sword is a mark of consummate skill.
- Many instructions might be given with regard to the cavalry. But as this branch of the service has been brought to perfection since the ancient writers and considerable improvements have been made in their drills and manoeuvres, their arms, and the quality and management of their horses, nothing can be collected from their works. Our present mode of discipline is sufficient.
- Dispositions for action must be carefully concealed from the enemy, lest they should counteract them and defeat your plans by proper expedients.

This abridgment of the most eminent military writers, invincible Emperor, contains the maxims and instructions they have left us, approved by different ages and confirmed by repeated experience. The Persians admire your skill in archery; the Huns and Alans endeavour in vain to imitate your dexterity in horsemanship; the Saracens and Indians cannot equal your activity in the hunt; and even the masters at arms pique themselves on only part of that knowledge and expertness of which you give so many instances in their own profession. How glorious it is therefore for Your Majesty with all these qualifications to unite the science of war and the art of conquest, and to convince the world that by your conduct and courage. You are equally capable of performing the duties of the soldier and the general.

CHAPTER 4

FREDERICK THE GREAT: INSTRUCTIONS

"In order to rest oneself it is necessary to keep the enemy occupied. This throws them back on the defensive, and once they are placed that way they can not rise up again during the entire campaign"

— Frederick the Great, 1712-1786

From Vegetius to Frederick II 'The Great', King of Prussia (1713-86) is a quantum jump from 390 AD to 1740 AD. But, as already mentioned earlier Vegetius had dominated military thought for over a thousand years; and it can be said that the turning point, or commencement of the modern era, started with Frederick the Great.[1]

It would be too simplistic, if not facile, to condense here the history of development of warfare from the time of Vegetius to Frederick the Great, in order to provide continuity or the necessary backdrop.[2] Much development in the conduct of warfare had taken place, the major one being due to the discovery of gun powder. There were many other technological innovations like the introduction of the crossbow. Chariots disappeared form the battlefield (they reappeared in the form of "tanks" in the First World War) and artillery came in as the third major "arm" in the battlefield.

Many techniques of warfare had been developed, for instance "siege warfare" and assaults against fortified towns or forts. The pendulum had swung from very heavily armoured knights or equally heavily armoured horses (during the Crusades and much of the medieval period) to lightly armoured and mobile cavalry. From heavy phalanxes and legions, "lines" were organized in a manner that fire could be best delivered. After the Roman legions (predominantly infantry) the battlefield came to be dominated by cavalry till about the 15th century. Infantry started slowly to regain its supremacy when Swiss pikemen proved that infantrymen could go into attack even against cavalry. Many great Captains had come on the scene, Jenghiz Khan, Sabutai (both masters of cavalry), Richard the Lionheart (in the

Crusades), Edward III (Battle of Crecy), Gustavus Adolphus, Cromwell, Marlborough and many others.

The career of Frederick defies a simple appreciation. He was a cultured individual who loved music, architecture and philosophy. At the same time he was also a brutal and cynical warmonger, who carried out a series of campaigns throughout his reign that emptied his treasury and caused the death of a large number of his subjects. His reputation as a military genius is, therefore, debatable. He did win a number of startling victories in war and hung onto his conquests against great odds. His military system perfected the existing art of war. Also, he pushed warfare to the limits of ruthlessness, within the prevailing code of conduct. He exhorted his generals to practice warfare with a ruthlessness that other rulers considered beyond proper. He also introduced a degree of conscription, something that was formally declared by the French Republic, in August 1793, when it was passed that: 'until the moment when enemies have been driven from the Republic's territory, all Frenchmen are permanently requisitioned for the service of the armies'. Frederick recruited the nucleus of his officer corps from the Teutonic Knights, which helped create a form of regimented army. It was this small army of highly disciplined regulars that frequently beat the armies of states much larger than his own.

Frederick's army reflected the state. The officers fought for honour, ambition and glory, while the soldiers enlisted for a source of livelihood. Recruits into the army were generally from the lowest strata of society. In order to retain them, governments built their morale through physical care of their well-being. The bonding of the officers and soldiers was carried out through discipline and training. Group cohesion became a major factor in the successful conduct of warfare. The state of Prussia owed its existence and identity to its army. In such a backdrop, military science, politics and economics were rolled into the mechanics of statecraft. The credo for the army was: "no one reasons; everyone executes". Everything flowed from the mind of the king or general. To achieve this mindset, training was essential, in order for the army to be completely responsive to commands: "Unless every man is trained beforehand in peacetime for that which he will have to accomplish in war, one has nothing but people who bear the name of a business without knowing how to practice it".

Frederick wrote "The Instructions of Frederick the Great for his Generals" around 1747 when he was convalescing from a bout of illness. He revised it in 1748 and called it "General Principles of War". It was classified "Secret" and written in French. Limited copies only were printed and given to his army commanders. A copy was found by the Austrians when they managed to capture General Czetteriz, in February 1760. It caused an immediate sensation and in the next few years, was translated into most of the European languages.

The book is a lengthy one. It is in the form of straight forward instructions as to what to do and what not to do, illustrated by examples and diagrams. In present day terminology it can be said that Frederick the Great drew "lessons" from various battles and instructed his commanders to follow them.

Frederick the Great covered a very wide canvas commencing from an analysis of Prussian troops, their deficiencies and advantages, capabilities and merits. It is followed by instructions as to how to plan a campaign. It is specific in nature, e.g. Frederick illustrated the planning of offensive action against Saxony, Bohemia and Moravia. One was expected to derive the general principles from these. His first instructions are to know one's enemy and the nature of the country. He cautions against over ambitious offensives involving deep penetration which cannot be sustained, as also, on a campaign based on absolute defensive techniques. "Thus I prefer to this conduct (implying defensive) the temerity of the offensive with the hazard of losing the battle since this will not be more fatal than your retreat and your trivial defensive".

He enjoins his generals to carefully study the frontiers and examine different points of attack and thus arrive at the locality through which the advance should take place. He propagated the idea of what today would be called offensive defence.[3] "I am now coming to what I call defensive which turns into offensive". He does that by giving two projects of defensive action—one for Silesia and the other for Brandenburg. But, before doing so, he also states: "the greatest secret of war and the masterpiece of a skilful general is to starve his enemy. Since it is very rare that a war is ended by the capture of a depot and matters are only decided by great battles, it is necessary to employ all these means to attain this object". Frederick was a great advocate of the offensive. It was always the offensive, in every situation, in the whole of the operation as well as battle, even in the presence of a superior enemy. He writes, "One should not embarrass oneself in the project of campaign with the number of the enemy, provided they do not extend you more than a third. That is to say, with 7,500 men, you can attack 10,00,00 in all security and even promise yourself to defeat them".

He continues with instructions on what today will be called" Administration and Logistics". These are headed "Subsistence and Commissary"; "Beer, Brandy and Sutlers"; "Green and Dry Forage"; "Encampments and Measures of Security taken for the Protection of the Camp".

He returns to strategy with an exposition on a general's coup d'oeil. According to him, it is "the talent which great men have of conceiving in a moment all the advantage of the terrain and the use they can make of it with their army". He follows with many instructions, basically dealing with tactics or miscellaneous matters like disposition of the troops, how detachments should be formed and deployed, ("None should be, except for good reasons, if you are acting offensively in open enemy country") – an indirect plea for concentration of force; how to march an army forward or in retreat and for relief, various formations to be adopted for retreat, how to deal with hussars, pandours,[4] lightly armed troops; and lines that can be used where one is weaker in order to defeat the enemy, and a host of other matters. Tactics and strategy[5] is so mixed in his instruction, it becomes difficult to sort them out fully without distorting their meaning.

Therefore, unlike the practice followed in the previous two chapters, no attempt will be made to summarize his writings. Instead some outstanding aspects will be highlighted.

Fredericks' tactics and strategy was based on mobility, on which he laid great emphasis; thus his detailed instructions on marches. He illustrated the composition of a marching army and showed how a balanced composition should be achieved. He left detailed instructions as to how to march through defiles, and protection of columns in retreat.[6] An innovation that he developed was forming divisions of armies so that they could march in a number of columns with less fatigue.

His exposition on how to prepare and defend entrenchments and how to overcome them remained the guidelines for many years to come. Frederick can also be credited with idea of winning the "fire fight" before an infantry assault.[7] He wrote: ". . . to attack the enemy without procuring oneself the advantage of superior , or at least equal fire, is to wish to fight against an enemy armed with clubs and this is impossible". He elaborated later: "Battles are won by superiority of fire".

Oblique order has more or less come to be synonymous with Frederick the Great. It was a very practical method of enveloping an enemy army, by appropriate placement of cavalry, infantry and horsed artillery at one of the flanks. It obviated a frontal clash between opposing forces. Its purpose was that, in case of success, a quick victory could be gained by rolling up the enemy flank; and, in case of failure, to minimize losses, since one wing could cover the withdrawal of the other. He illustrated his design (by actual drawings)[8] and by way of detailed explanation: "you see how I fortify my right with which I want to make my principle effort. I have placed a body of infantry on the flank of the cavalry to fire from the woods on the enemy cavalry. I have three lines of cavalry and three lines of infantry, and my left is only for the purpose of containing the enemy's right wing, while all my forces act on the right".

Although not entirely relevant, mention needs to be made of Frederick's exposition on what he termed as "the Talents that a General must have - ruses, stratagems of war, spies". He starts with: "A perfect General, like Plato's Republic, is a figment of imagination". He then goes on to expound many qualities that a general should have, his behaviour, the manner he should plan a campaign, and how to maintain morale. He also devoted a major portion of this chapter on ruses and stratagems a general should use to keep secrecy, and to achieve security to outwit the enemy.

Frederick also propagated the idea of "short and lively' wars where a speedy decision should be sought. He was also not in favour of full-size battles, as their outcome depended too much on chance (which was the opposite of rational calculation): "It is to be remarked, in addition, that most generals in love with battle resort to this expedient for want of other resources. Far from being considered a merit in them, this is usually thought a sign of the sterility of their talents".

Frederick's strategic objective during his campaigns was never the annihilation of the enemy's main combat force. His main purpose in battle was to force the enemy to move: "To win a battle means to compel your opponent to yield to you his position". He further added that, "manoeuvres in war turn upon the positions which a general may occupy with advantage and positions which a general may attack with the least loss".

Frederick the Great also warned that one should not follow rules, 'as a blind man follows a wall', and like all successful military commanders ignored the accepted principles of war when instinct and experience spoke otherwise. We do tend to read more about those who break the rules and succeed, because those who break them and fail tend to have very brief careers.

NOTES

1. Purely from the point of view of historiography, it would have been desirable to include Marshal Saxe before coming to Frederick the Great. In fact, it was the study carried out by Saxe and the innovations on marching and organizing that Saxe had arrived at, that paved the way for improvements in the art of war brought about by Frederick the Great. However, Saxe and Frederick the Great were rather close to each other. Saxe published his book in 1732, while Frederick the Great's instructions became well known by 1747. Frederick the Great has been chosen because he was a great admirer of Saxe and incorporated much of Saxe's teachings in his Instructions. Indeed, it can be said that Frederick was the inheritor and executor of Saxe's legacy.
2. Liddell Hart divides the period of development of strategy (up to the First World War) in three broad periods and categories: Greek and Roman Wars, ending with the Byzantine wars and exploits of Belisarius i.e. the ancient period; the medieval wars which he thought was only a link between the ancient and the modern history; and the commencement of the modern period with the Thirty Years War (1618-48).
3. This dictum needs to be seen in the light of the general practice followed in his days. Usually two armies manoeuvred, jockeying for position, even when they had encountered each other. It took days, weeks, even months before accepting an engagements or battle. Either side could refuse battle because they could get away while the opposing side was arranging their lines. Even Saxe was a great believer in positional warfare. Frederick changed this position by immediate attacks. However, in the medieval period, it was Machiavelli who advocated the reintroduction of the "battle". Frederick developed it further to mean battle and offensive action.
4. Hussars originally were the soldiers of national cavalry of Hungary (15th Century). It later came to mean Light Infantry. Pandours were Croatian infantry serving in the Austrian Army. Frederick used the term somewhat derogatively as many of them were bandits.
5. It needs to be remembered that Frederick combined in himself the national policy maker (The King), the strategist (as Supreme Commander) and the general who actually commanded in battle. Napoleon was possibly last of this line that did not have to deal with diverse authorities.
6. Because of Frederick's emphasis on the offensive, it is often forgotten that Frederick did lose quite a few battles. He had retreated from Libenther and Trantenea, both in 1745. Of course, it could be said that a part of his manoeuvre was retreat. According to many historians, he retreated to draw the enemy in and then administer a sharp blow or defeat, as in Cholusitz (Silesia).
7. This is one area where Frederick had diverted from Saxe. In the beginning, Frederick shared the belief with Saxe that firearms did not have much use; and his soldiers, as was the practice those days, carried their guns on their shoulders. Frederick's instructions, in fact till about 1758, were that "fire" should be used as little as possible in the attack. Later, he changed his idea. The idea of winning the battle or making a path for assaulting infantry by fire, of course, got fully developed by Napoleon and reached ridiculous proportions during the First World War.
8. Frederick had used the example to illustrate how the enemy can be defeated when you are weaker.

MILITARY INSTRUCTIONS
FREDERICK THE GREAT

THE KING OF PRUSSIA'S MILITARY INSTRUCTIONS TO HIS GENERALS

ARTICLE I
Of Prussian Troops, their Excellencies and their Defects

The strictest care and the most unremitting attention are required of commanding officers in the formation of my troops. The most exact discipline is ever to be maintained, and the greatest regard paid to their welfare; they ought also to be better fed than almost any troops in Europe.

Our regiments are composed of half our own people and half foreigners who enlist for money: the latter only wait for a favourable opportunity to quit a service to which they have no particular attachment. The prevention of desertion therefore becomes an object of importance.

Many of our generals regard one man as good in effect as another, and imagine that if the vacancy be filled up, this man has no influence on the whole; but one does not know how on this subject to make a proper application of other armies to our own.

If a deserter be replaced by a man as well trained and disciplined as himself, it is a matter of no consequence; but if a soldier, who for two years has been accustomed to arms and military exercise, should desert, and be replaced by a bad subject, or perhaps none at all, the consequence must prove eventually very material.

It has happened from the negligence of officers in this particular, that regiments have not only been lessened in number, but that they have also lost their reputation.

By accidents of this kind, the army becomes weakened at the very period when its completion is most essentially necessary, and unless the greatest attention is paid to the circumstance, you will lose the best of your forces and never be able to recover yourself.

Though my country be well peopled, it is doubtful if many men are to be met with of the height of my soldiers: and supposing ever that there was no want of them, could they be disciplined in an instant? It therefore becomes one of the most essential duties of generals who command armies or detachments, to prevent desertion. This is to be effected,

1. By not encamping too near a wood or forest, unless sufficient reason require it.
2. By calling the roll frequently every day.
3. By often sending out patrols of hussars, to scour the country round about the camp.
4. By placing chasseurs in the corn by night, and doubling the cavalry posts at dusk to strengthen the chain.
5. By not allowing the soldiers to wander about, and taking care that each troop be led regularly to water and forage by an officer.
6. By punishing all marauding with severity, as it gives rise to every species of disorder and irregularity.
7. By not drawing in the guards, who are placed in the villages on marching days, until the troops are under arms.
8. By forbidding, under the strictest injunctions, that any soldier on a march quit his rank or his division.
9. By avoiding night-marches, unless obliged by necessity.
10. By pushing forward patrols of hussars to the right and left, whilst the infantry are passing through a wood.
11. By placing officers at each end of a defile, to oblige the soldiers to fall into their proper places.
12. By concealing from the soldier any retrograde movement which you may be obliged to make, or giving some specious flattering pretext for doing so.
13. By paying great attention to the regular issue of necessary subsistence, and taking care that the troops be furnished with bread, flesh, beer, brandy, etc.
14. By searching for the cause of the evil, when desertion shall have crept into a regiment or company: enquiring if the soldier has received his bounty and other customary indulgencies, and if there has been no misconduct on the part of the captain. No relaxation of discipline is however on any account to be permitted. It may be said, that the colonel will take care of this business, but his efforts alone cannot be sufficient; for in an army, every individual part of it should aim at perfection, to make it appear to be the work of only one man.

An army is composed for the most part of idle and inactive men and unless the general has a constant eye upon them, and obliges them to do their duty, this artificial machine, which with the greatest care cannot be made perfect, will very soon fall to pieces, and nothing but the bare idea of a disciplined army will remain.

Constant employment for the troops is therefore indispensably necessary: the experience of officers who adopt such plan will convince them of its good effects, and they will also perceive that there are daily abuses to be corrected, which pass unobserved by those who are too indolent to endeavour to discover them.

This constant and painful attention may appear at first sight as rather a hardship on the general, but its consequences will make him ample amends. With troops so fine, so brave, and so well disciplined, what advantage can he not obtain? A general, who with other nations would be regarded as being rash or half mad, would with us be only acting by established rules. Any enterprise which man is capable of executing, may be undertaken by him. Besides this, the soldiers will not suffer a man to remain amongst them who has betrayed any symptoms of shyness, which would certainly not be regarded in other armies.

I have been an eye-witness to the conduct both of officers and private soldiers, who could not be prevailed on, though dangerously wounded, to quit their post, or fall into the rear to get themselves dressed. With troops like these the world itself might be subdued, if conquests were not as fatal to the victors as to the vanquished. Let them be but well supplied with provisions, and you may attempt any thing with them. On a march you prevent the enemy by speed; at an attack of a wood, you will force them; if you make them climb a mountain, you will soon disperse those who make any resistance, and it then becomes an absolute massacre. If you put your cavalry into action, they will charge through the enemy at the sword's point and demolish them.

But as it is not alone sufficient that the troops be good, and as the ignorance of a general may be the means of losing every advantage, I shall proceed to speak of the qualities which a general ought to possess, and lay down such rules as I have either learned from well-informed generals, or purchased dearly by my own experience.

ARTICLE II
Of the Subsistence of Troops, and of Provisions

It has been said by a certain general, that the first object in the establishment of an army ought to be making provision for the belly, that being the basis and foundation of all operations. I shall divide this subject into two parts: in the first I shall explain how and where magazines ought to be established, and in the latter, the method of employing, and transporting them.

The first rule is to establish the large magazines invariably in the rear of the army, and, if possible, in a place that is well secured. During the wars in Silesia and Bohemia, our grand magazine was at Breslau, on account of the advantage of being able to replenish it by means of the Oder. When magazines are formed at the head of an army, the first check may oblige you to abandon them, and you may be left without resource; whereas, if they Are established in the rear of each other, the war will be prudently carried on, and one small disaster will not complete your ruin.

Spandau and Magdebourg should be the chosen situations for magazines in the frontier of the Electorate. Magdebourg, on account of the Elbe, will be particularly serviceable in an offensive war against Saxony, and Schweidenitz against Bohemia.

You cannot be too cautious in the choice of commissaries and their deputies, for if they prove dishonest, the state will be materially injured. With this view, men of strict honour should be appointed as superiors, who must personally, frequently, and minutely examine and control the accounts.

There are two ways of forming magazines, either by ordering the nobility and peasants to bring their grain to the depot, and paying them for it according to the rate laid down by the chamber of finance, or by taking a certain quantity from them by requisition. It is the business of the commissary to settle and to sign all these agreements.

Vessels of a particular construction are built for the purpose of conveying corn and forage along the canals and rivers.

Purveyors are never to be employed but in cases of the last necessity, for even Jews [sic] are less exorbitant in their demands: they increase the price of provisions, and sell them out again at a most extravagant profit.

The magazines should be established at a very early period, that no kind of necessary may be wanting when the army leaves its quarters to being a campaign: if they be too long neglected, the frost will put a stop to water-carriage, or the roads will become so excessively deep and heavy, that their formation will be a business of the utmost difficulty.

Besides the regimental covered wagons which carry bread for eight days, the commissary is provided with conveniences for carrying provisions for a month.

The advantage of navigation is, however, never to be neglected, for without this convenience, no army can ever be abundantly supplied.

The wagons should be drawn by horses: trial has been made of oxen, but they do not answer the purpose.

The wagon-masters must be exceedingly careful that due attention be paid to their cattle. The general of an army must also have an eye to this circumstance, for the loss of horses will necessarily occasion a diminution of wagons, and consequently of provisions.

Moreover, unless they receive a proper quantity of good food, these horses will be unable to undergo the necessary fatigue. On a march, therefore, not only the horses will be lost, but also the wagons and their contents. The best concerted measures may be ruined by a repetition of such disasters. The general, therefore, must not neglect any of these circumstances, which are so materially important in all his operations.

In order to facilitate the carriage of provisions in a war against Saxony, advantage must be taken of the Elbe, and in Silesia of the Oder. The sea affords you this assistance in Prussia , but in Bohemia and Moravia, your only dependence is on carriages. It sometimes happens, that three or four depots of provisions are formed on the same line, as was the case with us in Bohemia in the year 1742. There was a magazine at Pardubitz, at Nienbourg, at Podjebrod, and at Brandies, to enable us to keep pace with the enemy, and follow him to Prague, if he had thought proper to have gone thither.

During the last campaign in Bohemia, Breslau furnished Schweidenitz, Schweidenitz supplied Jaromirez, and from thence provisions were carried to the army.

Besides the covered wagons which carry provisions, iron ovens always travel with the army, (the number of which has of late been very much augmented), and, on every halting day they are set to bake bread. On all expeditions, you should be supplied with bread or biscuit for ten days. Biscuits is a very good article, but our soldiers like it only in soup, nor do they know how to employ it to the best advantage.

On a march through an enemy's country, the depot of meal should ever be in a garrisoned town near the army. During the campaign of 1745, our depot was first at Neustadt, then at Jaromirez, and last at Trautenau. Had we been farther advanced, we could not have had a depot in security nearer than that at Pardubitz.

I have provided hand-mills for each company, which are found to be exceedingly useful, as they are worked by the soldiers, who carry the meal to the depot, and receive bread in return. With this meal, you are enabled to husband your magazines, and have it in your power to remain much longer in camp than you could without such supply. Moreover, fewer escorts, and a smaller number of convoys will also be found sufficient.

On the subject of convoys, I must enlarge a little. The strength of escorts depends on the fear which you entertain of the enemy. Detachments of infantry are sent into the towns through which the convoy will pass, to afford then a point of support. Large detachments to cover them are sometimes sent out, as was the case in Bohemia.

In all chequered countries, convoys should be escorted by the infantry, to which a few hussars may be added, in order to keep a lookout on the march, and inform themselves of all situations where the enemy may lie concealed.

My escorts have been formed of infantry in preference to cavalry even in a plain country, and in my own opinion, with very much advantage.

For what regards the minutiae of escorts, I refer you to my military regulation. The general of an army cannot be too anxious about the security of his convoys.

One good rule to attain this end is, to send troops forward for the purpose of occupying the defiles through which the convoy is to pass, and to push the escort a league in front towards the enemy. By this manoeuvre the convoys are masked, and arrive in security.

ARTICLE III
Of Sutlers, Beer, and Brandy

When you have it in contemplation to make any enterprise on the enemy, the commissary must be ordered to get together all the beer and brandy that he can lay his hands on, that the army may not want these articles, at least for the first days. As soon as the army enters an enemy's country, all the brewers and distillers who are in the neighbourhood must immediately be put in requisition: the distillers, in particular, must be instantly set to work, that the soldier may not lose his dram, which he can very badly spare.

Protection must be afforded to the sutlers, especially in a country whose inhabitants are fled, and where provisions cannot be had for money. At such a time we are justified in not being over nice with respect to the peasantry.

The sutlers and women must be sent out in search of vegetables and cattle. The price of provisions is however, a matter that requires much attention, as the soldier ought to be allowed to purchase at a reasonable price, and at the same time the sutler should derive an honest profit.

It may here be added, that the soldier receives gratis during a campaign two pounds of bread per day, and two pounds of flesh per week. It is an indulgence which the poor fellows richly deserve, especially in Bohemia, where the country is but little better than a desert.

Convoys for the army should ever be followed by herds of cattle, for the support and nourishment of the soldier.

ARTICLE IV
Of Dry and Green Forage

Oats, barley, hay, chopped straw, etc. compose what is called dry forage, and are carried to the magazine. If the oats be either fusty or moldy, the horses will contract the mange and farcy, and be so weakened as to be unserviceable even at the beginning of a campaign. Chopped straw is given because it is the custom, though it serves but barely to fill the belly.

The first object in collecting forage and carrying it to the magazine is, either to get the start of the enemy at the opening of a campaign, or to be prepared for some distant enterprise. But an army can seldom venture to move far from its magazines, as long as the horses are obliged to live on dry forage, on account of the inconvenience of moving it, as a whole province is sometimes unable to furnish a sufficient number of carriages. And in general, these are not the methods that we employ in an offensive war, unless there are no rivers, by means of which the forage can be transported.

During the campaign in Silesia, all my cavalry lived on dry forage, but we only marched from Strehla to Schwiednitz (where there was a magazine,) and from thence to Cracau, where we were in the neighbourhood of the Brieg and the Oder.

When any enterprise is about to take place in the winter, the cavalry should carry with them forage for five days, well bound together on their horses, if Bohemia or Moravia are to be the scene of action, unless you mean to destroy all your cavalry. We forage in the fields for corn and vegetables as long as any remain there, and thereafter the harvest in the villages.

When we encamp on a spot where we mean to make some stay, an account should be taken of the forage; and when its quantity be ascertained, a regular distribution of it should be made according to the number of days which we intend to remain.

All large foraging parties are escorted by a body of cavalry, the strength of which is proportioned to the vicinity of the enemy, and the fear which you entertain of him. Foraging is sometimes carried on by the wings, or even the whole of an army.

The foragers always assemble on the road which they intend taking, either on the wings, in front, or in the rear of the army.

The advanced guard is composed of hussars, who are followed by the cavalry in a plain country, but in irregular situations, the infantry go before them. The advanced guard is to precede the march of about a fourth part of the foragers, who are to be followed by a detachment of the escort, partly horse and partly foot; then another party of foragers, followed by a detachment of troops, and after them the remainder in the same order. The march of the rear guard is to be closed by a troop of hussars, who will form the rear of the whole column.

It is to be remembered, that in all escorts the infantry take their cannon with them, and the foragers their swords and carbines.

When arrived at the spot where they intend foraging, a chain is to be formed, and the infantry posted near the villages, behind the hedges, and in the hollow ways. Troops of cavalry joined with infantry should be formed into a reserve, and placed in the centre to be ready to support any point where the enemy may endeavour to make an impression. The hussars are to skirmish with the enemy, in order to amuse them and draw them off from the forage. As soon as the enclosure is complete, the foragers divide the ground by regiments. Great care must be taken by the officers commanding, that the trusses be made very large, and bound well together.

When the horses are laden, the foragers are to return to camp by troops, protected by small escorts, and as soon as they have all left the ground, the troops of the chain are to assemble and form the rear guard, followed by the hussars.

The method of foraging in villages differs from the foregoing only in this instance, viz. the infantry are posted round the village, and the cavalry behind them in a situation where they may be able to act. Villages are to be foraged one by one, to prevent the troops of the chain from being too much dispersed.

In mountainous countries, foraging becomes an arduous business, and on such occasions the greatest part of the escorts must be composed of infantry and hussars.

When we are encamped near the enemy, and intend remaining there some time, we must endeavour to secure the forage which is between the two camps. After that, we are to forage for two leagues round, beginning with the most distant fields, and preserving those that are near home till the last. If no stay be intended, we forage in the camp and in the neighbourhood.

When it becomes an object to secure a large quantity of green forage, I would rather send the parties out twice, than occupy too great an extent of country at once. By this means you will preserve your chain more snug and compact, and the foragers will be in much greater security: whereas if too great a space be occupied, the chain must consequently be weakened and rendered liable to be forced.

ARTICLE V
Of the Knowledge of a Country

The knowledge of a country is to be attained in two ways; the first (and that with which we ought to begin) is, by a careful and studious examination of a map of the country which is intended to be the scene of war, and by marking on it very distinctly the names of all the rivers, towns, and mountains that are of any consequence.

Having by this means gained a general idea of the country, we must proceed to a more particular and minute examination of it, to inform ourselves of the directions of the high roads, the situation of the towns, whether by a little trouble they can be made tenable, on what side to attack them if they are possessed by the enemy, and what number of troops are necessary for their defence.

We should also be provided with plans of the fortified towns, that we may be acquainted with their strength, and what are their most assailable parts. The course and depth of the large rivers should also be ascertained, how far they are navigable, and if shallow enough at any points to allow of being forded. It should also be known, what rivers are impassible in spring and dry in summer. This sort of enquiry must extend likewise to the marshes of any consequence that may be in the country.

In a flat, smooth country, the fertile parts should be distinguished from those that are not so, and we must be well acquainted with all the marches that either the enemy or ourselves can undertake, to pass from one great city or river to another. It will be necessary also to break up those camps, which are liable to be taken on that route.

A flat, open country can be reconnoitered presently, but the view is so confined in that which is woody and mountainous, that it becomes a business of much difficulty.

In order, therefore, to procure intelligence so highly important, we must ascend the heights, taking the map with us, and also some of the elders of the neighbouring villages, such as huntsmen and shepherds. If there be one mountain higher than another, that must be ascended, to gain an idea of a country which we wish to discover.

We must gain a knowledge of the roads, not only to be satisfied in how many columns we may march, but also that we may be enabled to plan a variety of projects, and be informed how we may reach the enemy's camp and force it, should any be established in the neighbourhood, or how place ourselves on his flank, should he alter his position.

One of the most material objects is, to reconnoitre situations that, in case of necessity, may serve as camps of defence, as well as a field of battle, and the posts that may be occupied by the enemy.

A just idea must be formed of all these matters of intelligence, as well as of the most considerable posts, the valleys, chief defiles, and all the advantageous situations which the country affords: and we must seriously reflect on every operation that may take place, so that by being prepared beforehand with a plan of arrangements, we may not be embarrassed when called into action. These reflections should be well connected, and maturely digested, with all the care and patience that an object of so much consequence requires; and unless we can arrange the matter to our satisfaction the first time, we must try it over again and again till we have got it perfect.

It is a general rule in the choice of all camps, whether for offence or defence, that both wood and water be near at hand, that the front be close and well covered, and the rear perfectly open.

If circumstances forbid the examination of a country in the manner laid down, clever, intelligent officers should be sent thither under any kind of excuse, or even in disguise if necessary. They are to be well informed of the nature of the observations which they are to make, and at their return, the remarks which they have made on the camps and different situations are to be noted on a map: but when we can make use of our own eyes, we ought never to trust to those of other people.

ARTICLE VI
Of the Coup d'oeil

The coup d'oeil may be reduced, properly speaking, to two points; the first of which is the having abilities to judge how many troops a certain extent of country can contain. This talent can only be acquired by practice, for after having laid out several camps, the eye will gain so exact an idea of space, that you will seldom make any material mistake in your calculations.

The other, and by far the most material point, is to be most material point, is to be able to distinguish at first sight all the advantages of which any given space of ground is capable. This art is to be acquired and even brought to perfection, though a man be not absolutely born with a military genius.

Fortification, as it possesses rules that are applicable to all situations of an army, is undoubtedly the basis and foundation of this coup d'oeil. Every defile, marsh, hollow way, and even the smallest eminence, will be converted by a skilful general, to some advantage.

Two hundred different positions may sometimes be taken up in the space of two square leagues, of which an intelligent general knows how to select that which is the most advantageous. In the first place, he will ascend even the smallest eminences to discover and reconnoitre the ground; and assisted by the same rules of fortification, he will be enabled to find out the weak part of the enemy's order of battle. If time permit, the general would do well to pace over the ground, when he has determined on his general position.

Many other advantages may also be derived from the same rules of fortification, such as, the manner of occupying heights, and how to choose them, that they may not be commanded by others; in what manner the wings are to be supported, that the flanks may be well covered; how to take up positions that may be defended, and avoid those which a man of reputation cannot, without great risk, maintain. These rules will also enable him to discover where the enemy is weakest, either by having taken an unfavourable position, distributed his force without judgment, or from the slender means of defence which he derives from his situation. I am led by these reflections to explain in what manner troops ought to be distributed so as to make the most of their ground.

ARTICLE VII
Of the Distribution of Troops

Though the knowledge and choice of ground are very essential points, it is of no less importance that we know how to profit by such advantages, so that the troops may be placed in situations that are proper and convenient for them.

Our cavalry, being designed to act with velocity, can only be made use of on a plain, whereas the infantry may be employed in every possible variety of ground. Their fire is for defence, and their bayonet for attack. We always begin by the defensive, as much caution is necessary for the security of a camp, where the vicinity of the enemy may at any moment bring on an engagement.

The greater part of the orders of battle now existing are of ancient date: we tread in the steps of our ancestors without regulating matters according to the nature of the ground, and hence it is that a false and erroneous application so often takes place.

The whole of an army should be placed in order of battle agreeably to the nature of ground which every particular part of it requires. The plain is chosen for the cavalry, but this is not all which regards them; for if the plain be only a thousand yards in front, and bounded by a wood in which we suppose the enemy to have thrown some infantry, under whose fire their cavalry can rally, it will then become necessary to change the disposition, and place them at the extremities of the wings of the infantry, that they may receive the benefit of their support.

The whole of the cavalry is sometimes placed on one of the wings, or in the second line; at other times, their wings are closed by one or two brigades of infantry.

Eminences, church-yards, hollow ways, and wide ditches are the most advantageous situations for an army. If, in the disposition of our troops, we know how to take advantage of these circumstances, we never need to fear being attacked.

If your cavalry be posted with a morass in it's front, it is impossible that it can render you any service: and if it be placed too near a wood, the enemy may have troops there, who may throw them into disorder and pick them off with their muskets, whilst they are deprived of every possible means of defence. Your infantry will be exposed to the same inconveniencies if they are advanced too far on a plain with their flanks not secured, for the enemy will certainly take advantage of such error, and make their attack on that side where they are unprotected.

The nature of the ground must invariably be our rule of direction. In a mountainous country I should place my cavalry in the second line, and never use them in the first line except they could act to advantage, unless it be a few squadrons to fall on the flank of the enemy's infantry who may be advancing to attack me.

It is a general rule in all well-disciplined armies, that a reserve of cavalry be formed if we are on a plain, but where the country is chequered and intersected, this reserve is formed of infantry, with the addition of some hussars and dragoons.

The great art of distributing troops on the field is, so to place them, that all have room to act and be uniformly useful. Villeroi, who perhaps was not well acquainted with this rule, deprived himself of the assistance of the whole of his left wing on the plain of Ramillies, by having posted them behind a morass, where it was morally impossible that they could manoeuvre, or render and sort of support to his right wing.

ARTICLE VIII
Of Camps

To be convinced that your camp be well chosen, you must discover, whether a trifling movement of yours will oblige the enemy to make one of greater consequence, or if after one march, he be under the necessity of making others. They who have the least occasion to move, are certainly the best situated.

The choice of situation for a camp should rest entirely with the general of an army, as it often becomes the field of battle, and the success of his enterprises so materially depends upon it.

As there are many observations to be made on this subject, I shall enter into it very particularly, saying nothing with respect to the method of placing troops in camp, but referring you on that head to my military regulation.

I now proceed to speak only of affairs of consequence, and of matters that more immediately concern the general himself.

All camps are designed to answer two purposes, defence and attack. The first class consists of those camps in which an army assembles where the sole object is the convenience and accommodation of the troops. They ought to be encamped in small bodies near the magazine, but so situate that they may readily be assembled in order of battle.

Camps of this kind are generally formed at such distance from the enemy as to be free from all alarm. The king of England, who neglected this caution, and imprudently encamped himself on the bank of the Mein opposite the French army, ran a very great risk of being defeated at Dettinghen.

The first rule to be observed in the marking out a camp is that both wood and water be at no great distance.

It is our custom to entrench camps, in the manner of the Romans, not only to secure ourselves against any enterprise which the numerous light troops of the enemy may attempt against us, but also to prevent desertion.

I have constantly observed, that fewer men have left us when the redans were joined by two lines that extended all round the camp, than when this caution has been neglected. This is a serious fact, however ridiculous or trifling it may appear.

Camps of repose are those, where we expect forage; on some occasions that are designed to watch the enemy, who have as yet made no movements, that we may be regulated by their manoeuvres. As relaxation is the only object in camps of this nature, they should be rendered secure by being in the rear of a large river or morass, or in short by any means that will render their front inaccessible. Of this description was our camp at Strehla.

If the brooks and rivers in front of the camp are too shallow, dams must be employed in order to deepen them.

Though there be no dread of the enemy to annoy us in camps of this kind, the general of an army must nevertheless on no account be idle. The leisure which he now has must be employed in paying attention to the troops, and re-establishing the usual discipline. He must examine if the service be carried on in strict conformity to order, if the officers on guard are attentive and well informed of the duties of their situation, and if the rules which I have laid down for the posting of cavalry and infantry guards be properly and strictly observed.

The infantry should go through their exercise three times a week, and the recruits once every day,: on some occasions also entire corps may perform their manoeuvres together. The cavalry must likewise go through their evolutions, unless they are employed in foraging; and the general, knowing the exact strength of each corps, should take particular care that the recruits and young horses be well drilled. He must also frequently visit the lines, commending those officers who pay attention to their troops, and severely rebuking those who appear to have neglected them, for it is not to be supposed that a large army can be self-animated. It will ever abound with idlers and malingerers, who require the general's attention to be put in motion and be obliged to do their duty.

Very great utility will be derived from camps of this sort, if they be employed in the manner which I have recommended, and the succeeding campaign will prove the good effects of their discipline and order.

We form our encampment, or we forage, near to the enemy, or at a considerable distance from him—I shall only speak of the former, where it is necessary that we make choice of the most fertile spots, and encamp in a situation which art or nature has rendered formidable.

When foraging camps are situate near the enemy, they should be very difficult of access, as foraging parties are regarded as detachments sent out against the enemy.

These parties may consist of a sixth part, or even half of an army. It would afford fine amusement to the enemy, if they were able on these occasions to attack us to our disadvantage, and it would certainly happen, but for the well-chosen situation of our camp.

But though the position is very good, and apparently there be nothing to fear from the enemy, there are, notwithstanding, other cautions which are by no means to be neglected. The most rigid secrecy must be observed both in regard to the time and place of foraging, nor should even the general who is to command on the occasion be acquainted with these circumstances till a late hour in the preceding evening.

We should send out as many detached parties as possible, to be more certainly informed of any movements which the enemy may make: and unless prevented by reasons that are very material, we may, to save trouble, forage on the same day that they do. We are not, however, to place too much confidence in this circumstance, as the enemy, by being apprized of our design, may countermand the order for foraging, and attack the main body.

The camp of Prince Charles of Lorraine under Koniginggraetz was inaccessible by nature, and extremely convenient for the purposes of foraging. That which we occupied at Cholm was made strong by art, viz. by the abattis which I ordered to be thrown up on our right wing and the redoubts which were in front of the infantry camp.

We entrenched a camp, when it is our intention to lay siege to a place, to defend a difficult pass, and supply the defects of the situation by throwing up works so as to be secure from every insult on the part of the enemy.

The rules which a general has to observe in the formation of all entrenchments are, to take advantage of every marsh, river, inundation, and abattis which may serve to render the extent of his entrenchments more difficult. They had better be too small than too large, for the progress of the enemy is not checked by the entrenchments themselves, but by the troops who defend them.

I would not wish to make entrenchments, unless I could line them with a chain of battalions, and had also at my disposal a reserve of infantry that could be moved to any point as occasion might require. Abattis are no longer of service than whilst they are defended by infantry.

The chief attention should be paid to the proper support of the lines of contravallation, which generally end in a river; and in such case the fosse should be carried some length into the river, and be so deepened as not to allow if being forded. If this precaution be neglected, you run the hazard of having your flank turned. It is necessary that you be abundantly supplied with provisions before you sit down behind the lines to besiege any place.

The flanks of entrenchments should be particularly strong, nor should there be a single point which the enemy might attack without being exposed to four or five cross fires. Infinite care and caution are required in the formation of entrenchments which are designed to defend the passes and defiles of mountains. The support of the flanks is here most essentially necessary, to accomplish which, redoubts are formed on the two wings: sometimes the whole entrenchment itself is made up of redoubts, so that the troops who defend it are in no danger of being turned.

Intelligent generals are well informed how to oblige the enemy to attack those points where the work is made strongest by the ditch being widened, deepened, and lined with palisades, *chevaux de frize* placed at the entrances, the parapet made cannon-proof, and pits dug in the places that are most exposed.

But for the covering of a siege, I would always prefer an army of observation to an entrenched camp, and for this plain reason, because we are taught by experience that the old method is not to be depended on.

The Prince of Conde saw his entrenchment which was before Arras forced by Turenne, and Conde (if I am not mistaken) forced that which Turenne had formed before Valenciennes—since that period, neither of these great masters in the military art have made any use of them, but, to cover a siege, have always employed armies of observation.

I shall now treat of defensive camps, which are only strong by situation, and intended solely to be secure from the attacks of the enemy.

To render these situations equal to the purposes for which they are designed, it is necessary, that the front and both flanks be of equal strength, and the rear perfectly free and open. Of such nature are those heights, whose front is very extensive, and whose flanks are covered by marshes, as was the camp of Prince Charles of Lorraine at Marschwitz, where the front was covered by a marshy river, and the flanks by lakes; or like that which we occupied at Konopist in the year 1744.

We may also shelter ourselves under the protection of some fortified place, as was done by the Marshal de Neipperg, who after being defeated at Mollwitz, took up an excellent position under the walls of Neiss. As long as a general can maintain his post in camps of this kind, he will be secure from attack; but as soon as the enemy is in motion with a view of turning him, he will no longer be able to remain. His arrangements should therefore be so settled before-hand, that if the enemy succeed in their attempt to turn him, he may have nothing to do but fall back, and take up another strong position in the rear.

Bohemia abounds in camps of this description, and as the country is so chequered by nature, we are often obliged to occupy some of them against our inclination.

I must again repeat how necessary it is for a general to be on his guard, lest he be led, by a bad choice of posts, into errors that cannot be remedied, or in a situation from which he has no means of escaping but by a narrow defile. For if he have a clever enemy to deal with, he will be so closely pent up, and so completely prevented from fighting by the nature of the ground, as to be obliged to submit to the greatest indignity which a soldier can suffer, that of laying down his arms without the power of defending himself.

In camps that are intended to cover a country, the strength of the place itself is not the object of attention, but those points which are liable to attack, and by means of which the enemy may penetrate. These should all be surrounded by the camp. Not that is necessary to occupy every opening by which the enemy may advance upon us, but that one only which would lead to his desired point, and that situation which affords us security, and from which we have it in our power to alarm him. In short, we should occupy that post, which will oblige the enemy to take circuitous routes, and enable us, by small movements, to disconcert his projects.

The camp at Newstadt defends the whole of the Lower Silesia against the attacks of an army that may be in Moravia. The proper position to take up, is to have the city of Neustadt and the river in front, and if the enemy show a design to pass between Ottmachau and Glatz, we have only to move between Neiss and Ziegenhals, and there take up an advantageous camp which will cut them off from Moravia.

For the same reason the enemy will not dare to stir on the side of Cosel, for by placing myself between Troppau and Jaegerndorff (where there are many very excellent positions,) I cut him off from his convoys.

There is another camp of equal importance between Liebau and Schaemberg, which secures all Lower Silesia against Bohemia.

In all these positions, the rules which I have laid down ought to be observed, as far as circumstances will allow. I must yet add one more, which is, that when you have a river in front, you never allow tents to be pitched on the ground which you intend for the field of battle at a greater distance than half musket-shot from the front of the camp.

The frontier of the electorate of Brandenberg is a country which no camp can cover, as it has six leagues of plain ground which is open the whole way. To defend it against Saxony, it is necessary to be possessed of Wittenberg, and either encamp there or adopt the plan of the expedition which took place there in the winter of the year 1745. The camp at Werben covers and defends all that part which is on the side of the country of Hanover.

The front and flanks of a camp for offence must be always closed; for unless the flanks, which are the weakest part of an army, are well closed, you have nothing to expect form your troops. This was the fault of our camp at Czaslaw, before the battle of the year 1742.

The village houses which are on the wings, or in the front of our camp, are always occupied by troops, except on fighting days, when they are called in, lest by the enemy's setting fire to such badly-constructed wooden buildings (as our own cottages and those of our neighbours generally are) the men may also be destroyed. There may, however, be an exception to this general rules, when any stone houses are in the villages, or any church-yards which do not communicate with wooden buildings.

But as it is our constant principle to attack, and not act on the defensive, this kind of post should never be occupied except it be at the head of the army, or in front of it's wings; in such situations it will afford much protection to our troops in the attack, and prove of great annoyance to the enemy during the action.

It is also a circumstance of material import, that the depth of the small rivers or marshes which are in front or on the flanks of our camp be well ascertained, lest by the rivers being fordable, or the marshes practicable, you discover too late that you have trusted to a false point of defence.

Villars was beaten at Malplaquet by conceiving that the marsh on his right was impracticable, which proved to be only a dry meadow, which our troops passed to take him in the flank. Every thing should be examined by our own eyes, and no attentions of this nature treated on any account as matters of indifference.

ARTICLE IX
How to Secure a Camp

The front of the first line must be defended by the regiments of infantry, and if a river be there, piquets must be posted on its banks. The rear of the camp is to be guarded by piquets from the second line. These piquets are to be covered by redans, joined by slight entrenchments, by means of which the camp will be entrenched after the manner of the Romans. We must occupy the villages which are on the wings, or even to the distance of half a league from thence, if they serve to defend any other passages.

The cavalry guards are to be posted agreeably to the rules laid down in my military regulation. We seldom had more than 300 *maitres de garde* amongst 80 squadrons, unless we were very near to the enemy, as when we marched to Schweidenitz between the battle of Hohen-Freidberg, and again when we marched into Lusatia in order to go to Naumbourg. These advanced guards should be composed of all sorts of troops, for example, 2000 hussars, 1500 dragoons, and 2000 grenadiers. The general who has the command of bodies of men that are advanced, should be a man of sound understanding, and as it is his object to gain intelligence, not expose himself to action, his camps should be chosen with judgment, having in their front either woods or defiles with which he is well acquainted. He must also send out frequent patrols for the purpose of gaining information that he may know at every instant what is going forward in the camp of the enemy.

If in the mean time you employ the hussars who remain with you to patrol in the rear and on the wings of the camp, you have taken all possible precautions to be guarded against any hostile enterprises.

Should a considerable body of troops endeavour to slide in between you and your rear guard, you may be assured that they have formed some design against it, and you are therefore to hasten to its support.

To conclude all that I have to say on this subject, it must be added, that if those generals who canton their troops wish to be free from danger and alarm, they should only occupy those villages which are between the two lines.

ARTICLE X
In what Manner and for what Reason we are to send out Detachments

It is only repeating an ancient maxim in war to say, "That he who divides his force will be beaten in detail." If you are about to give battle, strain every nerve to get together as many troops as you possibly can, for they never can be employed to better purpose. Almost every general who has neglected this rule has found ample reason to repent of it.

Albemarle's detachment, which was beaten at Oudenarde, lost the great Eugene the whole campaign; and Gen. Stahrenberg was beaten at the battle of Villa Viciosa in Spain, by being separated from the English troops.

Detachments have also proved very fatal to the Austrians in the latter campaigns that they have made in Hungary. The Prince of Hildbourghausen was defeated at Banjaluka, and General Wallis suffered a check on the banks of the Timok. The Saxons also were beaten at Kesseldorf, for want of having joined Prince Charles, as they could have done. I should have been defeated at Sohr, and deservedly too, if presence of mind in my generals, and valour in my troops, had not rescued me from such misfortune. It may be asked, are we then never to send out detachments? My reply is, that it is a business of so delicate a nature, as never to be hazarded but on the most pressing necessity, and for reasons of the utmost importance.

When you are acting offensively, detachments ought never to be employed, and even though you are in an open country, and have some places in your possession, no more troops are to be spared than are barely sufficient to secure your convoys.

Whenever war in made in Bohemia or Moravia, necessity requires that troops be sent out to insure the arrival of provisions. Encampments must be formed on the chain of mountains which the convoys are obliged to pass, and remain there till you have collected provisions for some months, and are possessed of some strong place in the enemy's country that with serve as a depot.

Whilst these troops are absent on detachments, you are to occupy advantageous camps, and wait for their return.

The advanced guard is not reckoned as a detachment, because it should ever be near the army, and not ventured on any account too near the enemy.

It sometimes happens that when we are acting on the defensive, we are forced to make detachments. Those which I had in Upper Silesia were in perfect safety by confining themselves, as I have already observed, to the neighbourhood of fortified places.

Officers, who have the command of detachments, should be men of prudence and resolution, for though they receive general instructions from their chief, it remains for themselves to consult on the propriety of advancing or retreating, as occasion may require.

When the force of the opponents is too strong, they should fall back, but on the other hand, they should well know how to take advantage, if the superiority happens to be on their own sides.

If the enemy approach by night, they will sometimes retire, and whilst they are supposed to be put to flight, return briskly to the charge and defeat them.

No regard whatever is to be paid to the light troops.

The first thing to be attended to by an officer, who commands a detachment, is his own safety, and when that is secured, he is at liberty to form schemes against the enemy. To ensure rest to himself, he must keep his adversary constantly awake, by continually contriving plans against him, and if he succeeds in two or three instances, the enemy will be obliged to keep on the defensive.

If these detachments be near the army, they will establish a communication with it by means of some town or neighbouring wood.

In a war of defence, we are naturally induced to make detachments. Generals of little experience are anxious to preserve every thing, whilst the man of intelligence and enterprise regards only the grand point, in hopes of being able to strike some great stroke, and suffers patiently a small evil that may secure him against one of more material consequence.

The army of the enemy should be the chief object of our attention, it's designs must be discovered, and opposed as vigorously as possible. In the year 1745 we abandoned Upper Silesia to the ravages of the Hungarians that we might be better enabled to thwart the intentions of Prince Charles of Lorraine, and we made no detachments until we had defeated his army. When that was done, General Nassau in fifteen days cleared the whole of Upper Silesia of the Hungarians.

It is a custom with some generals to detach troops when they are about to make an attack, to take the enemy in the rear during the action, but much danger attends a movement of this kind, as the detachments generally lose their road, and arrive either too early or too late. The detachment which Charles XII sent out on the evening before the battle of Pultawa lost it's way, and was the cause of the army's being beaten. Prince Eugene's design of surprising Cremona failed also from the too late arrival of the detachment of the Prince of Vaudemont, which was intended to attack the gate of Po.

Detachments should never take place on the day of battle, unless it be in the manner of Turenne near Colmar, where he presented his first line to the army of the Elector Frederick William, whilst the second line passing through defiles attacked him in flank and routed him. Or we may copy the example of the Marshal de Luxembourg at the battle of Fleury, in the year 1690, who posted a body of infantry in some high corn on the Prince of Waldeck's flank, and by that manoeuvre gained the battle.

After a victory, but never till then, troops may be detached for the protection of convoys, but even in this case they should not proceed a greater length than half a league from the army.

I shall conclude this article by saying, that detachments which weaken the army one half, or even a third part, are excessively dangerous, and strongly to be disapproved.

ARTICLE XI
Of the Tricks and Stratagems of War

In war, the skin of a fox is at times as necessary as that of the lion, for cunning may succeed when force fails. Since, therefore, force may at one time be repelled by force, and at another be obliged to yield to stratagem, we ought to be well acquainted with the use of both, that we may on occasion adopt either.

I have no wish to recite here the almost infinite list of stratagems, for they have all the same end in view, which is, to oblige the enemy to make unnecessary marches in favour of our own designs. Our real intentions are to be studiously concealed, and the enemy misled by our affecting plans which we have no wish to execute.

When our troops are on the point of assembling, we countermarch them in a variety of ways, to alarm the enemy, and conceal from him the spot where we really wish to assemble and force a passage.

If there be fortresses in the country, we choose to encamp in a situation that threatens three or four places at the same time. Should the enemy think proper to throw troops into all these places, the consequence will be, that his force will be so weakened, that we shall have a good opportunity of falling on him: but if one point only has been the object of his attention, we lay siege to that which is the most defenceless.

If the object be to pass a river, or be possessed of some post of importance, you must withdraw to a great distance both from the post and from the spot where you mean to pass, in order to entice the enemy after you. And when every thing is arranged and your march concealed, you are to betake yourself suddenly to the settled point and possess yourself of it.

If you wish to come to an action, and the enemy seems disposed to avoid it, you must appear to be in dread of the force which is opposed to you, or spread a report that your army is much weakened. We played this game before the battle of Hohen-Friedburg. I caused all the roads to be repaired as if I meant, at the approach of Prince Charles, to march to Breslau in four columns: his self-confidence seconding my design, he followed me into the plain, and was defeated.

Sometimes we contract the dimensions of the camp, to give it the appearance of weakness, and send out small detachments, (that we affect to be of great consequence,) in order that the enemy may hold us cheap, and neglect an opportunity which he might improve. In the campaign of 1745, if it had been my intention to take Konigingraetz and Pardubitz, I had only to make two marches through the country of Glatz on the side of Moravia, as that would certainly have alarmed Prince Charles and brought him thither, to defend the place from which, after leaving Bohemia, he drew all his provisions. You will be sure of creating jealousy in the enemy, if you threaten places that either communicate with the capitol or serve as depots for his provisions.

If we have no inclination to fight, we put a bold face upon the business, and give out that we are much stronger than we really are. Austria is a famous school for this sort of manoeuvre, for with them the art is brought to its greatest perfection.

By keeping up a bold and determined appearance, you give the idea of wishing to engage, and occasion a report to be circulated that you are meditating some very bold and daring enterprise: by means of which the enemy, in dread of the consequences of an attack, will frequently remain on the defensive.

It is an essential object in a war of defence, to know how to make a good choice of posts, and to maintain them to the last extremity: when forced to retire, the second line begins to move, followed insensibly by the first, and as you have defiles in your front, the enemy will not be able to take advantage of you in the retreat.

Even during the retreat, the positions that are taken up should be so oblique as to keep the enemy as much as possible in the dark. The more he endeavours to discover your designs, the more he will be alarmed, whilst you indirectly obtain the object of your wishes.

Another stratagem of war is, to show to the enemy a front of very great extent, and if he mistakes a false attack for a real one, he will inevitably be defeated.

By means of tricks also, we oblige the enemy to send out detachments, and when they are marched, take the opportunity of falling on him.

The best stratagem is, to lull the enemy into security at the time when the troops are about to disperse and go into winter quarters, so that by retiring, you may be enabled to advance on them to some good purpose. With the view, the troops should be so distributed, as to assemble again very readily, in order to force the enemy's quarters. If this measure succeeds, you may recover in a fortnight the misfortunes of a whole campaign.

Peruse with attention the two last campaigns of Turenne, for they are the *chefs d'oeuvres* of the stratagems of this age.

The schemes which our ancestors employed in war are now only in use amongst the light troops, whose practice it is to form ambuscades, and endeavour by a pretended flight to draw the enemy into a defile, that they may cut them in pieces. The generals of the present day seldom manage their matters so badly as to be taken in by such contrivances. Nevertheless, Charles XII was betrayed at Pultawa through the treachery of one of the Cossack chiefs. The same accident also befell Peter I on the Pruth, owing to the misconduct of a prince of that country. Both these men had promised a supply of provisions which it was not in their power to furnish.

As the method of making war by parties and detachments is fully laid down in my Military Regulation, I refer to that work all those who wish to refresh their memories, as it is a subject on which I have nothing farther to advance.

To be informed of the method to oblige the enemy to make detachments, we have only to read over the glorious campaign of 1690, made by the Marshal de Luxembourg against the King of England, which concluded with the battle of Neerwinde.

ARTICLE XII
Of Spies, how they are to be employed on every Occasion, and in what Manner we are to learn Intelligence of the enemy

If we were acquainted beforehand with the intentions of the enemy, we should always be more than a match for him even with an inferior force. It is an advantage which all generals are anxious to procure, but very few obtain.

Spies may be divided into several classes: 1st, common people who choose to be employed in such concern; secondly, double spies; thirdly, spies of consequence; fourthly, those who are compelled to take up the unpleasant business.

The common gentry, viz. peasants, mechanics, priests, etc. which are sent into the camp, can only be employed to discover where the enemy is: and their reports are generally so incongruous and obscure, as rather to increase our uncertainties than lessen them.

The intelligence of deserters is, for the most part, not much more to be depended on. A soldier knows very well what is going forward in his own regiment, but nothing farther. The hussars being detached in front, and absent the greatest part of their time from the army, are often ignorant on which side it is encamped. Nevertheless, their reports must be committed to paper, as the only means of turning them to any advantage.

Double spies are used to convey false intelligence to the enemy. There was an Italian at Schmiedeberg, who acted as a spy to the Austrians, and being told by us, that when the enemy approached we should retire to Breslau, he posted with the intelligence to Prince Charles of Lorraine, who narrowly escaped being taken in by it.

The post-master at Versailles was a long time in the pay of Prince Eugene. This unfortunate fellow opened the letters and orders which were sent from the court to the generals, and transmitted a copy of them to Prince Eugene, who generally received them much earlier than the commanders of the French army.

Luxembourg had gained over to his interest a secretary of the King of England, who informed him of all that passed. The king discovered it, and derived every advantage from it that could be expected in an affair of such delicacy: he obliged the traitor to write to Luxembourg, informing him that the allied army would be out the day following on a large foraging party. The consequence was that the French very narrowly escaped being surprised at Steinquerque, and would have been cut to pieces if they had not defended themselves with extraordinary valour. It would be very difficult to obtain such spies in a war against Austria: not that the Austrians are less alive to bribery than other people, but because their army is surrounded by such a cloud of light troops, who suffer no creature to pass without being well searched. This circumstance suggested to me the idea of bringing over some of their hussar officers, by means of whom a correspondence might be carried on in the following manner. It is a custom with hussars, when opposed to each other as skirmishing parties, to agree every now and then to a suspension of arms, which opportunity might be employed in conveying letters.

When we wish to gain intelligence of the enemy, or give him a false impression of our situation and circumstances, we employ a trusty soldier to go from our camp to that of the enemy, and report what we wish to have believed. He may also be made the bearer of hand-bills calculated to encourage desertion. Having completed his business, he may take a circuitous march and return to camp.

There is yet another way to gain intelligence of the enemy when milder methods fail, though I confess it to be a harsh and cruel practice. We find out a rich citizen who has a large family and good estate, and allow him a man who understands the language of the country dressed as a servant, whom we force him to take along with him into the enemy's camp, as his valet or coachman, under pretence of complaining of some injuries which he has received; he is to be threatened also at the same time, that if he does not return after a certain period, and bring the man with him, that his houses shall be burned, and his wife and children hacked in pieces. I was obliged to have recourse to this scheme at . . . and it succeeded to my wish.

I must further add, that in the payment of spies we ought to be generous, even to a degree of extravagance. That man certainly deserves to be well rewarded, who risks his neck to do your service.

ARTICLE XIII
Of certain Marks, by which the Intentions of the Enemy are to be discovered

The knowledge of the spot which the enemy has chosen as a depot for his provisions is the surest means of discovering his intentions before the campaign opens. For example, if the Austrians establish their magazines at Olmutz, we may be assured that they mean to attack Upper Silesia: if at Konigingraetz, we may be convinced that part of Schweidenitz is threatened. When it was the wish of the Saxons to invade the frontier of the Electorate, their magazines marked their intended route, for they were established at Zittau, Goerlitz, and at Guben, which are on the road leading to Crossen.

The first object of intelligence should be, on what side and in what situations the enemy means to fix his magazines.

The French played a double game, by forming depots on the Meuse and on the Scheld, in order to conceal their intentions.

When the Austrians are encamped, it is easy to discover when they intend moving, by their custom of cooking on the days of march. If, therefore, much smoke be perceived in their camp at five or six o'clock in the morning, you may take it for granted on that day they mean to move.

Whenever the Austrians intend fighting, all their strong detachments of light troops are called in; and when you have observed this, it behooves you to be very well upon your guard.

If you attack a post which is defended by their Hungarian troops, without being able to make any impression on it, you may be satisfied that the army is near at hand to support them.

If their light troops endeavour to post themselves between your army and the body of men which you have detached, you may be assured that the enemy has a design on that detachment, and your measures must be taken accordingly.—It must be added, that if the same general be always opposed to you, his designs will be readily discovered, and his plan of conduct very soon become familiar.

After mature reflection on the nature of the country which is the scene of war, the state of the army which you command, the safety of the magazines, the strength of the fortified places, the means which the enemy may be able to employ in order to gain possession of them, the mischief which the light troops may do by posting themselves on your flanks, rear, and other parts, or if the enemy should employ them to make a diversion; I say, after having well deliberated on all these points, you may conclude that an intelligent enemy will attempt that enterprise which is likely to give you the greatest annoyance, at least that such will be his intention, to frustrate which your every effort must be exerted.

ARTICLE XIV
Of our own Country, and that which is either neutral or hostile; of the Variety of Religions, and of the different Conduct which such Circumstances require

War may be carried on in three different kinds of country: either in our own territories, those belonging to neutral powers, or in the country of an enemy.

If glory were my only object, I would never make war but in my own country, by reason of it's manifold advantages, as every man there acts as a spy, nor can the enemy stir a foot without being betrayed.

Detachments of any strength may boldly be sent out, and may practice in safety all the manoeuvres of which war is capable.

If the enemy have the advantage, every peasant turns soldier and lends a hand to annoy him, as was experienced by the Elector Frederick William after the battle of Fehrbelin, where a greater number of Swedes was destroyed by the peasants than fell in the engagement. After the battle of Hohen-Friedberg, also, I observed that the mountaineers in Silesia brought into us the runaway Austrians in great abundance.

When war is carried on in a neutral country, the advantage seems to be equal, and the object of attention then is, to rival the enemy in the confidence and friendship of the inhabitants. To attain this end, the most exact discipline must be observed, marauding and every kind of plunder strictly forbidden, and its commission punished with exemplary severity. It may not be amiss also, to accuse the enemy of harbouring some pernicious designs against the country.

If we are in a protestant country, we wear the mask of protector of the Lutheran religion, and endeavour to make fanatics of the lower order of people, whose simplicity is not proof against our artifice.

In a catholic country, we preach up toleration and moderation, constantly abusing the priests as the cause of all the animosity that exists between the different sectaries, although, in spite of their disputes, they all agree upon material points of faith.

The strength of the parties you may be required to send out, must depend on the confidence that can be placed in the inhabitants of the country. In our country you may run every risk, but more caution and circumspection are necessary in a neutral country, at least till you are convinced of the friendly disposition of the whole, or the greatest part of the peasantry.

In a country that is entirely hostile, as Bohemia and Moravia, you are to hazard nothing, and never send out parties, for the reasons already mentioned;

as the people there are not to be trusted any farther than you can see them. The greater part of the light troops is to be employed in guarding the convoys, for you are never to expect to gain the affection of the inhabitants of this country. The Hussites in the circle of Konigingraetz are the only people that can be induced to render us any sort of service. The men of consequence there, though seemingly well disposed towards us, are arrant traitors, nor are the priests or magistrates at all better. As their interest is attached to that of the house of Austria, whose views do not altogether clash with ours, we neither can nor ought to repose any sort of confidence in them.

All that now remains for our management is fanaticism, to know how to inspire a nation with zeal for the liberty of religion, and hint to them in a guarded manner, how much they are oppressed by their great men and priests. This may be said to be moving heaven and hell for one's interest.

Since these notes have been put together, the empress queen has materially increased the taxes in Bohemia and Moravia: advantage may be taken of this circumstance to gain the good-will of the people, especially if we flatter them that they shall be better treated if we become masters of the country.

ARTICLE XV
Of every Kind of March, which it can be necessary for an Army to make

An army moves for the purposes of advancing in an enemy's country, to take possession of an advantageous camp, join a reinforcement, give battle, or retire before the enemy.

When the camp is properly secured, the next object is, to reconnoitre the whole neighbourhood and every road that leads from it to camp, that we may be enabled to make the necessary arrangements, as a variety of circumstances may require.

With this view and under various pretences we send out large detachments, accompanied by some engineers and quarter-masters, who are to pry into every place that is capable of being occupied by troops. They are also to take up the situation of the country, and reconnoitre the roads by which the troops can march. A certain number of chasseurs should follow them, who are to observe the roads very attentively, that they may be able to lead the columns, provided that the general marches thither.

On their return, the aforesaid officers are to make their report concerning the situation of the camp, the roads that lead to it, the nature of the soil, the woods, mountains, and rivers that are situate thereabouts; and the general, being well informed of all these particulars will make his dispositions accordingly. When the camp is not too near the enemy, the following arrangement may take place:—

> I suppose that the camp may be approached in four different ways. The advanced guard, composed of six battalions of grenadiers, one regiment of infantry, two of dragoons, (consisting of five squadrons each,) and two regiments of hussars, under the command of General N. N. will depart at eight o'clock this evening. All the encampments of the army are to follow this advanced guard, which is to take their tents only with them, leaving their heavy baggage with the army.

These troops are to march four leagues in front and occupy the defile, river, height, town, village, etc. which may be objects of attention, and wait there the arrival of the army, after which they are to enter into the camp which has been already marked out.

On the following morning the army, marching in four columns, is to move forward after the advanced guard: those men who have been posted as guards in the villages, falling in with their respective regiments. The cavalry of the two lines of the right wing, marching by it's right, will form the first column: the infantry of the two lines of the right wing, marching by it's right, will form the second: the infantry of the two lines of the left wing, filing by it's right, will form the third; and the cavalry of the left wing, filing by it's right, will form the fourth column. The infantry regiments N. N. of the second line, and the three regiments of hussars under the command of General N. N. will escort the baggage, which is to march in the rear of the two columns of infantry.

Four *aides-de-camp* are to command this party, who are to take particular care that the carriages follow each other in order, allowing as little interval as possible.

If the general commanding the rear guard should be in want of support, he is immediately to apply to the commander in chief.

The chasseurs that have reconnoitered the roads are to conduct the four columns.

A detachment of carpenters, with wagons laden with beams, joists, and planks, should precede each column, to throw bridges over the small rivers.

The heads of columns must be careful not to go before each other without allowing any intervals. Officers commanding divisions must be attentive in observing their distances.

When you have to pass a defile, the heads of columns must march very slowly, or halt now and then to allow the rear to recover its situation.

It is thus that the order of march is to be conducted.

When mountains, woods, or defiles, are met with on the march, the columns are to be divided, and the head, which consists of the infantry, is to be followed by the cavalry, who will close the march.

If there be a plain in the centre, it is to be assigned to the cavalry, and the infantry formed into columns on the two extremities, are to traverse the wood; but this is only to be understood of a march which is made not too near the enemy. In that situation, we are content to place some battalions of grenadiers at the head of each column of cavalry, that they may preserve the order of battle.

The most certain way to insure the safe arrival of a reinforcement is, to march through a difficult road to meet it, and to retire from the enemy to avoid an engagement. By means of the superiority which you gain by the arrival of this succour, you will soon recover that ground, which you have, as it were, only lent to the enemy.

When we are obliged to march parallel to the enemy, it must be done in two lines, either by the right or by the left, and each line must form a column, with an advanced guard in front. In other respects, those rules which I have just laid down, may also here be employed.

All the marches which we made from Frankenberg to Hohen-Friedberg were directed in this manner, marching to the right.

I prefer these dispositions to any others, because the army can be formed in order of battle by one to the right or one to the left, which is much the readiest way of collecting them, and I would ever practice this method, if I had my choice in attacking the enemy, though I lost the advantage of it at Sohr and at Hohen-Friedberg. In this sort of march, care is to be taken that the flank be never shown to the enemy.

When the enemy begins a march in preparation for an action, you are to disencumber yourself of all your heavy baggage, and send it under escort to the nearest town. The advanced guard is then to be formed, and pushed forward to the distance of a short half league.

When the army marches in front against the enemy, care must be taken not only that the columns do not go before each other, but also that when they draw near to the field of battle, they extend themselves in such a manner, that the troops do not take up more or less ground than they will occupy when they are formed. This is a business of much difficulty, as some battalions are generally too much crowded, and others have too much ground allotted them.

Marching by lines is attended with no sort of inconvenience, and on that account has by me ever been preferred.

When we expect to be engaged upon a march, great precaution is required, and it is necessary that the general be very much upon his guard. He should reconnoitre the ground, without exposing himself, from point to point, so as to have an idea of different positions, if the enemy should come to attack him.

Steeples and heights are to be made use of in order to reconnoitre the ground, and the road which leads to them is to be cleared by light troops, detached from the advanced guard.

Retreats are generally conducted in the following manner: A day or two before we depart, the heavy baggage is got together, and sent away under a strong escort.

The number of columns is then to be determined by the number of roads that can be made use of, and the march of the troops regulated by the nature of the ground. In a plain, the advanced guard is formed by the cavalry; if it be a chequered country, that post belongs to the infantry in a plain country, the army will march in four columns.

The infantry of the second line of the right wing, filing by it's right, and followed by the second line of the cavalry of the same wing, will form the fourth column. The infantry of the first line of the right wing, filing by it's right, will be followed by the first line of cavalry of that wing, and form the third column.

The infantry of the second line of the left wing, followed by the cavalry of that same line, will form the second column. The infantry of the first line of the left wing will be followed by the cavalry of that same line, forming together the first column.

In this manner the rear guard will be formed by the whole of the cavalry, which may be supported, for security sake by the hussars of the army.

If, during the retreat, it be necessary to pass any defiles, the infantry must occupy them the evening before we depart, and be so posted as to cover the troops, in order that the passage of the defile may remain open.

Supposing that the army marches in two columns, the cavalry of the right will file by its left, the second line moving first, and taking the lead of the second column: the infantry of the second line, followed by the first, will place itself in the rear and follow this cavalry.

The cavalry of the left wing will file by its left, the second line moving first, and heading the first column. This will be joined by the infantry of the left wing, (whose second line will also move before the first,) and thus the first column will be formed.

Six battalions of the rear of the first line, supported by ten squadrons of hussars will form the rear guard. These six battalions are to place themselves in order of battle in front of the defile in two lines, as the chequered disposition.

Whilst the army is passing the defile, the troops that are posted in front must cover and protect by their fire those which still remain on the other side of it.

When the whole army shall have come up, the first line of the advanced guard is to throw itself into the defile, having passed through the intervals of the second line; and when it is gone on, the second line will follow in the same manner, under cover of the fire of those who are posted on the other side, who are to follow last, and will form the rear guard.

The most difficult of all manoeuvres is that of passing a river during a retreat in presence of the enemy. On this subject I cannot quote a better example that our repassing the Elbe at Kolin in the retreat of 1744.

But as towns are not always in the neighbourhood of such situations, I will suppose that your only resource is in two bridges. In such a case a large entrenchment is to be thrown up which will include both bridges, leaving a small opening at the head of each of them.

This being done, we are to send across the river several pieces of cannon with a certain number of troops, and post them on the opposite bank, which should on no account be too steep, but sufficiently elevated to command that which is on the other side. The large entrenchment is then to be lined with infantry, and after such a disposition, the infantry are to be the first to pass over, whilst the cavalry, forming the rear guard, retire in a chequered way through the entrenchment.

When all are passed, the two small heads of the bridge are to be skirted by the infantry, whilst those who are in the entrenchment leave it, in order to retire.

If the enemy has any inclination for a pursuit, he will be exposed to the fire from both heads of the bridge, and from the troops who are posted on the other side of the river.

The infantry who were placed in the entrenchment having passed the river, the bridge is to be destroyed, and the troops who defended the heads of the bridge, are to pass over in boats, under cover of those who are posted on the other side of the river, whose duty it is to advance in order to support them.

When the pontoons are placed on the carriages, the last troops put themselves in motion.

Fougasses may also be formed at the angles of the entrenchments, which may be set on fire by the last grenadiers at the moment that they have passed the river.

ARTICLE XVI
On the Precautions necessary to be taken in a Retreat against Hussars and Pandours

The hussars and *pandours* are dreadful only to those who do not know them. They are never brave but when animated by the hope of plunder, or when they can annoy others without exposing themselves. The first species of their bravery they exercise against convoys and baggage, and the other against troops who are obliged to retire, whom they endeavour to tease in their retreat.

Our troops have nothing serious to dread from them, but as a march is often retarded by their manner of skirmishing, and as some men will unavoidably be lost, and that too at a very inconvenient season, I shall explain the best method that I am acquainted with of getting rid of these gentry.

When we retreat through plains, the hussars are to be driven away by a few discharges of cannon, and the *pandours* by means of the dragoons and hussars, of whom they are in a very great dread. The most difficult retreats, and those in which the *pandours* have it in their power to do the greatest mischief are those where we have to pass woods, defiles, and mountains. In such cases, the loss of some men is almost inevitable.

In these situations, then, the heights should be occupied by the advanced guard with their front towards the enemy, and at the same time troops are to be detached on the flank of the line of march, who keeping along on the side of the army will always pass over the heights or through the woods. Some squadrons should also be at hand to be employed where the ground will allow of it.

On these occasions, we are never to halt, but keep constantly moving, for halting would certainly be an unseasonable sacrifice of some of your men.

The *pandours* fire as they lie down, and by that means keep themselves concealed; and when the marching of the army makes it necessary for the rear guard and the small parties that were detached to quit the heights and follow the main body, they then possess themselves of those situations, and being under cover, pick off those who are retreating. Neither musketry or cannon loaded with cartridge can do them much mischief, as they are scattered and concealed behind the heights and trees.

I made two retreats of this kind in the year 1745; one by the valley of Liebenthal, when marching to Staudenitz, and the other from Trautenau to Schatzlar. Notwithstanding every possible precaution, we lost sixty men killed and wounded in the first retreat, and more than two hundred in the second.

When we have to retreat through difficult ways, our marches should be very short, that we may be the more readily and perfectly on our guard. The longest march should not exceed two leagues, or one German mile, and as then we are not hurried, we are sometimes able to force the *pandours*, especially if they are imprudent enough to take shelter in a wood, which it is in our power to turn.

ARTICLE XVII
Of the Method in which the Light Prussian Troops conduct themselves when engaged with the Hussars and *Pandours*

Our plan in forcing a post which is occupied by the enemy's light troops is, to attack it hastily, for as they disperse in their mode of fighting, they cannot stand against the attack of our regular troops, who are never to mince the matter with them.

We have only to detach a few troops to cover the flanks of the party which marches against them, and then attack them with spirit, to insure their running away.

Our dragoons and hussars attack them closely formed and sword in hand, and as this is a sort of *rencontre* which they cannot endure, it has always happened that we have beaten them, without paying any regard to the superiority of their numbers.

ARTICLE XVIII
By what Movements on our Side the Enemy may also be Obliged to Move

We are egregiously mistaken, if we suppose that the mere movement of an army will oblige the enemy also to put himself in motion. This is to be effected not simply by moving, but by the manner in which it is conducted. An intelligent enemy will not be induced to stir on account of any specious manoeuvres which you may think proper to practice: settled positions must be taken up that will oblige him to reflect, and reduce him to the necessity of decamping.

For this reason we should be well informed of the nature of the country, the abilities of the general to whom we are opposed, the situation of his magazines, the towns that are most convenient to him, and those from which he draws his forage, and when these various circumstances are well combined together, the plan is to be formed and maturely digested.

That general who has the most fertile imagination, and attempts the most frequently to distress his enemy, will eventually rival his antagonist in glory.

He who at the opening of a campaign is the most alert in the assembling his troops, and marches forward to attack a town or occupy a post, will oblige his adversary to be regulated by his motions, and remain on the defensive.

You must always be possessed of very good reasons for wishing to oblige the enemy to move during a campaign: whether with a view of taking a town near where he is encamped, driving him to a barren country where he will hardly be able to exist, or with the hope of bringing on an engagement which will prove of material advantage. Induced by reasons of this nature, you set about arranging your plan, taking care that the marches which you are to make, and the camps which you are to occupy, do not lead you into greater inconveniencies than the enemy will suffer, by drawing you away from your depot, which may be in a place but badly fortified, and liable to be plundered by the light troops during your absence; by taking up a position where you may be cut off from all communications with your own country, or by occupying a situation which you will soon be obliged to abandon for want of subsistence.

After serious deliberation on these objects, and after having calculated the chances of enterprise on the part of the enemy, your plan is to be arranged, either for the purpose of encamping on one of his flanks, approaching the provinces whence he draws his subsistence, cutting him off from his capitol, threatening his depots, or in short, taking up any position by which you deprive him of his provisions.

To give an instance with which the greatest part of my officers are well acquainted-I had formed a plan by which I had reason to hope that I should oblige Prince Charles of Lorraine to abandon Konigingraetz and Pardubitz in the year 1745.

When we quitted the camp at Dubletz, we ought to have gone to the left, passed along by the country of Glatz, and marched near Hohenmauth. By this manoeuvre we should have forced the Austrians, whose magazines were at Teutschbrod, and whose provisions were, for the most part, drawn from Moravia, to have marched to Landscron, leaving to us Konigingraetz and Pardubitz. The Saxons, being cut off from their home, would have been obliged to quit the Austrians, in order to cover their own country.

What prevented my making this manoeuvre at that period was, that I should have profited nothing if I had gained Koenigingraetz, as I must have sent detachments to the support of the Prince of Anhalt, in case that the Saxons had returned home. Besides this circumstance, the magazines at Glatz were not equal to the subsistence of my army during the whole of the campaign.

The diversions that are made by detaching troops, will also sometimes oblige the enemy to decamp, for generally speaking, every kind of enterprise that comes on him unawares will have the effect of deranging him, and obliging him to quit his position.

Of such nature are the passing of mountains which the enemy deems impassible, and the crossing of rivers without his knowledge.

Sufficient information is to be gained on this head by reading the campaign of Prince Eugene in the year 1701. The confusion of the French army when it was surprised by Prince Charles of Lorraine; who had crossed the Rhine, is a matter sufficiently well understood.

I shall conclude by saying, that the execution of enterprises of this nature should always correspond with the design, and as long as the general's dispositions are wise and founded on solid principles, so long will he have it in his power to give the law to his enemy, and oblige him to keep on the defensive.

ARTICLE XIX
Of the Crossing of Rivers

As long as the enemy remains on the other side of a river which you wish to cross, all force is useless, and recourse must be made to stratagem. To be informed how we are to pass a large river, we have only to consult Caesar's passage of the Rhine, that of the Po by Prince Eugene, or of the Rhine by Prince Charles of Lorraine. These generals sent out detachments to impose upon the enemy, and conceal the spot where they intended to pass. They made every preparation for the building of bridges in places where they had no idea of employing them, whilst the main body of the army, by a night march, gained a considerable distance from the enemy, and had time to pass the river before the troop, who were to dispute their passage, could be put in order to prevent them.

We generally choose to cross rivers at those parts where there are some small islands, as they forward the business very materially. We wish also to meet on the other side with woods or other obstacles that may prevent the enemy from attacking us before we have had time to get into proper order.

The most prudent measures and the most particular attention are required in enterprises of this nature. The boats or pontoons with every other article of necessary apparatus must be at the rendezvous by the appointed hour, and every boatman well instructed what generally attends expeditions by night. Everything being arranged, the troops are to pass over and establish themselves on the other side of the river.

Whenever rivers are to be crossed, care should be taken that the two heads of the bridge be entrenched, and well furnished with troops. The islands which are in the neighbourhood should be fortified, in order to support the entrenchments, and prevent the enemy, during your operations, from seizing or destroying the bridges.

If the rivers be narrow, we choose our passage at those parts where they form angles, and where the bank, by being a little more elevated, commands that on the opposite side.

On this spot we place as many cannon, with a proportionate number of troops, as the ground will allow, under the protection of which the bridges are to be built; and as the ground grows narrower on account of the angle, we are to advance but very little, and insensibly gain ground as the troops pass.

If there be any fords, we slope the ground leading to them, to enable the cavalry to pass.

ARTICLE XX
Of the Manner in which the Passage of Rivers is to be Defended

Nothing is more difficult, not to say impossible, than to defend the passage of a river, especially when the front of attack be of too great an extent. I would never undertake a commission of this kind, if the ground which I had to defend was more than eight German miles in front, and unless there were two or three redoubts established on the bank of the river within this distance; neither should any other part of the river be fordable.

But supposing the situation to be exactly as I have stated, time must always be required to make the necessary preparations against the enterprises of the enemy, the disposition of which should be nearly as follows:—

All the boats and barks which can be found upon the river should be got together and conveyed to the two redoubts, that the enemy may not have it in his power to make use of them.

Both the banks of the river are to be reconnoitre, that you may discover and destroy those parts of them where it would be possible to pass.

The ground which might protect the passage of the enemy is to be particularly attended to, and your plans of attack must be regulated by the nature and situation of each part of it.

Roads sufficiently wide to admit of many columns are to be made along the whole front of the river which you are to defend, that you may march against the enemy free of every impediment.

These precautions being taken, the army is to be encamped in the centre of the line of defence that you may have but four miles to march to either extremity. Sixteen small detachments are then to be formed, and commanded by the most active, intelligent officers of dragoons and hussars; eight of which, under the orders of a general officer, are to have charge of the front of attack on the right, whilst the other eight, commanded in like manner, take care of the left.

These detachments will be designed to give information of the enemy's movements, and of the spot where it will be his intention to pass.

During the day, guards are to be posted to discover what is going forward, and by night patrols are to go out every quarter of an hour near to the river, and not retire till they have distinctly seen that the enemy has made a bridge, and that the head has passed.

The aforesaid generals and commanding officers of redoubts are to send their reports to the commander in chief four times a day.

Fresh horses should be stationed between them and the army, in order to hasten the arrival of their dispatches, and inform the general as immediately as possible when the enemy is about to pass. As it is the duty of the general to repair thither at a moment's warning, his baggage should be sent away beforehand, that he may be ready for every event.

The different dispositions for each part of the ground being already made, the generals are appointed by the commander in chief to those which regard the points of attack. No time is to be lost in marching, (the infantry taking the lead of the columns,) as you are to suppose that the enemy are entrenching themselves. When arrived, the attack is to be made instantly and with great spirit, as the only means of promising to yourself brilliant success.

The passages of small rivers are still more difficult to defend; their fords are to be rendered impassible, if possible, by throwing in of trees. But if the enemy's bank commands yours it is vain to attempt resistance.

ARTICLE XXI
Of the Surprise of Towns

A town must be badly guarded and weakly fortified that suffers a surprise;

and if it's ditches be filled with water, the success of such enterprises must depend on a wintry season and hard frost.

Towns may be surprised by a whole army, as was the case at Prague in the year 1741, or the accident may happen from the garrison having been lulled into security by a long continued blockade, as was effected by Prince Leopold d'Anhalt at Glogau. Detachments also sometimes have the desired effect, as was attempted by Prince Eugene at Cremona, and as succeeded with the Austrians at Cosel.

The principal rule in making dispositions for surprise is, to be well informed of the nature of the fortifications and of the interiors of the place, so as to direct your attack to any particular spot.

The surprise of Glogau was a *chef d'oeuvre*, and is well worth the imitation of those who attempt such enterprises. There was nothing so extraordinary in the surprise of Prague, as it was impossible by such a variety of attacks must carry a place, where the garrison had so great an extent to defend. Cosel and Cremona were betrayed; the first by an officer who deserted and informed the Austrians that the excavation of the ditch was not quite completed, by which means they got over, and the place was carried.

If we wish to take small places, we batter some of the gates with mortars, whilst detachments are sent to the others to prevent the garrison from saving themselves.

If cannon are to be employed, they must be so placed that the artillerymen be not exposed to the fire of the musketry; otherwise the guns will be in danger of being lost.

ARTICLE XXII
Of Combats and Battles

The Austrian camp is surrounded by such a number of light troops, as to render a surprise a work of very great difficulty.

If two armies keep near to each other, the business will very soon be decided, unless one of them occupies an inaccessible post that will secure it from surprises; a circumstance which seldom takes place between armies, though it be nothing uncommon between detachments.

To have it in our power to surprise an enemy in his camp, it is necessary that he relies entirely either on the superiority of his troops, the advantageous situation of his post, the reports of his emissaries, or lastly, on the vigilance of his light troops.

The nature of the country and the position of the enemy should be perfectly well understood prior to the formation of any plan.

The roads leading to camp must be well examined, and the general disposition of things formed from thence, being regulated in every point by the particular and exact knowledge of all attendant circumstances.

The most intelligent chasseurs, which are best acquainted with the roads, should be appointed to conduct the columns.

Be particularly careful to conceal your design, for secrecy is the soul of all enterprises.

The light troops should take the lead on the march, for which regulation various reasons may be assigned, though the real one be to prevent any scoundrel of a deserter from betraying you. They will also be of service by preventing the enemy's patrols from approaching too nearly and discovering your movements.

The generals who are under your orders must be well instructed of all events that may happen, and how to act when any accident occurs.

If the enemy's camp be situated in a plain, an advanced guard may be formed of dragoons, who, being joined by the hussars, will enter the enemy's camp on full speed, throw it into confusion, and cut down whatever comes in their way.

The whole army should support these dragoons, and the infantry being at the head of it, should be particularly employed in attacking the wings of the enemy's cavalry.

The advanced guard should begin the attack half an hour before day, but the army should not be more than eight hundred yards in its rear.

During the march the most profound silence is to be observed, and the soldiers must be forbidden to smoke tobacco.

When the attack has commenced and the day appears, the infantry, formed into four or six columns, must march straight forward to the camp, in order to support it's advanced guard.

No firing is to be allowed before day-light, as it might prove the means of destroying our own people: but as soon as the day is broke, we should fire on all those places into which the advanced guard has not penetrated, especially on the wings of the cavalry, that we may oblige the troopers, who have not time to *accoutre* their horses, to abandon them and fly.

The enemy is to be followed even out of their camp, and the whole of the cavalry should be let loose after them to take advantage of their disorder and confusion.

If the enemy have abandoned their arms, a strong detachment must be left in charge of the camp, whilst the remainder of the army, instead of amusing themselves with plunder, pursue the enemy with all possible ardour;

the more so, as a like opportunity of entirely routing them, may not soon present itself, and we may, by so doing, have the upper hand during the whole campaign, and be able to act just as we think proper.

Fortune intended to favour me with an opportunity of this kind before the battle of Mollwitz: we approached the army of the Marshal de Neuperg without being perceived, as they were cantoned in three villages; but at that time I wanted information how to profit by such circumstance.

My business then was, to have surrounded the village of Mollwitz by two columns, and to have attacked it. At the same moment I should have detached some dragoons to the other two villages where the Austrian cavalry lay, in order to throw them into confusion, whilst the infantry who followed them would have prevented the cavalry from mounting. By this method I am persuaded the whole army would have been destroyed.

I have already shown the necessary cautions that respect our camp, and the manner in which it is to be protected: but if in spite of all our care, the enemy should approach the army, I would advise that the troops be formed in order of battle on the ground which is allotted to them, and that the cavalry remain firm on their posts, firing by platoons till daybreak. The generals are then to examine whether it be advisable to advance, if the cavalry has been victorious or suffered a repulse, and what farther methods are to be pursued.

On such occasions, each general should know how to act independently, without being obliged to wait for the instructions of the commander in chief.

For my own part, I am determined never to attack by night, on account of the confusion which darkness necessarily occasions, and because the major part of the soldiery require the eye of their officers, and the fear of punishments, to induce them to do their duty.

Charles XII in the year 1715, attacked the Prince of Anhalt in the night, though he was but just disembarked on the island of Rugen. The King of Sweden had reason for so doing, as daylight would have discovered the weakness of his army. He came with four thousand men to attack five times the number, and of course was defeated.

It is an invariable axiom of war, to secure your flanks and rear, and endeavour to turn those of your enemy. This may be done in different ways, though they all depend on the same principle.

When you are obliged to attack an entrenched enemy, it should be done instantly, without allowing him time to finish his works. What would be of advantage to-day, may not be so to-morrow.

But before you set about making the attack, the enemy's position must be well reconnoitred with your own eyes, and your first dispositions of attack will convince you whether your scheme will be easily put into execution, or become a work of labour and difficulty.

The want of sufficient support is the chief reason that entrenchments are taken. The entrenchment of Turenne was carried, as was also that of Stralsund because there was sufficient ground to enable the Prince of Anhalt to turn it. That of Malplaquet was turned by the wood which was on the Marshal Villers' left. Had the allies been aware of this circumstance at the beginning of the battle, it would have saved their army fifteen thousand men.

If a fordable river supports the entrenchment, it must be attacked on that side. The work at Stralsund, conducted by the Swedes, was carried because the attack was made on the sea-side, where it happened to be fordable.

If the enemy's entrenchments are of too great an extent, so that the troops are obliged to occupy more ground than they can well defend, we attack at several points, and provided we can keep our designs secret from the enemy, (which will prevent his meeting us with a sufficient force), we shall certainly get possession of the works.

Sketch 1 will explain the following dispositions of an attack on an entrenchment, where I shall form the line with thirty battalions, and strengthen the left wing by the river N. N. The attack on the left, where I wish to penetrate, shall be made by twelve battalions and that on the right by eight. The troops destined for the attack are to be formed in a chequered way, with the allowance of proper intervals. The remainder of the infantry is to throw themselves into the third line, and behind them, at the distance of four hundred yards, the cavalry should be posted. By this means my infantry will

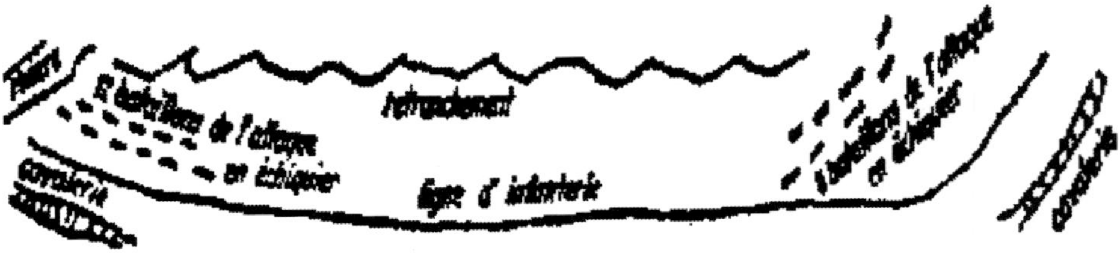

riviere – river
12 bataillons de l'attaque en echiquier – 12 attack battalions in checquerboard
retranchment – entrenchment
ligne d'infanterie – line of infantry
8 bataillons de l'attaque en echiquier – 8 attack battalions in checquerboard
cavalerie - cavalry

Sketch 1

keep the enemy in check, and be ready to take advantage of any false movement which he may make.

Care must be taken that each of these attacks be followed closely by a number of pioneers with shovels, pick-axes, and fascines to fill up the ditch, and make a road for the cavalry, when the entrenchment shall have been forced.

The infantry who form the attack are not to fire till the work is carried, and they are drawn up in order of battle on the parapet.

The cavalry are to enter through the openings made by the pioneers, and attack the enemy as soon as they find themselves of sufficient force. If the cavalry be repulsed, they must rally under the cover of the infantry's fire until the whole army has got in, and the enemy is entirely routed.

I must here repeat, that I would never entrench my army unless I had a siege in contemplation; and I am not decided, whether it be not the best plan to go on before the army that comes to relieve a place.

But supposing for a moment, that we have an inclination to entrench ourselves; to execute such intention, the following method appears to me the most advantageous.

We contrive to have two or three large reserves, which are to be sent out during the attack to those points where the enemy is making his greatest efforts.

The parapet is to be lined by battalions, and a reserve placed behind them, to be at hand in case of necessity. The cavalry should be ranged in one line behind these reserves.

The entrenchments should be very well supported, and if it be joined by a river, the ditch should be carried some distance into it, to prevent its being turned.

If it be strengthened by a wood, it should be closed at that end by a redoubt, and a large abbatis of trees should also be made in the wood.

Particular regard must be paid to the flanking of the *redans*.

The ditch should be very deep and wide, and the entrenchments must be improved every day, either by strengthening the parapet, placing palisades at the entrance of the barriers, digging of pits, or furnishing the whole of the camp with *chevaux de frize.*

The greatest advantage you have is, in the choice of your work, and in the observance of certain rules of fortification which will oblige the enemy to attack you on a small front, and that only in the principle points of your entrenchment.

Sketch 2 will give you a more exact idea of this business. The army,

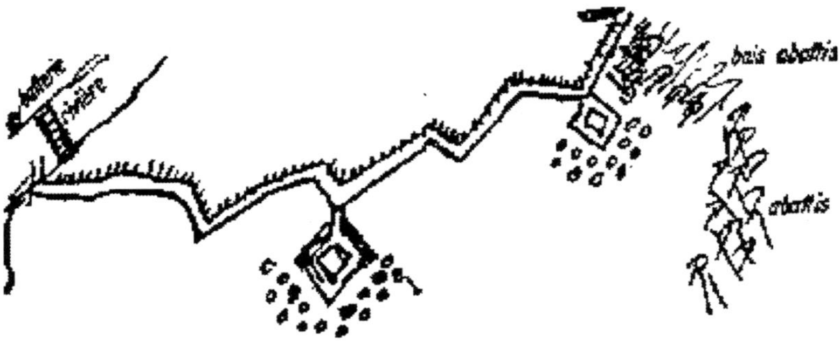

batterie – battery
riviere – river
bois abattis – woods, abattis

Sketch 2

which is there placed at the head of the entrenchment is thrown back on one side by the river, so that you present a projecting front to the enemy who comes to attack you. Your right is safe from attack by means of the batteries placed at the extremities of that wing, which would play upon the enemy's flank, whilst the centre redoubt would take him in the rear. The only point liable to attack therefore is the centre redoubt, and even here he will be obliged to cut his way through the abbatis.

In your preparations for this attack it behooves you therefore to strengthen the fortifications of this redoubt, and as you have but one point which demands your particular attention, that one will consequently be more perfect and complete.

Sketch 3 exhibits entrenchments of a different kind, which are composed of projecting and receding redoubts, which cross each other, and are connected by entrenchments.

By this method of fortification, those that project from the point of attack,

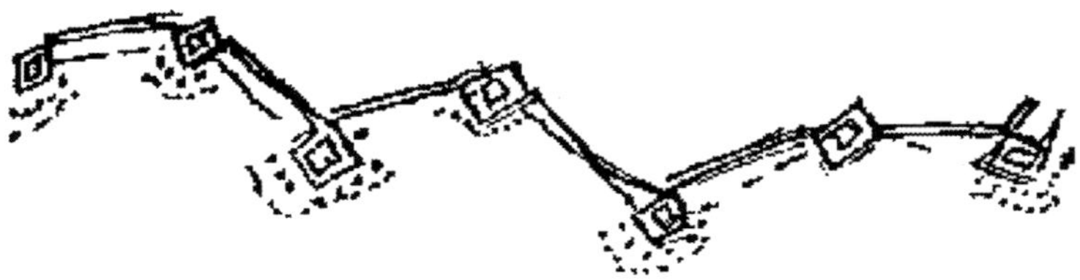

Sketch 3

and as they are but few of them, much less time is required in completing them, than if the whole front was to be equally well fortified.

In these projecting redoubts, the fire of the musketry must always cross each other, and for this reason they should never be more than six hundred yards apart.

Our infantry defend an entrenchment by the fire of entire battalions, and every soldier should be provided with one hundred rounds. This, however, is not to prevent the placing as many cannon as we can between the battalions and the projecting redoubts.

Whilst the enemy is at a distance, we fire shot, but when they approach within four hundred yards, we have recourse to cartridges.

If, notwithstanding the strength of your entrenchment, and the smartness of your fire, the enemy should make any impression, the reserve of infantry must march forward to repel him, and if they also be obliged to fall back, your last effort to put him to the route must depend upon your cavalry.

The principal reasons why entrenchments are carried are these, the want of attention to proper rules in their construction, or the troops being turned or panic struck: the superior freedom and boldness with which the attackers are able to conduct themselves, gives them this advantage.

Examples have already shown that when an entrenchment is forced, the whole army is discouraged and put to flight: I have a better opinion of my troops, and am persuaded that they would repel the enemy; but what end would this answer, if the entrenchments prevent their profiting by such advantages?

As there are so many inconveniencies attending entrenchments, it naturally follows that lines are still more useless. The fashion of our day is that which was practiced by Prince Louis de Baden, whose first lines were made on the side of Briel. The French also employed them after that in Flanders. I maintain that they are of no service whatever, since they compass more ground than the troops can possibly defend; they allow of a variety of attacks being made on them, and tempt the enemy to force a passage. On this account they do not cover the country, but, on the contrary, ensure the loss of reputation to the troops who have to defend them.

Although a Prussian army should be inferior to that which is opposed to them, they are not to despair of success, as the general's management will supply the want of numbers.

An army that is weak should always make choice of a difficult, mountainous country, where the ground narrows, so that the superior number of the enemy, not being able to pass their wings, becomes useless, and often an encumbrance to them.

It may here be added, that in a country which is close and hilly, the wings can better be supported than when we are on a plain. We should not have gained the battle of Sohr but for the advantage of the ground, for though the Austrian army doubled ours, they were not able to break through our wings, as the ground rendered both the armies nearly equal.

The choice of ground is my first object, and my second the disposition of the battle itself; it is here that my oblique order of battle may be employed to advantage, for you to refuse one wing to the enemy, whilst you strengthen that which ought to make the attack. By this means you turn all your force on that wing of the enemy which you wish to take in flank.

An army of ten thousand men, if it's flanks are turned, will very soon be defeated. Every thing is done by my right wing. A body of infantry will move by degrees into the wood, to attack the flanks of the enemy's cavalry, and protect the onset of our own: some regiments of hussars should be ordered to take the enemy in the rear whilst the army advances, and when their cavalry are routed, the infantry who are in the wood must take the enemy's infantry in flank, whilst the remainder are attacking them in front.

My left wing will not stir till the enemy's left wing is entirely defeated.

By this disposition you will gain the following advantages: 1st, that of making head with a small force against a much superior number; secondly, of attacking the enemy at a point which will decide the business; thirdly, if your wing should chance to be beaten, as only a small part of your army has been engaged, three fourths of your troops, who are fresh, will be ready to support you in your retreat. See Sketch 4.

If you wish to attack an enemy that is advantageously posted, you must carefully examine both his strong and weak side before you make your dispositions for attack, and always choose that point where you expect to meet with the least resistance.

So many men are lost in the attacks on villages that I have vowed never to undertake them, unless obliged by absolute necessity, for you run the hazard of losing the flower of your infantry.

It is said by some generals, that the most proper point of attack is the centre of a post. Sketch 5 will represent the situation of such a post, where I suppose the enemy to have two large towns and two villages on its wings. The wings must certainly be lost, when you have forced the centre, and by similar attacks, the most complete victories may be obtained.

If must be added to the plan which I here lay down, that you must double your attack when you have once made an impression, in order to force the enemy to fall back both on his right and upon his left.

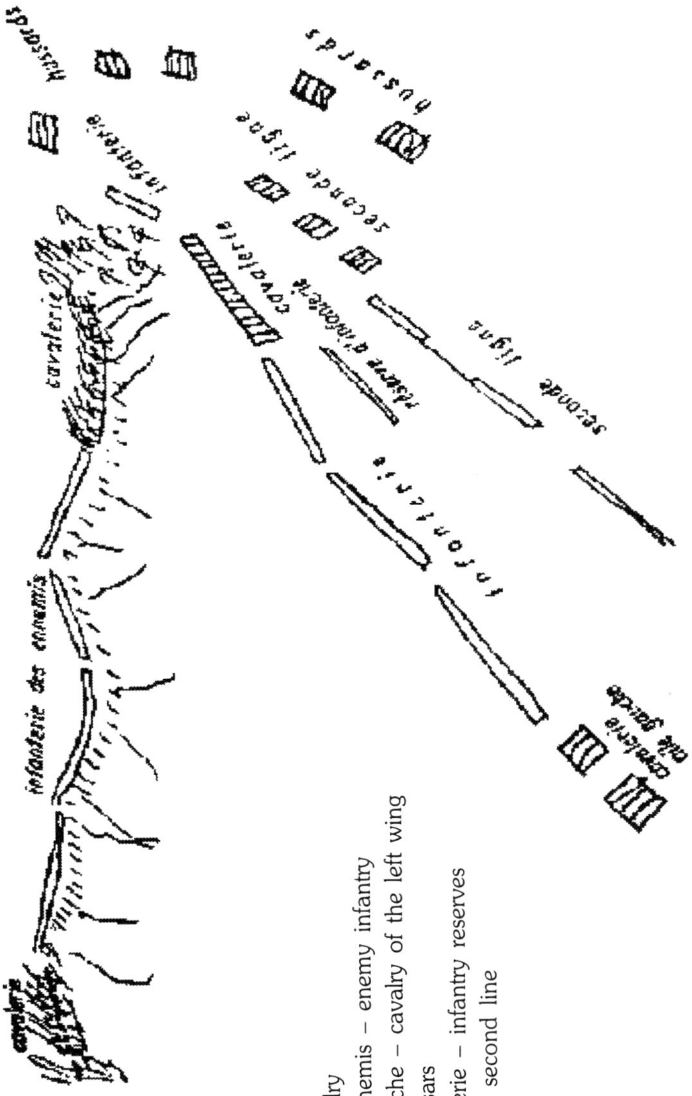

Sketch 4

cavalerie – cavalry
infanterie des enemis – enemy infantry
cavalry aile gauche – cavalry of the left wing
hussards – hussars
reserve d'infanterie – infantry reserves
seconde ligne – second line

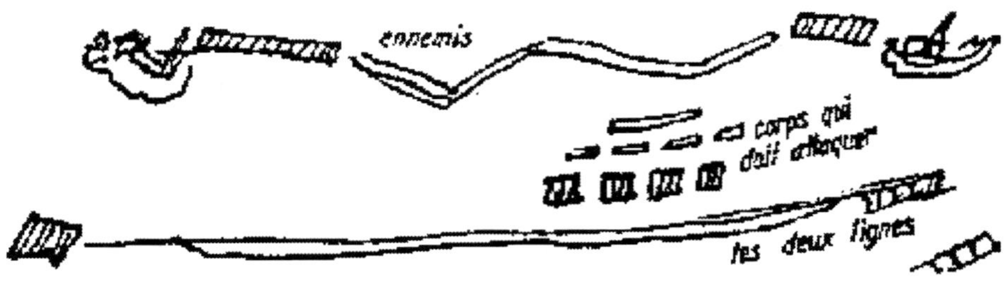

enemis – enemy
corps qui doit attaquer – force which is to attack
les deux lignes – the two lines

Sketch 5

Nothing is so formidable in the attack of a post, as the discharge of cartridges from the batteries, which made a terrible havoc amongst the battalions. I witnessed the attacks on the batteries of Sohr and Kesseldorf, and shall here communicate the idea suggested by my reflections on that business, supposing that we wish to be possessed of a battery mounted with fifteen pieces of cannon, which it is not in our power to turn.

I have remarked, that the fire of cannon and of infantry who defend a battery render it inaccessible. We cannot make ourselves masters of the enemy's batteries but through their own fault: finding our infantry who attacked half destroyed and giving way, the infantry of the enemy quit their post to follow them, and being by this movement deprived of the use of their cannon, when they return to their batteries, our people enter with them and take possession. See Sketch 6.

The experience of those two battles gave me the idea, that in similar cases we should copy the example of our troops on this occasion, viz. to form the attack in two lines in a chequered way, and to be supported in the third line by some squadrons of dragoons.

The first line should be ordered to attack but faintly, and fall back through the intervals of the second, so that the enemy, deceived by this sham retreat, may abandon his post in order to pursue us.

This movement of theirs is to be our signal to advance and make a vigorous attack.

It is my principle, never to place my whole confidence in one post, unless it can be physically proved to be safe from any attack.

The great dependence of our troops is in attacking, and we should act very foolish part to give up this point without good reason.

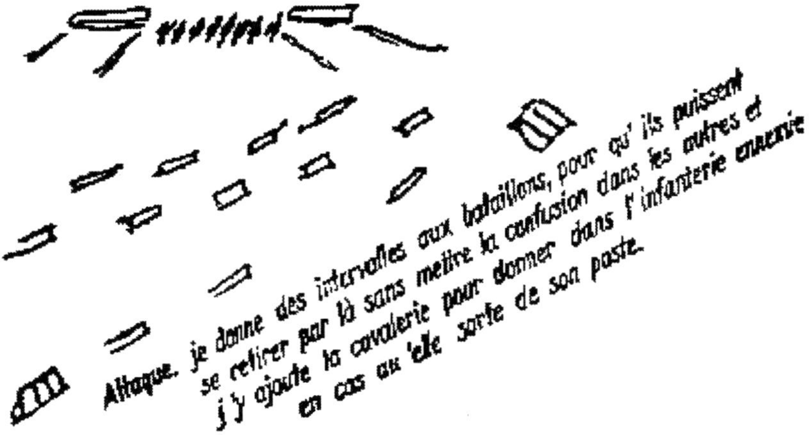

Attack. I place intervals between battalions so that they can retire through them without creating confusion in the others and I add the cavalry to charge the enemy infantry in case it leaves its position.

Sketch 6

But if it be necessary that posts should be occupied, we remember to get possession of the heights, and make our wings sufficiently strong.

I would burn every village which is at the head or on the wings of the army, if the wind did not drive the smoke into the camp.

If there were any strong stone houses in front, I would defend them by the infantry, in order to annoy the enemy during the action.

Great care should be taken, not to place troops on ground where they cannot act; it was this which made our position at Grotkau in the year 1741 worth nothing, for the centre and left wing were posted behind impassible bogs. The only ground that would admit of being manoeuvred on, was that which was occupied by a part of the right wing.

Villeroy was beaten at Ramillies for the very reason that I have just mentioned, as his right wing was rendered entirely useless, and the enemy crowded all it's force against the right wing of the French which could make no resistance.

I allow the Prussian troops to take possession of advantageous posts as well as other troops, and to make use of them in favour of any movement, or to take advantage of their artillery; but they must quit this post instantly to march against the enemy, who instead of being allowed to begin the attack, is attacked himself, and sees all his projects miscarry. Every movement which we make in presence of the enemy without his expecting it, will certainly produce a good effect.

We must rank battles of this kind amongst the best, always remembering to attack the weakest point.

On these occasions, I would not permit the infantry to fire, for it only retards their march, and the victory is not decided be the number of slain, but by the extent of territory which you have gained.

The most certain way of insuring victory is, to march briskly and in good order against the enemy, always endeavouring to gain ground. It is the custom to allow fifteen yards of interval between squadrons in a difficult, intersected country, but where the ground is good and even, they form in a line entire.

No greater interval is to be allowed between the infantry than is sufficient for the cannon. It is only in attacks of entrenchment, batteries, and villages, and in the formation of the rear guard in a retreat, that the cavalry and infantry are placed in a chequered way, in order to give an immediate support to the first line by making the second fall into it's intervals, so that the troops may retire without disorder, and be a mutual support to each other. This is a rule never to be neglected.

An opportunity offers itself here of giving you some principle rules on what you are to observe when you range the army in order of battle, whatever the ground may happen to be. See Sketch 7.

The general must be particularly careful that he does not suffer the troops to take up a wrong position.

It is not always necessary to defer the attack till the whole army can engage, as opportunity may present advantages which would be lost by a little delay.

A great part of the army, however, ought to be engaged, and the first line should be the chief object in the regulation of the order of battle. If all the regiments of that line are not present, they should be replaced by the same number of the second.

The wings should always be well supported; especially those which are expected to make the greatest exertions.

In an open country, the order of battle should be equally strong throughout, for as the enemy's movements are unconfined, he may have reserved a part of his army which he may make use of to cut you out a little employment.

In case that one of the two wings should not be properly supported, the general who commands the second line should send some dragoons thither, (without waiting for an order on the occasion) to extend the first line, and the hussars taken from the third line should replace the dragoons.

The reason for so doing, is, that if the enemy make a movement to take

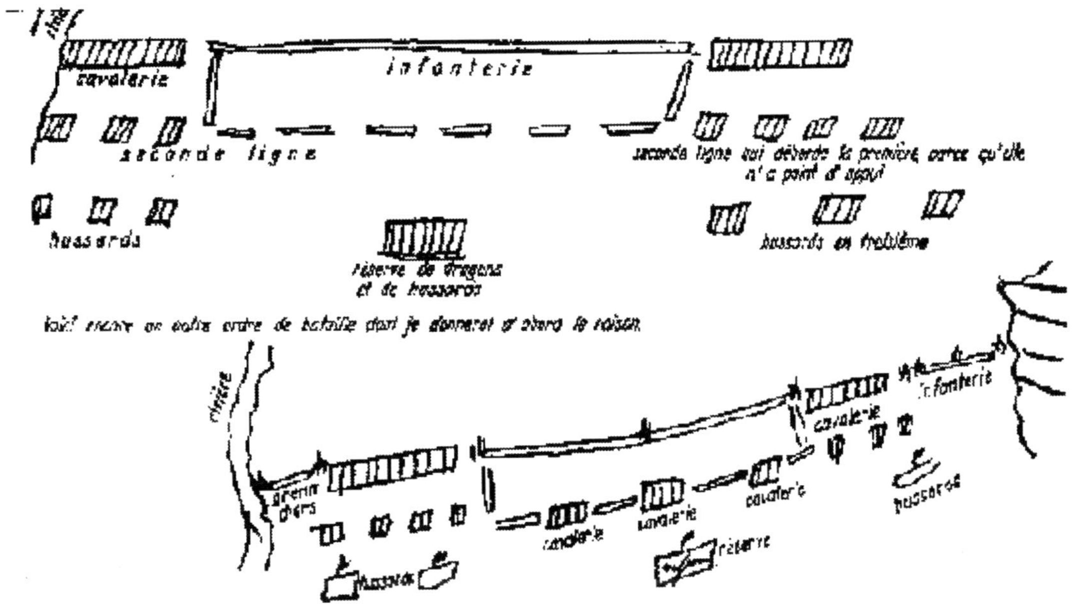

riviere – river
cavalerie – cavalry
seconde ligne – second line
hussards – hussars
seconde ligne qui deborde la premiere, parce qu'elle n'a point d'appui – second line which extends beyond the first because it has no point of support
Voici encore un autre ordre de bataille don't je donnerai d'abord laraison – Here is another order of battle for which I shall first give the reason
reserve de dragons et de hussards – reserve of dragoons and hussars
grenadiers - grenadiers

Sketch 7

the cavalry of the first line in flank, your dragoons and hussars may be able in turn to repay the compliment.

You will see that I place three battalions in the interval between the two lines of the left wing, the better to support it: for supposing your cavalry to be beaten, these battalions will always prevent the enemy from falling foul on the infantry, an instance of which we witnessed at Mollwitz.

The general commanding the second line must preserve a distance of three hundred paces from the first, and if he perceives any intervals in the first line, he is to fill them up with battalions from the second.

In a plain, a reserve of cavalry should always be placed in the rear of the centre of the battalions, and be commanded by an officer of address, as he is to act from himself, either in support of a wing that he sees hardly pressed, or by flanking the enemy who are in pursuit of the wing that is thrown into disorder, that the cavalry may in the mean time have an opportunity of rallying.

The affair should be begun by the cavalry on full gallop, and the infantry also should march on briskly towards the enemy. Commanding officers are to take care that their troops penetrate and entirely break through the enemy, and that they make no use of their fire arms till their backs are turned.

If the soldiers fire without the word of command, they are to be ordered to shoulder arms, and proceed without any halting.

When the enemy begins to give way, we fire, by battalions, and a battle conducted in this manner will very soon be decided.

A new order of battle which differs from the others in having bodies of infantry placed at the extremities of the wings of the cavalry. The battalions are intended to support the cavalry, by playing with their own cannon and those belonging to the wings of the cavalry, on the enemy's cavalry, at the beginning of the affair, that our own may have a better game to play during the attack. Another reason is, that supposing your wings to be beaten, the enemy dare not pursue, for fear of being between two fires.

When your cavalry, to all appearance, has been victorious, this infantry is to approach that of the enemy, and the battalions which are in the intervals must make a quarter-wheel and place themselves on your wings, to take the enemy's infantry in flank and rear, and enable you to make a handsome business of it.

The conquering wing of your cavalry must not allow the enemy's cavalry to rally, but pursue them in good order, and endeavour to cut them off from the infantry. When the confusion becomes general, the commanding officer should detach the hussars after them, who are to be supported by the cavalry. At the same time some dragoons should be sent to the roads which the infantry have taken, in order to pick them up, and by cutting off their retreat, make a great number of them prisoners.

There is another difference in this order of battle, which is, that the squadrons of dragoons are mixed with the infantry of the second line: this is done, because I have remarked in all the affairs which we have had with the Austrians, that after the fire of their musketry has continued for about a quarter of an hour, they get together round their colours; at Hohen Friedburg our cavalry charged many of these round-about parties, and made a great number of them prisoners. The dragoons, being near at hand, are to be let loose instantly, and they never fail to give a very good account of them.

It will be said, that I never employ my small arms, but that it is my wish in all these dispositions to make use of may artillery only: to this I answer, that one of the two accidents which I suppose will unavoidably happen, either that my infantry fire in spite of my orders to the contrary, or that they obey my commands, and the enemy begins to give way. In either case, as soon as you perceive any confusion amongst their troops, you are to detach the cavalry after them, and when they find themselves attacked in flank on one side, charged in front, and their second line of cavalry cut off by the rear, the greatest part of them will be sure to fall into your hands.

It then cannot be called a battle, but an entire destruction of your enemies, especially if there be no defile in the neighbourhood to protect their flight.

I shall close this article with a single reflection, viz. if you march to battle in column, whether by the right or by the left, the battalions or divisions must follow each other closely, that when you begin to deploy, you may have it in your power readily to engage. But if you march in front, the distances of the battalions must be well attended to, that they be not too close or too far from each other.

I make a distinction between the heavy cannon and the field pieces attached to the battalions, as the former should be planted on the heights, and the latter fifty paces in front of the battalions. Both the one and the other should be well pointed and well fired.

When we are within five hundred yards of the enemy, the field pieces should be drawn by men that they may fire without intermission as we advance.

If the enemy begins to fly, the heavy cannon are to move forward and fire a few rounds, by way of wishing them a good journey.

Six gunners and three regimental carpenters should be attached to every piece in the first line.

I had omitted saying, that at the distance of three hundred and fifty yards, the cannon should begin to fire cartridges.

But to what end serves the art of conquest, if we are ignorant how to profit by our advantage? To shed the blood of soldiers when there is no occasion for it, is to lead them inhumanly to the slaughter; and not to pursue the enemy on certain occasions, to increase their fear and the number of our prisoners, is leaving an affair to future chance which might be determined at the present moment. Nevertheless, you may sometimes be prevented from pursuing your conquest by a want of provisions, or the troops being too much fatigued.

It is always the fault of the general in chief if an army wants provisions. When he gives battle, he has a design in so doing: and if he has a design, it is his duty to be provided with every thing necessary for the execution of it, and of course he ought to be supplied with bread or biscuit for eight or ten days.

With respect to fatigues, if they had not been too excessive, they must not be regarded, as on extraordinary occasions extraordinary feats should be performed.

When victory is perfectly decided, I would recommend a detachment to be made of those regiments who have been the greatest sufferers, to take care of the wounded, and convey them to the hospitals, which ought to be already established. Though our own wounded are to be the first objects of our attention, we are not to forget our duty to the enemy.

In the mean time the army is to pursue the enemy to the nearest defile, which in the first transport of their alarm they will not tarry to keep possession of, if you take care not to allow them sufficient time to recover their wind.

When you have attended to all these circumstances, the camp is to be marked out, paying strict regard to the established rules, and not allowing yourself to be lulled with too great an idea of security.

If the victory has been complete, we may send out detachments either to cut off the enemy's retreat, seize his magazines, or lay siege to three or four towns at the same time.

On this article, general rules only can be given, as a great deal must depend on fortuitous circumstances. You are never to imagine that every thing is done as long as any thing remains undone; nor are you to suppose but that a cunning enemy, though he may have been beaten, will keep a sharp look-out to take advantage of your negligence or errors.

I pray to heaven, that the Prussians never may be beaten, and dare affirm that such an accident never will happen if they are well led on and well disciplined.

But should they meet with a disaster of such a nature, the following rules are to be observed in order to recover the misfortune. When you see that the battle is inevitably lost, and that it is not in your power to oppose the enemy's movements, or even resist them much longer, you are to send the second line of infantry to any defile that may be near, and place them in it agreeably to the disposition which I have given under the article of retreats, sending thither at the same time as many cannon as you can spare.

If there be no defile in the neighbourhood, the first line must retire through the interval of the second, and place itself in order of battle three hundred yards behind them.

All the remains of your cavalry must be got together, and if you choose it, they may be formed into a square to protect your retreat.

History furnishes us with accounts of two remarkable squares: one that was formed by General Schullembourg after the battle of Frauenstadt, by means of which he retired across the Oder without being forced by Charles XII.; the other by the Prince of Anhalt when General Stirum lost the first battle of Hochstaedt. This Prince traversed a plain of two leagues, and the French cavalry did not dare to molest him.

I shall conclude with saying, that though we are defeated, there is no occasion for running away forty leagues, but that we are to halt at the first advantageous post, and put a bold face upon the business, in order to collect the scattered army, and encourage those who are dispirited.

ARTICLE XXIII
Of the Reasons which should induce us to give Battle, and in what Manner it is to be conducted

Battles determine the fate of nations. It is necessary that actions should be decisive, either to free ourselves from the inconveniencies of a state of warfare, to place our enemy in that unpleasant situation, or to settle a quarrel which otherwise perhaps would never be finished. A man that is wise will make no sort of movement without good reason; and a general of an army should never be engaged without some design of consequence. If he be forced into an engagement by his adversary, his former errors must have reduced him to that situation, and given his enemy the power of dictating the law to him.

On the present occasion it will be seen, that I am not writing my own panegyric: for out of five battles which my troops have given to the enemy, three of them only were premeditated, and I was forced by the enemy into the other two. At the affair of Mollwitz the Austrians had posted themselves between my army and Wohlau, where I kept my provisions and artillery. At that of the Sohr, the enemy had cut me off from the road to Trautenau, so that I was obliged to fight, or run the risk of losing my whole army. But how great is the difference between forced and premeditated battles! How brilliant was our success at Hohen-Friedberg, at Kesseldorf, and also at Czaslau, which last engagement was the means of procuring us peace!

Though I am here laying down rules for battles, I do not pretend to deny that I have often erred through inadvertence; my officers, however, are expected to profit by my mistakes, and they may be assured, that I shall apply myself with all diligence to correct them.

It sometimes happens that both the armies wish to engage, and then the business is very soon settled.

Those battles are the best into which we force the enemy, for it is an established maxim, to oblige him to do that for which he has no sort of inclination, and as your interest and his are so diametrically opposite, it cannot be supposed that you are both wishing for the same event.

Many are the reasons that may induce us to give battle, such as, a desire to oblige the enemy to raise the siege of any place that may prove of convenience to yourself, to drive him out of a province which he possess, penetrate his country, enable yourself to lay a siege, correct him for his stubbornness if he refuse to make peace, or make him suffer for some error that he has committed.

You will also oblige the enemy to come to action when, by a forced march, you fall upon his rear and cut off his communications, or by threatening a town which it is his interest to preserve.

But in this sort of manoeuvre great care is to be taken that you do not get into the same embarrassed situation, or take up a position which enables the enemy to cut you off from your magazines.

The affairs which are undertaken against rear guards are attended with the least danger.

If you entertain a design of this nature, you are to encamp near the enemy, and when he wishes to retire and pass the defiles in your presence, make an attack upon his rear. Much advantage is often gained by engagements of this kind.

It is also a custom to tease and tire the enemy, in order to prevent different bodies from forming a junction. The object in view sufficiently warrants such attempt, but a skilful enemy will have the address to get out of your way by a forced march, or escape the accident by taking up an advantageous position.

Sometimes when you have no inclination to fight, we are induced to it by the misconduct of the enemy, who should always be punished for his faults, if we can profit by so doing.

It must be urged, in addition to all these maxims, that our wars should ever be of short duration, and conducted with spirit, for it must always be against our interest to be engaged in a tedious affair. A long war must tend insensibly to relax our admirable discipline, depopulate our country, and exhaust its resources.

For this reason, generals commanding Prussian armies should endeavour, notwithstanding their success, to terminate every business prudently and quickly. They must not argue, as the Marshal de Luxembourg did in the Flanders wars, who when he was told by his son, "Father, it appears to me, that we could still take another town," replied, "Hold your tongue, you little fool! Would you have us go home to plant cabbages?" In a word, on the subject of battles, we ought to be guided by the maxim of Sannerib of the Hebrews, "that it is better one man perish than a whole people."

With regard to punishing an enemy for his fault, we should consult the relation of the battle of Senef, where the Prince of Conde brought on an affair of the rear guard against the Prince of Orange or the Prince of Waldeck, who had neglected to occupy the head of a defile, in order to facilitate his retreat.

The accounts of the battle of . . . ., gained by the Marshal de Luxembourg, and that of Raucoux, will also furnish you with other examples.

ARTICLE XXIV
Of the Hazards and Unforeseen Accidents which Happen in War

This article would be of a melancholy length, if it was my intention to treat of all the accidents which might happen to a general in war. I shall cut the matter short by saying, that it is necessary a man should have both address and good fortune.

Generals are much more to be pitied than is generally imagined. The entire world condemns them unheard. They are exposed in the gazette to the judgment of the meanest plebeian, whilst amongst many thousand readers there is not one perhaps who knows how to conduct the smallest detachment.

I shall not pretend to excuse those generals who have been in fault; I shall even give up my own campaign of 1744, but I must add, that though I have many times erred, I have made some good expeditions; for example, the siege of Prague, the defence and the retreat of Koelin, and again the retreat in Silesia. I shall not enter farther into these actions, but must observe, that there are accidents which neither the most mature reflection nor keenest human foresight can possibly prevent.

As I write at present solely for my own generals, I shall not quote other examples than what have occurred to me. When we were at Reichenbach, I intended to have reached the river Neiss by a forced march, and to have posted myself between the town of that name and the army of General de Neuperg, in order to cut off his communication. All the necessary dispositions were arranged for such operation, but a heavy fall of rain came on which made the roads so very bad, that our advanced guard with the pontoons were unable to proceed. During the march of the army also so thick a fog arose, that the troops who were posted as guards in the villages wandered about without being able to join their respective regiments. In short, every thing turned out so ill, that instead of arriving at four o'clock A.M. as I had intended, we did not get there till midnight. The advantages to be derived from a forced march, were then out of the question, the enemy had the start of us, and defeated our project.

If, during your operations, disease should break out amongst your troops, you will be obliged to act on the defensive, which was the case with us in Bohemia in the year 1741, on account of the badness of the provisions with which the troops were furnished.

At the battle of Hohen-Friedberg, I ordered one of my aide de camp (flugel-adjutants) to go to Margrave Charles, and tell him to place himself, as eldest general, at the head of my second line, because General Kalckstein had been detached to the command of the right wing against the Saxons: this aide de camp mistook the business entirely, and ordered the margrave to form the first line into the second. By great good fortune I discovered the mistake, and had time to remedy it.

Hence we see the necessity of being always on our guard and of bearing in mind that a commission badly executed may disconcert all our intentions.

If a general fall sick, or be killed, at the head of a detachment of any importance, many of your measures must consequently suffer a very material derangement. To act offensively, requires generals of sound understanding and genuine valour, the number of which is but very small: I have at the most but three or four such in my whole army.

If, in spite of every precaution, the enemy should succeed in depriving you of some convoy, your plans will again be disconcerted, and your project either suspended or entirely overset.

Should circumstances oblige the army to fall back, the troops will be very much discouraged.

I have never been so unhappy as to experience a situation of this sort with my whole army, but I remarked at the battle of Mollwitz, that it required a length of time to reanimate troops who had been disheartened. At that time my cavalry was so weakened, that they looked on themselves as merely led to the slaughter, which induced me to send out small detachments to give them spirits, and bring them forward to action. It is only since the battle of Hohen-Friedberg, that my cavalry are become what they ever ought to be, and what they are at present.

If the enemy should discover a spy of any consequence in their camp, the compass is lost which was to have directed you, and you are unable to learn any thing of the enemy's movements but from your own eyes.

The negligence of officers who are detached to reconnoitre may render your situation very distressed and embarrassing. It was in this way that Marshal de Neuperg was surprised; the hussar officer who was sent forward on the look-out, had neglected his duty, and we were close upon him before he had the least suspicion of it. It was also owing to the carelessness of an officer of the regiment of Ziethen in making his patrole by night, that the enemy built his bridges at Selmitz, and surprised the baggage.

Hence will appear the truth of my assertion that the safety of a whole army should never be entrusted to the vigilance of an individual officer. No one man or subaltern officer should be charged with a commission of such material consequence. Treasure up, therefore, carefully in your mind what I have said on this subject under the article, "Of the Defence of Rivers."

Too much confidence must not be reposed in patrols and reconnoitering parties, but in measures of more surety and solidity.

The greatest possible misfortune that can attend an army is treason. Prince Eugene was betrayed in the year 1733 by General Stein who had been corrupted by the French. I lost Cosel through the treachery of an officer of the garrison who deserted and conducted the enemy thither. Hence we are taught, that even in the height of our prosperity, it is not safe to trust to good fortune, or wise to be too much elevated with success; we should rather recollect, that the slender portion of genius and foresight which we may possess is at best but a game of hazard and unforeseen accidents, by which it pleases, I know not what destiny, to humble the pride of presumptuous man.

ARTICLE XXV
If it be absolutely necessary that the General of an Army should hold a Council of War

It was a saying of Prince Eugene, "that if a general did not wish to fight, he had nothing more to do than hold a council of war;" and his assertion is proved, by the general voice of councils of war being against engaging. Secrecy, so necessary in war, can here be no longer observed.

A general, to whom his sovereign has entrusted his troops, should act for himself, and the confidence placed in him by his king is a sufficient warrant for such conduct.

Nevertheless, I am persuaded that a general ought not to be inattentive to the advice of even a subaltern officer, as it is the duty of a good citizen to forget himself when the welfare of his country is at stake, and not regard who furnishes the advice that may be productive of happy, wished-for consequences.

ARTICLE XXVI
Of the Manoeuvres of an Army

It will be seen by the maxims which I have laid down in this work, on what the theory turns of those evolutions which I have introduced amongst my troops. The object of these manoeuvres is to gain time on every occasion, and decide an affair more quickly than has heretofore been the custom; and, in short, to overset the enemy by the furious shocks of our cavalry. By means of this impetuosity, the coward is hurried away, and obliged to do his duty as well as the bravest; no single trooper can be useless. The whole depends on the spirit of the attack.

I therefore flatter myself that every general, convinced of the necessity and advantage of discipline, will do every thing in his power to preserve and improve it, both in time of war and of peace.

The enthusiastic speech made by Vegece respecting the Romans, will never leave my memory: "And at length," says he, "the Roman discipline triumphed over the hordes of Germans, the force of the Gauls, the German cunning, the barbarian swarm, and subdued the whole universe." So much does the prosperity of a state depend on the discipline of it's army.

ARTICLE XXVII
Of Winter Quarters

When a campaign is ended, we think of winter quarters, which must be arranged according to the circumstances in which we find ourselves.

The first thing to be done is, the forming the chain of troops who are to cover these quarters, which may be effected in three different ways, either behind a river, taking advantage of posts that are defended by mountains, or under the protection of some fortified towns.

In the year 1741-2, my troops who wintered in Bohemia, took up their position behind the Elbe. The chain which covered them began at Brandeis, and extending along by Nienbourg, Koelin, Pojebrod, and Pardubitz, ended at Konigingraetz.

I must add here, that rivers must not be too much confided in, as when frozen they can be crossed at any point. Care should be taken to post hussars in every part of the chain to watch the enemy's movements, for which purpose, they should patrol frequently in front to observe if all be quiet, or if the enemy be assembling troops.

Besides the chain of infantry, there should be placed also brigades of cavalry and infantry here and there, to be in readiness to lend assistance wherever it might be wanted.

In the winter of 1744-5, the chain of quarters was formed the whole length of those mountains which separate Silesia from Bohemia, and we guarded very particularly the frontiers of our quarters, that we might remain in quiet.

Lieutenant-General de Trusches had to take charge of the front of Lusatia as far as the country of Glatz, the town of Sagan, and the posts from Schmiedberg to Friedland, which last place was fortified by redoubts. There were also some other small entrenched posts on the roads of Schatzlar, Liebau, and Silberberg. The general had likewise contrived a reserve to support that post which might be first insulted by the enemy. All these detachments were covered by abbatis made in the woods, and all the roads leading into Bohemia were rendered impassible. Every post was also supplied with hussars, for the purpose of reconnoitering.

General Lehwald covered the country of Glatz with a detachment of the same nature, and with the same prudent cautions. These two generals lent each other assistance in such a way, that if the Austrians had marched against General Trusches, General Lehwald would have entered Bohemia to take the enemy in the rear, and Trusches would have returned the favour had Lehwald been attacked.

The towns of Tropau and Jagerndorf were our biggest points in Upper Silesia, and the communication was by way of Zeigenhals and Patchskau to Glatz, and by Neustadt to Neiss.

It must be observed here, that we are not to trust too much to the security of mountains, but remember the proverb, "that wherever a goat can pass a soldier can."

With regard to the chains of quarters that are supported by fortresses, I refer you to the winter quarters of Marshal Saxe. They are the best, but it is not in our power to choose, as the chain must be made according to the nature of the ground which we occupy.

I shall lay it down here as a maxim, that we are never to fancy ourselves perfectly secure from the enemy's annoyance in any one town or post, but that our attention must be constantly alive to the keeping of winter quarters quiet.

Another maxim to be observed in winter quarters is, to distribute the regiments by brigades that they may be always under the eyes of the generals.

Our service also requires that the generals should, if possible be with their own regiments: but there may be exceptions to this rule, of which the general commanding the army will be the best judge.

Here follow the rules that are to be observed respecting the maintenance of troops in winter quarters.

If circumstances absolutely require that we take up winter quarters in our own country, the captains and subaltern officers are to receive a gratuity proportionate to the common allowance which they receive in winter quarters. This is to be furnished with his bread and meat at free cost.

But if the winter quarters are in an enemy's country, the general in chief of the troops shall receive 15,000 florins, the generals of the cavalry and infantry 10,000 each, lieutenant-generals 7000, major-generals (camp marshals) 5000, captains of cavalry 2000, of infantry 1800, and the subaltern officers 1000 ducats or from 4 to 500 florins. The country is to supply the soldier with bread, flesh, and beer gratis, but he is to have no money, as that only tends to favour desertion.

The general in chief is to take care that this business be properly arranged, and that no pillaging is allowed, but he is not to be too strict with an officer who has it in his power to make any trifling, fair advantage.

If the army be quartered in an enemy's country, it is the duty of the general commanding to see that the necessary number of recruits be furnished: (such distribution should obtain in the circles that three regiments, for example, should be assigned to one, and four to the other.) Each circle should also be subdivided into regiments, as is done in the enrolling cantonments.

If the recruits are furnished voluntarily by the states of the country, so much the better; if not, compulsive methods must be used. They ought to arrive very early, that the officer may have time to drill them and make them fit for duty the following spring. This, however, is not to prevent the captain from sending out recruiting parties.

As the general in chief ought to interest himself in the whole of this economy, he should be particularly careful that the artillery horses and the provisions, which are a tribute of the country, are furnished in kind or in hard cash.

All the baggage wagons, and in short, the whole apparatus of an army, is also to be repaired at the enemy's cost.

Minute attention must be paid by the general that the cavalry officers repair their saddles, bridles, stirrups, and boots, and that the officers of infantry provide their men with shoes, stockings, shirts, and gaiters for the ensuing campaign. The soldier's blankets and tent should also be repaired, the cavalry swords filed, and the arms of the infantry put in good condition. The artillery, likewise, must prepare the necessary quantity of cartridges for the infantry.

It still remains to be seen by the general that the troops which form the chain are well provided with powder and ball, and in short, that nothing be wanting in the whole army.

If time allows, the general would do well to visit some of his quarters, to examine into the state of the troops, and satisfy himself that the officers attend to the exercising of their men, as well as to every other part of their duty; for it is necessary that the old soldiers should be employed in this way as well as the recruits, in order to keep them in practice.

At the beginning of a campaign, we change the cantoning quarters, and distribute them according to the order of battle, viz. the cavalry on the wings, and the infantry in the centre. These cantonments generally extend nine or ten leagues (from four to five miles) in front, to four (two) in depth, and when the time of encamping draws near, they are to be contracted a little.

I find it very convenient in cantonments to distribute the troops under the orders of the six eldest generals: one, for example, shall command all the cavalry of the right wing, and another that of the left, in the first line, whilst two others shall command that of the second. In this method, all orders will more quickly be executed, and the troops be more easily formed into columns to go to camp.

On the subject of winter quarters, I must again advise you to be very careful of not going into them before you are well convinced that the enemy's army is entirely separated. Keep always in your recollection the misfortune which befell the Elector Frederick William, when he was surprised by the Marshal de Turenne in his quarters at Alsace.

ARTICLE XXVIII
Of Winter Campaigns in Particular

Winter campaigns ruin the troops, both on account of the diseases which they occasion, and by obliging them to be constantly in motion, which prevents their being well clothed or recruited. The same inconvenience attends the carriage of ammunition and provisions. It is certain, that the best army in the world cannot long support campaigns of this kind, for which reason they ought ever to be avoided, as being, of all expeditions, the most to be condemned. Accidents, however, may occur, which will oblige a general to undertake them.

I believe that I have made more winter campaigns than any general of this age, and that I shall do right to explain the motives which induced me to such undertakings.

At the death of the Emperor Charles VI in the year 1740, there were but two Austrian regiments in all Silesia. Having determined to make good the claims of my house on that duchy, I was obliged to make war in winter, that I might profit by every favourable circumstance, and carry the theatre of war to the Neiss.

If I had delayed my project till the spring, the war would have been established between Crossen and Glogau, and it would have required three or four hard campaigns to effect that which we accomplished by one simple march. This reason appeared to me sufficiently cogent.

If I did not succeed in the winter campaign which I made in the year 1742 to relieve the country from the Elector of Bavaria, it was because the French behaved like fools, and the Saxons like traitors.

My third winter campaign in the year 1741-2 was forced upon me, as I was obliged to drive the Austrians from Silesia, which they had invaded.

From the beginning of the winter 1745-6, the Austrians and Saxons wished to introduce themselves into my hereditary dominions, that they might put every thing to fire and sword. I acted according to my usual principle, and got the start of them by making war in the middle of winter in the very heart of their own country.

Should similar circumstances occur, I should not hesitate to pursue the same plan, and shall applaud the conduct of my generals who shall follow my example. But I must ever blame those who, without the concurrence of such reasons, shall undertake a war at that season of the year.

In regard to the detail of winter campaign, the troops are always to be as close to each other as possible in their cantonments, and two or three regiments of cavalry, mixed with infantry, should be lodged in one village, if it be large enough to hold them. Sometimes all the infantry are quartered in one town, as the Prince of Anhalt did at Torgau, Eilenbourg, Meissen, and two or three other small towns (whose names I forget) in Saxony, after which he encamped himself.

When we come near the enemy, a rendezvous is to be appointed to the troops, who are to continue marching as before in several columns; and when about to make any decisive movement, such as, storming the enemy's quarters, or marching against him to engage, we arrange ourselves in order of battle, remaining under the canopy of heaven, each company kindling a large fire, by which to pass away the night. But as such fatigues are too distressing to be long endured; all possible dispatch should be employed in enterprises of this nature. We must not stand contemplating our danger or hesitating about it, but form our resolution with spirit and execute it with firmness.

Be careful of undertaking a winter campaign in a country which is crowded with fortified places, for the season will prevent your setting down seriously before a place which you cannot carry by surprise. We may be assured beforehand that such project will miscarry, as it is morally impossible it should be otherwise.

If it be left to our choice, the troops should have as much rest during the winter as possible, and the time should be employed tot he best advantage in recovering the army, that at the opening of the campaign they may get the start of their adversaries.

These are nearly the principal rules of the grand manoeuvres of war, the particulars of which have been explained as much as was in my power. I have taken particular care that what I have said should be clear and intelligible, but if any parts should, in your idea, still remain obscure, I shall be favoured by your communicating them, that I may either explain myself more fully, or subscribe to your opinion, if it prove better than mine own.

The small experience of war which has fallen to my share, convinces me, that it is an art never to be exhausted, but that something new will ever reward his labour who studies it with serious application.

I shall not think my moments misemployed, if what I have said should stimulate my officers to the study of that science, which will afford them the most certain opportunity of acquiring glory, rescuing their names from the rust of oblivion, and securing by their brilliant actions a glorious and immortal fame.

CHAPTER 5

NAPOLEON: MAXIMS

"Anyone can plan a campaign, but few are capable of waging war, because only a true military genius can handle the developments and circumstances."

— Napoleon Bonaparte, 1769-1821

What is a maxim? As defined by the American Heritage Dictionary of the English Language, a maxim is "a succinct formulation of some fundamental principle or rule of conduct." This is the primary definition and the one that applies here. For a soldier it is a saying that is widely accepted on its own merits.

These maxims do not constitute a complete collection of Napoleon's maxims. As with many of his other accomplishments, his maxims were prolific and those included here probably represent only the proverbial "drop in the bucket."

In Paragraph 8 of his Will, which he wrote very shortly before his death at St. Helena, Napoleon stated: "I disavow the *Manuscript of St. Helena*, and other works, under the title of *Maxims, Sayings*, etc., which persons have been pleased to publish for the last six years."

Assuming that the above statement was factual within Napoleon's mind, it is apparent from the following maxims that he did adhere to some of them in principal, and also that he violated many. When and where the maxims were spoken or written, is largely speculative. For the most part, they are phrases taken out of context and; therefore, since there is no point of true reference to associate them with, many are open to interpretation by the reader.

Born Napoelon Buonaparte in Ajaccio, Corsica in 1769, the second son of an impecunious lawyer, Napoleon lost his father when he was only 15. At school, he distinguished himself in mathematics and science in particular.

Having entered the Ecole Militaire in 1784 he was, a year later, commissioned into the artillery. In between discharging his professional duties and visiting his impoverished family in Corsica, he undertook an intensive study of military history and theory. Indeed on moving to Auxonne, France's premier artillery school at the time, Bonaparte became acquainted with, among other military thinkers, the commandant, Baron du Teil, a celebrated gunner who, recognizing his potential, took a keen, paternal interest in his training.

Although once an ardent Corsican nationalist, Bonaparte was gradually alienated by separatist sentiments and eventually moved his family to France. In the interim, he witnessed the fall of the Bourbons in 1792, developing an ever deeper loathing for the disorder that followed the storming of the Tuileries. One the other hand, the French Revolution provided Captain Bonaparte with the perfect opportunity to make a name for himself. His skilful handling of the artillery at the siege of Toulon in 1793 was duly rewarded with promotion to brigadier general. He quickly fell from favour, however. A friend of Robespierre's brother, he was arrested following the coup d'etat of 9 Thermidor and imprisoned for a time. Thereafter, he found himself unemployed and was considering emigrating when the political pendulum swung in his favour. A Directory member, Paul Barras, ordered Bonaparte to defend the Convention from a hostile crowd. This he did with a show of force, dispersing the mob with a 'whiff of grapeshot'. He was rewarded with the command of the Army of the Interior.

Early in 1798 he was appointed to lead the Army of Italy, which he did with conspicuous success. His victories induced the Austrians to conclude the Peace of Campo Formio (1797), and Paris turned its attention to Britain. Having judged the Royal Navy's mastery of the English Channel to be incontestable, an invasion was deemed impracticable, but a blow against British trading interests through an Egyptian expedition seemed to have much to recommend it. Accordingly, in 1798, forces under Bonaparte sailed from Toulon, captured Malta, and landed in Egypt. Defeating the Mamelukes at the battle of the Pyramids, Bonaparte took Cairo only to have his maritime communications severed by Nelson's destruction of the French flotilla at Aboukir Bay. Invading Syria in 1799, he endeavoured to capture Acre before turning back into Egypt, where at Aboukir, he routed a Turkish army which had recently arrived from Rhodes.

This strengthened the French grip on Egypt. However, Bonaparte returned to France, which was being menaced by the forces of the Second Coalition. Publication of the news of his recent triumph at Aboukir raised his standing with the public still further – so much so that, on his return, the Directory, corrupt and discredited, felt threatened by him. Their fears were not to prove groundless; in the coup of d'etat of Brumaire 1799 they were overthrown and Bonaparte became one of the three consuls, He wasted no time in establishing himself as first Consul and persuading the other two to withdraw into private life, leaving him as France's de facto ruler.

In order to consolidate his own position and reinvigorate his war weary country Napoleon had to give France a period of peace. In 1800, Napoleon set out in search of a decisive confrontation with France's principal opponent, Austria, and embarked on a second Italian campaign. It was a mercurial, brilliant affair which culminated in his victory at Marengo. Defeated in Germany, too, the Austrians ratified the Treaty of Luneville, dismembering the Second Coalition. Britain's Prime Minister, Willam Pitt 'the younger', resigned and his successor quickly sought an agreement with France.

With the signing of the Peace of Amiens, ten years of incessant conflict came to an end and Napoleon's popularity reached new heights. With peace, he carried out a series of domestic reforms; the state bureaucracy was overhauled; a Concordat with the Pope was reached, restoring some legitimacy and tranquility to France's relations with Rome and by extension to those between Napoleon's Catholic subjects and his regime; a scientifically uniform and versatile set of weights and measures was created; the Bank of France was established to support business and regulate the state's finances; a metal-based currency was started with the franc's value fixed at 5 grains of silver; French law in its entirety was codified; international industrial exhibitions were staged and economic development encouraged; and the control of education was centralized, with emphasis being placed on the creation of elitist secondary schools – the *lycees* – which drew pupils primarily from middle class families and prepared them for a life of public service.

All of this helped strengthen Napoleon's own position. He was proclaimed emperor in December 1804, and also proclaimed king of Italy, while his siblings and marshals were granted titles and lands as part of his policy of creating a new, imperial aristocracy. The dynasty was further underpinned by the institution of a system of civil and military awards, notably the Legion d'Honneur

Britain resumed hostilities against France in 1803 and, over the next ten years, orchestrated the formation of a further four coalitions against her. The first three of these were shattered by Napoleon in a series of dazzling campaigns which firmly established him as the pre-eminent commander of his age and as one of the greatest military leaders in history. So spectacular was his success that by the beginning of 1810, he found himself presiding over the largest empire Europe had seen since Roman times. Napoleon thus posed a threat to the whole European order. His opponents, particularly Britain, were unwilling to grant him a lengthy period of peace in which to consolidate his gains and France found herself in an attritional struggle which proved unsustainable. The Spanish Peninsular War of 1807-14 was already bleeding France white when the Russian debacle of 1812 jeopardized the whole of Napoleon's gains in central Europe. Victorious at Leipzig, the Sixth Coalition's armies invaded France in 1814, securing Napoleon's abdication and restoring the Bourbons.

Exiled to Elba, Napoleon staked all on one last desperate gamble. Landing in France, in March 1815, he deposed the Bourbons in a bloodless revolution. A renewal of the war was unavoidable, and the Allies promptly formed the Seventh Coalition. Although the Campaign of the Hundred Days began well, Napoleon was defeated at Waterloo, abdicated a second time and was confined on St. Helena where he remained until his death. Victorious in nearly all of the 50 battles he fought in his career, for contemporary military theorists, notably Clausewitz and Jomini, Napoleon was the very 'God of War', an operational commander of the premier rank.

Actually, there should be no need to introduce Napoleon. He has been claimed to be the greatest of European soldiers. He fought more battles than Alexander, Hannibal and Caesar combined. Indeed, he was the first great strategist of the Western World; his battles came about as a result of carefully calculated strategic movements. But Napoleon was not a theoretician. He never wrote out his theories or principles or maxims on the conduct of war – though he often had expressed his desire to do so. He was fond of saying that everyone would be surprised at how simple are the principles of winning wars.

Although Napoleon did not write out his theories, the art of conducting war, or strategy as developed by later thinkers had their foundation and inspiration from Napoleonic practices. Most notable amongst them are Jomini and Clausewitz.[1] Baron Jomini was the chief expounder of Napoleon's methods and it is said that Jomini's book became the text book for the American Civil War. Clausewitz, of course, became the seer whose influence can be found even today; although it was most profound in the Franco-Prussian war (1870) and in the First World War.

While Napoleon may not have been a great military theoretician, his genius as a great Captain lay in achieving the synthesis between strategy and grand tactics. He was able to develop the systems and procedures introduced by his predecessors, and formulate a system of strategy ending with a matching system of tactics. He was able to perceive the possibilities of new organisations[2] and weapons and achieved the required synthesis. His manoeuvre and marching plans ensured that he could concentrate his forces much more rapidly and thus surprise his opponents. This, of course, is nothing new; but what Napoleon was able to achieve was to make his plan of battle, a part of his plan of march. He was able to turn his enemy's flank by secretly marching past them, thus forcing his opponents to turn around and fight at a disadvantage. Napoleon had been able to perceive the importance of the communication and the effect it was to have on campaigns. His other innovation was the use of artillery *enmasse* to break the opponent's line and thereby prepare the way for his infantry.[3]

There is also a view that a lot of what Napoleon had to say was influenced by the writings of Marshal Maurice de Saxe (1696-1750). Saxe was the greatest European general and military intellectual of his times. He wrote his famous *Mes reveries*, published in English as *Reveries upon the Art of War* in 1757. The work is not just one of military theory, but also a treatise on military life, that draws heavily on Machiavelli.

There have been many collections of Napoleon maxims and sayings, some large, some small. The one used here was made by General Burnod and first published in 1827. Amongst the smaller collections, it is still considered to be one of the best compilations of Napoleon's thoughts.

The collection is in two parts, although the parts by themselves do not form any subject-wise division. The collections are apparently random. Also, tactics, strategy, man management, and logistics are mixed. Like all aphorisms, each one has to be read independently and interpreted suitably. However, there are some lengthy ones, number 37 for example, which deals with river crossing. In it there is a modicum of explanation as to why some action should be taken: "When a river is less than a hundred and twenty yards wide in breadth, and you can command the opposite bank, the troops that are thrown over to other side derive such advantage from the protection afforded by the artillery . . ." The last maxim (115) is also a fairly lengthy one, which compares land warfare with warfare on the seas and the qualities that a general and an admiral should have.[4] In another one (39) he gives an example as to how Turenne[5] fought a battle to bring out a lesson forming bridgeheads across a river.

Not unnaturally, much of his thoughts were on how to organize an invasion of another country: An army invading a country may either have its two wings resting on neutral countries or on great natural obstacles, such as rivers or chains of mountains".[6] He also goes on to elaborate as to how a general should manage if the flanks were to be open. "He must keep his different corps resting well on his centre and never allow them to separate from it ....." He clearly spelt out how lines of advance should be decided. "It may be laid down as a principle that in invading a country with two or three armies, each of which has its own distinct line of operations, extending towards a fixed point at which all are to unite, the union of the different corps should never be ordered to take place in the vicinity of the enemy, as by concentrating his forces he may not only prevent their junction, but also defeat them one by one".

Napoleon had perceived and preached the true interpretation of concentration of force. "The strength of an army, like momentum in mechanics, is estimated by the weight multiplied by the velocity". His other saying "big battalions always win" of course has now become more or less a truism. There are others: "It is a violation of correct principles to cause corps to act separately, without communication with each other".

Considerable thought had been given to seige warfare fortification.[7] Although he said "Fortresses are useful in offensive as well as defensive war" his main advocacy is for the offensive and how to conduct a siege of a fortified place. Also, one can discern the shades of Vegetius in: "The keys of a fortified place are ample compensation for permitting the garrison to retire unmolested, whenever the latter evince a determination to die rather than accept less favourable terms. It is always better, therefore, to grant an honourable capitulation to a garrison which has resisted vigorously than to run the risk of an attempt to storm".

Napoleon was the first great captain who truly exploited the full potential of the artillery. He was the first one to perceive the inter se relationship between artillery and other two arms: "The principle part of artillery should be with the divisions of infantry and of cavalry, whether marching or in position:"

A good deal of Napoleon's thoughts went towards the qualities of a general, his knowledge, conduct, how to "calculate", what the general must do, how to organize reconnaissance, and many others. Though not strictly relevant to the subject in hand, it is too tempting not to quote a maxim, whose relevance probably troubles generals even today: "A general in chief cannot exonerate himself from the responsibility for his faults by pleading an order of his sovereign or the minister, when the individual from whom it proceeds is at a distance from the field of operations, and but partially, or not at all, acquainted with the actual conditions of things. Hence, it follows that every general in chief who undertakes to execute a plan which he knows to be bad, is culpable. He should communicate his reasons, insist on a change of plan and finally resign his commission rather than become the instrument of his army's ruin".

According to Napoleon, "the art of war is simple; everything is a matter of execution". The one concept that dominated his actions was to be as strong for a battle as possible, even if it meant leaving his bases or lines of communication unguarded. The relationship between offensive and defensive had also engaged the attention of Napoleon. He had realized that strategically speaking there is no real difference between the two: "Defensive war does not exclude attacking, just as offensive war does not exclude defending, although its aim may be to force the frontiers and invade the enemy's country".

Liddell Hart had termed these maxims as trite. Possibly Napoleon did not bring out anything fundamentally original – and his loud thinking could well have been wrongly recorded. His own maxims were overshadowed by his interpreters (Jomini and Clausewitz), but their value remains.

NOTES

1. Instead of the Maxims of Napoleon, they could well have been on Jomini and Clauzewitz, both being great exponents and analysers of Napoleon's method. Jomini had studied Napoleon's campaigns, discerned their essence, and written his book by 1804. This is discussed in the next chapter. A discourse on Clauzewitz follows in a later chapter.
2. The main organisational development was that of forming permanent divisional structures. Mention has already been made of Frederick's innovation of forming divisional columns for marching. Marshal de Broglie had worked out permanent divisional organisations and introduced them in the French Army in 1759. Marshal de Broglie had also developed the principles of dispersion with units remaining in supporting distance, and rapid concentration on the battlefield. Technological innovations had reduced the weight of artillery trains and increased their mobility as well artillery could be made to manoeuvre with infantry.
3. It is relevant that the practice is followed even today. In fact it is a basic doctrine which has not changed since that time, though its application has varied. In the First

World War artillery preparation or softening up of the defences went on for days. During the Second World War, it varied from a few hours to minutes. It can be said that carpet bombing by air force, developed during the Second World War, is also an extension and application of the same precept.

4. Napoleon places the general well above the admiral; "The art of war on land is an art of genius, of inspiration. On the sea everything is definite and a matter of experience". Napoleon's reasons for placing the general well over the admiral are not far to seek – Trafalgar.
5. Possibly the most famous soldier of the 17th century, Marshal Henri de La Turenne (1611-1675), started his military career at he age of 14 under his uncle during the Dutch War. He was made a Marshal of France at the age of 32 by the redoubtable Cardinal Richelieu, and commanded the French Army in Italy. He also commanded the combined armies of France and the "Weimar" Republic during the concluding part of the Thirty Years War. He was made the Marshal General of France by Louis XIV. He seemed to have been fighting almost continuously, but his military career was somewhat uneven – he lost quite a few battles, just as he won many more. His most famous and daring campaign was a secret march in mid-winter across the Vosges mountains thereby gaining complete surprise and the regaining of Alsace after the battle of Turkhheim (January 1675). He was killed in the battle of Sassbah (July 1675). He was one of the most admired and read generals during the 17th and 18th centuries.
6. France and Britain tried this in both the First and Second world wars. The concept is applicable even today.
7. Marshal Saxe and Frederick the Great were equally concerned about seige warfare. Fortification and seige warfare gained prominence with the introduction of gun powder and development of the cannon. One could say that science and technology entered the arena of battle from this time (15th and 16th Century). Seige cannons had been fully developed by early 17th century. In keeping with the development of the cannon, the design and techniques of constructing forts and entrenchments, also progressed and brought about the science of military architecture. There developed in France a school of fortification, whose titular founder is Errad who published a book on it around 1594. The process continued till the 18th century. Napoleon was greatly influenced by the writings of the great military engineer, de Vauban, who served Louis XIV.

MILITARY MAXIMS
NAPOLEON

MAXIM I

The frontiers of states are either large rivers, or chains of mountains, or deserts. Of all these obstacles to the march of an army, the most difficult to overcome is the desert; mountains come next, and broad rivers occupy the third place.

MAXIM II

In forming the plan of a campaign, it is requisite to foresee everything the enemy may do, and to be prepared with the necessary means to counteract it. Plans of campaign may be modified, ad infinitum, according to circumstances — the genius of the general, the character of the troops, and the topography of the theater of action.

MAXIM III

An army which undertakes the conquest of a country has its two wings resting either upon neutral territories, or upon great natural obstacles, such as rivers or chains of mountains. It happens in some cases that only one wing is so supported, and in others that both are exposed.

MAXIM IV

When the conquest of a country is undertaken by two or three armies, which have each their separate line of operation, until they arrive at a point fixed upon for their concentration, it should be laid down as a principle, that the union of these different corps should never take place near the enemy: because the enemy, in uniting his forces, may not only prevent this junction, but may beat the armies in detail.

MAXIM V

All wars should be governed by certain principles, for every war should have a definite object, and be conducted according to the rules of art. (A war should only be undertaken with forces proportioned to the obstacles to be overcome.)

MAXIM VI

At the commencement of a campaign, to advance or not to advance is a matter for grave consideration; but when once the offensive has been assumed, it must be sustained to the last extremity. However skillful the manoeuvres in a retreat, it will always weaken the morale of an army, because in losing the chances of success these last are transferred to the enemy. Besides, retreats always cost more men and material than the bloodiest engagements; with this difference, that in a battle the enemy's loss is nearly equal to your own—whereas in a retreat the loss is on your side only.

MAXIM VII

An army should be ready every day, every night and at all times of the day and night, to oppose all the resistance of which it is capable. With this view, the soldier should always be furnished completely with arms and ammunition; the infantry should never be without its artillery, its cavalry, and its generals; and the different divisions of the army should be constantly in a state to support, to be supported, and to protect itself. The troops, whether halted, or encamped, or on the march, should be always in favourable positions, possessing the essentials required for a field of battle; for example, the flanks should be well covered, and all the artillery so placed as to have free range, and to play with the greatest advantage. When an army is in column of march, it should have advanced guards and flanking parties, to examine well the country in front, to the right, and to the left, and always at such distance as to enable the main body to deploy into position.

MAXIM VIII

A General-in-Chief should ask himself frequently in the day, "What should I do if the enemy's army appeared now in my front, or on my right, or my left?" If he has any difficulty in answering these questions, his position is bad, and he should seek to remedy it.

MAXIM IX

The strength of an army, like the power in mechanics, is estimated by multiplying the mass by the rapidity; a rapid march augments the morale of an army, and increases its means of victory. Press on!

MAXIM X

When an army is inferior in number, inferior in cavalry, and in artillery, it is essential to avoid a general action. The first deficiency should be supplied by rapidity of movement; the want of artillery, by the nature of the manoeuvres; and the inferiority in cavalry, by the choice of positions. In such circumstances the morale of the soldier does much.

MAXIM XI

To direct operations with lines far removed from each other, and without communications, is to commit a fault which always gives birth to a second. The detached column has only its orders for the first day. Its operations on the following day depend upon what may have happened to the main body. Thus this column either loses time upon emergency, in waiting for orders, or it will act without them, and at hazard. Let it therefore be held as a principle, that an army should always keep its columns so united as to prevent the enemy from passing between them with impunity. Whenever, for particular reasons, this principle is departed from, the detached corps should be independent in their operations. They should move toward a point fixed upon for their future junction. They should advance without hesitating and without waiting for fresh orders; and every precaution should be taken to prevent an attack upon them in detail.

MAXIM XII

An army ought to have only one line of operation. This should be preserved with care, and never abandoned but in the last extremity.

MAXIM XIII

The distances permitted between corps of an army upon the march must be governed by the localities, by circumstances, and by the object in view.

MAXIM XIV

Among mountains, a great number of positions are always to be found very strong in themselves, and which it is dangerous to attack. The character of this mode of warfare consists in occupying camps on the flanks or in the rear of the enemy, leaving him only the alternative of abandoning his position without fighting, to take up another in the rear, or to descend from it in order to attack you. In mountain warfare, the assailant has always the disadvantage; even in offensive warfare in the open field, the great secret consists in defensive combats, and in obliging the enemy to attack.

MAXIM XV

The first consideration with a general who offers battle should be the glory and honour of his arms; the safety and preservation of his men is only the second; but it is in the enterprise and courage resulting from the former that the latter will most assuredly be found. In a retreat, besides the honour of the army, the loss of life is often greater than in two battles. For this reason, we should never despair while brave men are to be found with their colours. It is by this means we obtain victory, and deserve to obtain it.

MAXIM XVI

It is an approved maxim in war, never to do what the enemy wishes you to do, for this reason alone, that he desires it. A field of battle, therefore, which he has previously studied and reconnoitered, should be avoided, and double care should be taken where he has had time to fortify and entrench. One consequence deducible from this principle is, never to attack a position in front which you can gain by turning.

MAXIM XVII

In a war of march and manoeuvre, if you would avoid a battle with a superior army, it is necessary to entrench every night, and occupy a good defensive position. Those natural positions which are ordinarily met with are not sufficient to protect an army against superior numbers without recourse to art.

MAXIM XVIII

A general of ordinary talent occupying a bad position, and surprised by a superior force, seeks his safety in retreat; but a great captain supplies all deficiencies by his courage, and marches boldly to meet the attack. By this means he disconcerts his adversary; and if the latter shows any irresolution in his movements, a skillful leader, profiting by his indecision, may even hope for victory, or at least employ the day in manoeuvring—at night he entrenches himself, or falls back to a better position. By this determined conduct he maintains the honour of his arms, the first essential to all military superiority.

MAXIM XIX

The transition from the defensive to the offensive is one of the most delicate operations in war.

MAXIM XX

It may be laid down as a principle, that the line of operation should not be abandoned; but it is one of the most skillful manoeuvres in war, to know how to change it, when circumstances authorize or render this necessary. An army which changes skilfully its line of operation deceives the enemy, who becomes ignorant where to look for its rear, or upon what weak points it is assailable.

MAXIM XXI

When a army carries with it a battering train, or large convoys of sick and wounded, it cannot march by too short a line upon its depots.

MAXIM XXII

The art of encamping in position is the same as taking up the line in order of battle in this position. To this end, the artillery should be advantageously placed, ground should be selected which is not commanded or liable to be turned, and, as far as possible, the guns should cover and command the surrounding country.

MAXIM XXIII

When you are occupying a position which the enemy threatens to surround, collect all your force immediately, and menace him with an offensive movement. By this manoeuvre you will prevent him from detaching and annoying your flanks, in case you should judge it necessary to retire.

MAXIM XXIV

Never lose sight of this maxim, that you should establish your cantonments at the most distant and best protected point from the enemy, especially where a surprise is possible. By this means you will have time to unite all your forces before he can attack you.

MAXIM XXV

When two armies are in order of battle, and one has to retire over a bridge, while the other has the circumference of the circle open, all the advantages are in favour of the latter. It is then a general should show boldness, strike a decided blow, and manoeuvre upon the flank of his enemy. The victory is in his hands.

MAXIM XXVI

It is contrary to all true principle to make corps, which have no communication with each other, act separately against a central force whose communications are cut off.

MAXIM XXVII

When an army is driven from a first position, the retreating columns should rally always sufficiently in the rear, to prevent any interruption from the enemy. The greatest disaster that can happen is when the columns are attacked in detail, and before their junction.

MAXIM XXVIII

No force should be detached on the eve of a battle, because affairs may change during the night, either by the retreat of the enemy, or by the arrival of large reinforcements to enable him to resume the offensive, and counteract your previous arrangements.

MAXIM XXIX

When you have resolved to fight a battle, collect your whole force. Dispense with nothing. A single battalion sometimes decides the day.

MAXIM XXX

Nothing is as rash or so contrary to principle as to make a flank march before an army in position, especially when this army occupies heights at the foot of which you are forced to defile.

MAXIM XXXI

When you determine to risk a battle, reserve to yourself every possible chance of success, more particularly if you have to deal with an adversary of superior talent; for if you are beaten, even in the midst of your magazines and your communications, woe to the vanquished!

MAXIM XXXII

The duty of an advanced guard does not consist of advancing or retiring, but in manoeuvring. An advanced guard should be composed of light cavalry, supported by a reserve of heavy cavalry, and by battalions of infantry, supported also by artillery. An advanced guard should consist of picked troops, and the general officers, officers and men should be selected for their respective capabilities and knowledge. A corps deficient in instruction is only an embarrassment to an advanced guard.

MAXIM XXXIII

It is contrary to the usages of war to allow parks or batteries of artillery to enter a defile, unless you hold the other extremity. In case of retreat, the guns will embarrass your movements, and be lost. They should be left in position under a sufficient escort, until you are master of the opening.

MAXIM XXXIV

It should be laid down as a principle, never to have intervals by which the enemy can penetrate between corps formed in order of battle, unless it be to draw him into a snare.

MAXIM XXXV

Encampments of the same army should always be formed so as to protect each other.

MAXIM XXXVI

When the enemy's army is covered by a river, upon which he holds several *tetes de pont*, do not attack in front. This would divide your force and expose you to be turned. Approach the river in echelon of columns; in such a manner that the leading column shall be the only one the enemy can attack, without offering you his flank. In the meantime, let your light troops occupy the bank, and when you have decided on the point of passage, rush upon it and fling across your bridge. Observe that the point of passage should be always at a distance from the leading echelon, in order to deceive the enemy.

MAXIM XXXVII

From the moment you are master of a position which commands the opposite bank, facilities are acquired for effecting the passage of the river; above all, if this position is sufficiently extensive to place upon it artillery in force. This advantage is diminished if the river is more than three hundred *toises* (or six hundred yards) in breadth, because the distance being out of the range of grape, it is easy for the troops which defend the passage to line the bank and get under cover. Hence it follows that if the grenadiers, ordered to pass the river for the protection of the bridge, should reach the other side, they would be destroyed by the fire of the enemy; because his batteries, placed at the distance of two hundred *toises* from the landing, are capable of a most destructive effect, although removed above five hundred *toises* from the batteries of the crossing force. Thus the advantage of the artillery would be exclusively his. For the same reason, the passage is impracticable, unless you succeed in surprising the enemy, and are protected by an intermediate island, or unless you are able to take advantage of an angle in the river, to establish a cross-fire upon his works. In this case the island or angle forms a natural *tete de pont,* and gives the advantage in artillery to the attacking army. When a river is less than sixty *toises* (or one hundred and twenty yards) in breadth, and you have a post upon the other side, the troops which are thrown across derive such advantages from the protection of your artillery, that, however small the angle may be, it is impossible for the enemy to prevent the establishment of a bridge. In this case, the most skillful generals, when they have discovered the project of their adversary, and brought their own army to the point of crossing, usually content themselves with opposing the passage of the bridge, by forming a semicircle round its extremity, as round the opening of a defile, and removing to the distance of three or four hundred *toises* from the fire of the opposite side.

MAXIM XXXVIII

It is difficult to prevent an enemy supplied with pontoons from crossing a river. When the object of an army which defends the passage is to cover a siege, the moment the general has ascertained his inability to oppose the passage, he should take measures to arrive before the enemy, at an intermediate position between the river he defends and the place he desires to cover.

MAXIM XXXIX

In the campaign of 1645, Turenne was attacked with his army before Philipsburg by a very superior force. There was no bridge here over the Rhine, but he took advantage of the ground between the river and the place to establish his camp. This should serve as a lesson to engineer officers, not merely in the construction of fortresses, but of "*tetes de pont*". A space should always be left between the fortress and the river, where an army may form and rally without being obliged to throw itself into the place, and thereby compromise its security. An army retiring upon Mayence before a pursuing enemy, is necessarily compromised; for this reason, because it requires more than a day to pass the bridge, and because the lines of Cassel are too confined to admit an army to remain there without being blocked up. Two hundred *toises* should have been left between that place and the Rhine. It is essential that all "*tetes de pont*" before great rivers should be constructed upon this principle; otherwise they will prove a very inefficient assistance to protect the passage of a retreating army. "*Tetes de pont*", as laid down in our schools, are of use only for small rivers, the passage of which is comparatively short.

MAXIM XL

Fortresses are equally useful in offensive and defensive warfare. It is true they will not in themselves arrest an army, but they are an excellent means of retarding, embarrassing, weakening, and annoying a victorious enemy.

MAXIM XLI

There are only two ways of insuring the success of a siege. The first, to begin by beating the enemy's army employed to cover the place, forcing it out of the field, and throwing its remains beyond some great natural obstacle, such as a chain of mountains, or large river. Having accomplished this object, an army of observation should be placed behind the natural obstacle, until the trenches are finished and the place taken.

But if it be desired to take the place in presence of a relieving army, without risking a battle, then the whole materiel and equipment for a siege are necessary to begin with, together with ammunition and provisions for the presumed period of its duration, and also lines of contravallation and circumvallation, aided by all the localities of heights, woods, marshes, and inundations.

Having no longer occasion to keep up communications with your depots, it is now only requisite to hold in check the relieving army. For this purpose, an army of observation should be formed, whose business it is never to lose sight of that of the enemy, and which, while it effectively bars all access to the place, has always time enough to arrive upon his flanks or rear in case he should attempt to steal a march.

It is to be remembered, too, that by profiting judiciously by the lines of contravallation, a portion of the besieging army will always be available in giving battle to the approaching enemy.

Upon the same general principle, when a place is to be besieged in presence of an enemy's army, it is necessary to cover the siege by lines of circumvallation.

If the besieging force is of numerical strength enough (after leaving a corps before the place four times the amount of the garrison) to cope with the relieving army, it may remove more than one day's march from the place; but if it be inferior in numbers after providing for the siege as above stated, it should remain only a short day's march from the spot, in order to fall back upon its lines, if necessary, or receive succour in case of attack. If the investing corps and army of observation are only equal when united to the relieving force, the besieging army should remain entire within, or near its lines, and push the works and the siege with the greatest activity.

MAXIM XLII

Feuquiere says that "we should never wait for the enemy in the lines of circumvallation, but we should go out and attack him." He is in error. There is no authority in war without exception; and it would be dangerous to proscribe the principle of awaiting the enemy within the lines of circumvallation.

MAXIM XLIII

Those who proscribe lines of circumvallation, and all the assistance which the science of the engineer can afford, deprive themselves gratuitously of an auxiliary which is never injurious, almost always useful, and often indispensable. It must be admitted at the same time, that the principles of field-fortification require improvement. This important branch of the art of war has made no progress since the time of the ancients. It is even inferior at this day to what it was two thousand years ago. Engineer officers should be encouraged in bringing this branch of their art to perfection, and in placing it upon a level with the rest.

MAXIM XLIV

If circumstances prevent a sufficient garrison being left to defend a fortified town which contains a hospital and magazines, at least every means should be employed to secure the citadel against a coup de main.

MAXIM XLV

A fortified place can only protect the garrison and detain the enemy for a certain time. When this time has elapsed, and the defences of the place are destroyed, the garrison should lay down its arms. All civilized nations are agreed on this point, and there never has been an argument except with reference to the greater or less degree of defence which a governor is bound to make before he capitulates. At the same time, there are generals—Villars among the number—who are of opinion that a governor should never surrender, but that in the last extremity he should blow up the fortifications, and take advantage of the night to cut his way through the besieging army. Where he is unable to blow up the fortifications, he may always retire, they say, with his garrison, and save the men. Officers who have adopted this line of conduct have often brought off three-fourths of their garrison.

MAXIM XLVI

The keys of a fortress are well worth the retirement of the garrison, when it is resolved to yield only on those conditions. On this principle it is always wiser to grant an honourable capitulation to a garrison which has made a vigorous resistance, than to risk an assault.

MAXIM XLVII

Infantry, cavalry, and artillery are nothing without each other; therefore they should always be so disposed in cantonments as to assist each other in case of surprise.

MAXIM XLVIII

The formation of infantry in line should be always in two ranks, because the length of the musket only admits of an effective fire in this formation. The discharge of the third rank is not only uncertain, but frequently dangerous to the ranks in its front. In drawing up infantry in two ranks, there should be a supernumerary behind every fourth of fifth file. A reserve should likewise be placed twenty-five paces in rear of each flank.

MAXIM XLIX

The practice of mixing small bodies of infantry and cavalry together is a bad one, and attended with many inconveniences. The cavalry loses its power of action. It becomes fettered in all its movements. Its energy is destroyed; even the infantry itself is compromised, for on the first movement of the cavalry its left without support. The best mode of protecting cavalry is to cover its flank.

MAXIM L

Charges of cavalry are equally useful at the beginning, the middle, and the end of a battle. They should be made always, if possible, on the flanks of the infantry, especially when the latter is engaged in front.

MAXIM LI

It is the business of cavalry to follow up the victory, and to prevent the beaten enemy from rallying.

MAXIM LII

Artillery is more essential to cavalry than to infantry, because cavalry has no fire for its defence, but depends upon the saber. It is to remedy this deficiency that recourse has been had to horse-artillery. Cavalry, therefore, should never be without cannon, whether when attacking, rallying, or in position.

MAXIM LIII

During a march, or in position, the greater part of the artillery should be with the divisions of infantry and cavalry. The rest should be in reserve. Each gun should have with it three hundred rounds, without including the limber. This is about the complement for two battles.

MAXIM LIV

Artillery should always be placed in the most advantageous positions, and as far in front of the line of cavalry and infantry as possible, without compromising the safety of the guns.

Field batteries should command the whole country round from the level of the platform. They should on no account be masked on the right and left, but have free range in every direction.

MAXIM LV

A general should never put his army into cantonments when he has the means of collecting supplies of forage and provisions, and of thus providing for the wants of the soldier in the field.

MAXIM LVI

A good general, a well-organized system, good instructions, and severe discipline, aided by effective establishments, will always make good troops, independently of the cause for which they fight.

At the same time, a love of country, a spirit of enthusiasm, a sense of national honour, and fanaticism will operate upon young soldiers with advantage.

MAXIM LVII

When a nation is without establishments and a military system, it is very difficult to organize an army.

MAXIM LVIII

The first qualification of a soldier is fortitude under fatigue and privation. Courage is only the second; hardship, poverty, and want are the best school for the soldier.

MAXIM LIX

There are five things the soldier should never be without—his musket, his ammunition, his knapsack, his provisions (for at least four days), and his entrenching tool. The knapsack may be reduced to the smallest size possible, if it be thought proper, but the soldier should always have it with him.

MAXIM LX

Every means should be taken to attach the soldier to his colours. This is best accomplished by showing consideration and respect to the old soldier. His pay likewise should increase with his length of service. It is the height of injustice not to pay a veteran more than a recruit.

MAXIM LXI

It is not set speeches at the moment of battle that render soldiers brave. The veteran scarcely listens to them, and the recruit forgets them at the first discharge. If discourses and harangues are useful, it is during the campaign; to do away with unfavourable impressions, to correct false reports, to keep alive a proper spirit in the camp, and to furnish materials and amusement for the bivouac. All printed orders of the day should keep in view these objects.

MAXIM LXII

Tents are unfavourable to health. The soldier is best when he bivouacs, because he sleeps with his feet to the fire, which speedily dries the ground on which he lies. A few planks, or a little straw, shelter him from the wind.

On the other hand, tents are necessary for the superior officers, who have to write and to consult their maps. Tents should therefore be issued to these, with directions to them never to sleep in a house. Tents are always objects of observation to the enemy's staff. They afford information in regard to your numbers and the ground you occupy, while an army bivouacking in two or three lines is only distinguishable from afar by the smoke which mingles with the clouds. It is impossible to count the number of the fires.

MAXIM LXIII

All the information obtained from prisoners should be received with caution, and estimated at its real value. A soldier seldom sees anything beyond his company; and an officer can afford intelligence of little more than the position and movements of the division to which his regiment belongs. On this account the general of an army should never depend upon the information derived from prisoners, unless it agrees with the reports received from the advanced guards, in reference to the position, etc., of the enemy.

MAXIM LXIV

Nothing is so important in war as an undivided command; for this reason, when war is carried on against a single power, there should be only one army, acting upon one base, and conducted by one chief.

MAXIM LXV

The same consequences which have uniformly attended long discussions and councils of war will follow at all times. They will terminate in the adoption of the worst course, which in war is always the most timid, or, if you will, the most prudent. The only true wisdom in a general is determined courage.

MAXIM LXVI

In war the general alone can judge of certain arrangements. It depends on him alone to conquer difficulties by his own superior talents and resolution.

MAXIM LXVII

To authorize generals or other officers to lay down their arms in virtue of a particular capitulation, under any other circumstances than when they are composing the garrison of a fortress, affords dangerous latitude. It is destructive of all military character in a nation to open such a door to the cowardly, the weak, or even to the misdirected brave. Great extremities require extraordinary resolution. The more obstinate the resistance of an army, the greater the chances of assistance or of success.

How many seeming impossibilities have been accomplished by men whose only resolve was death!

MAXIM LXVIII

There is no security for any sovereign, for any nation, or for any general, if officers are permitted to capitulate in the open field, and to lay down their arms in virtue of conditions favourable to the contracting party, but contrary to the interests of the army at large. To withdraw from danger, and thereby to involve their comrades in greater peril, is the height of cowardice. Such, conduct should be proscribed, declared infamous, and made punishable with death. All generals, officers, and soldiers who capitulate in battle to save their own lives should be decimated.

He who gives the order and those who obey are alike traitors, and deserve capital punishment.

MAXIM LXIX

There is but one honourable mode of becoming prisoner of war. That is, by being taken separately; by which is meant, by being cut off entirely, and when we can on longer make use of our arms. In this case, there can be no conditions, for honour can impose none. We yield to an irresistible necessity.

MAXIM LXX

The conduct of a general in a conquered country is full of difficulties. If severe, he irritates and increases the number of his enemies. If lenient, he gives birth to expectations which only render the abuses and vexations inseparable from war the more intolerable. A victorious general must know how to employ severity, justness, and mildness by turns, if he would allay sedition or prevent it.

MAXIM LXXI

Nothing can excuse a general who takes advantage of the knowledge acquired in the service of his country, to deliver up her frontier and her towns to foreigners. This is a crime reprobated by every principle of religion, morality, and honour.

MAXIM LXXII

A general-in-chief has no right to shelter his mistakes in war under cover of his sovereign, or of a minister, when these are both distant from the scene of operation, and must consequently be either ill informed or wholly ignorant of the actual state of things.

Hence it follows, that every general is culpable who undertakes the execution of a plan which he considers faulty. It is his duty to represent his reasons, to insist upon a change of plan—in short, to give in his resignation rather than allow himself to be made the instrument of his army's ruin. Every general-in-chief who fights a battle in consequence of superior orders, with the certainty of losing it, is equally blamable.

In this last-mentioned case, the general ought to refuse obedience; because a blind obedience is due only to a military command given by a superior present on the spot at the moment of action. Being in possession of the real state of things, the superior has it then in his power to afford the necessary explanations to the person who executes his orders.

But supposing a general-in-chief to receive a positive order from his sovereign, directing him to fight a battle, with the further injunction, to yield to his adversary, and allow himself to be defeated — ought he to obey it? No. If the general should be able to comprehend the meaning or utility of such an order, he should execute it; otherwise, he should refuse to obey it.

MAXIM LXXIII

The first qualification in a general-in-chief is a cool head—that is, a head which receives just impressions, and estimates things and objects at their real value. He must not allow himself to be elated by good news, or depressed by bad.

The impressions he receives either successively or simultaneously in the course of the day should be so classed as to take up only the exact place in his mind which they deserve to occupy; since it is upon a just comparison and consideration of the weight due to different impressions that the power of reasoning and of right judgment depends.

Some men are so physically and morally constituted as to see everything through a highly coloured medium. They raise a picture in the mind on every slight occasion, and give to every trivial occurrence a dramatic interest. But whatever knowledge, or talent, or courage, or other good qualities such men may possess, Nature has not formed them for the command of armies, or the direction of great military operations.

MAXIM LXXIV

The leading qualifications which should distinguish an officer selected for the head of the staff are, to know the country thoroughly; to be able to conduct a reconnaissance with skill; to superintend the transmission of orders promptly; to lay down the most complicated movements intelligibly, but in a few words, and with simplicity.

MAXIM LXXV

The commandant of artillery should understand well the general principles of each branch of the service, since he is called upon to supply arms and ammunition to the different corps of which it is composed. His correspondence with the commanding officers of artillery at the advanced posts should put him in possession of all the movements of the army, and the disposition and management of the great park of artillery should depend upon this information.

MAXIM LXXVI

The qualities which distinguish a good general of advanced posts are: to reconnoiter accurately defiles and fords of every description; to provide guides that may be depended on; to interrogate the cure and postmaster; to establish rapidly a good understanding with the inhabitants; to send out spies; to intercept public and private letters; to translate and analyse their contents; in a word, to be able to answer every question of the general-in-chief when he arrives with the whole army.

MAXIM LXXVII

Generals-in-Chief must be guided by their own experience, or their genius. Tactics, evolutions, the duties and knowledge of an engineer or artillery officer, may be learned in treatises, but the science of strategy is only to be acquired by experience, and by studying the campaigns of all the great captains.

Gustavus Adolphus, Turenne, and Frederick, as well as Alexander, Hannibal, and Caesar have all acted upon the same principles. These have been — to keep their forces united; to leave no weak part unguarded; to seize with rapidity on important points.

Such as the principles which lead to victory, and which, by inspiring terror at the reputation of your arms, will at once maintain fidelity and secure subjection.

MAXIM LXXVIII

Peruse again and again the campaigns of Alexander, Hannibal, Caesar, Gustavus Adolphus, Turenne, Eugene, and Frederick. Model yourself upon them. This is the only means of becoming a great captain, and of acquiring the secret of the art of war. Your own genius will be enlightened and improved by this study, and you will learn to reject all maxims foreign to the principles of these great commanders.

MAXIM LXXIX

The first principle of a general-in-chief is to calculate what he must do, to see if he has all the means to surmount the obstacles with which the enemy can oppose him and, when he has made his decision, to do everything to overcome them.

MAXIM LXXX

The art of a general of the advance guard or the rear guard is, without compromising himself, to contain the enemy, to delay him and to force him to take three or four hours to advance a mile. Tactics supplies the only means to attain such great results. It is more necessary for the cavalry than for the infantry, for an advance guard or for a rear guard, than for any other position.

MAXIM LXXXI

It is exceptional and difficult to find all the qualities of a great general combined in one man. What is most desirable and distinguishes the exceptional man, is the balance of intelligence and ability with character or courage. If courage is predominant, the general will hard far beyond his conceptions; and on the contrary, he will not dare to accomplish his conceptions if his character or his courage are below his intelligence.

MAXIM LXXXII

With a great general there is never a continuity of great actions which can be attributed to chance and good luck; they always are the result of calculation and genius.

MAXIM LXXXIII

A general in chief should never allow any rest either to the conquerors or to the conquered.

MAXIM LXXXIV

An irresolute general who acts without principles and without plan, even though he lead an army numerically superior to that of the enemy, almost always finds himself inferior to the later on the field of battle. Fumblings, the *mezzo termine* (middle course) lose all in war.

MAXIM LXXXV

A general of engineers who must conceive, propose and direct all the fortifications of an army, needs, good judgement and a practical mind above all.

MAXIM LXXXVI

A cavalry general should be a master of practical science, know the value of seconds, despise life and not trust to chance.

MAXIM LXXXVII

A general in the power of the enemy has no more orders to give; whoever obeys him is a criminal.

MAXIM LXXXVIII

The heavy cavalry should be with the advance guard, with the rear guard and on the wings and in reserve to support the light cavalry.

MAXIM LXXXIX

To wish to hold the cavalry in reserve for the end of the battle, is to have no idea of the power of combined cavalry and infantry charges either for attack or for defence.

MAXIM XC

The power of cavalry is in its impulsion. But it is not only its velocity that insures success; it is order, formation and proper employment of reserves.

MAXIM XCI

The cavalry should compose a quarter of the army in Flanders or Germany, in the Pyrenees or in the Alps, a twentieth; in Italy or in Spain, a sixth.

MAXIM XCII

In a battle like in a siege, skill consists in covering a mass of fire on a single point; once the combat is opened, the commander who is adroit will suddenly and unexpectedly open fire with a surprising mass of artillery on one of these points, and is sure to seize it.

MAXIM XCIII

The better the infantry is, the more it should be used carefully and supported with good batteries.

Good infantry is, without doubt, the sinew of an army; but if it is forced to fight for a long time against very superior artillery, it will become demoralized and will be destroyed. It is possible that a general who is more skillful and a better manoeuvrer than his adversary, having better infantry, will gain success during a part of the campaign although his artillery park is very inferior; but, on a decisive day in a general action, he will feel his inferiority in artillery cruelly.

MAXIM XCIV

A good army of 35,000 men should in a few days, especially when supported by a fortress or a large river, make its camp unassailable by an army double in force.

MAXIM XCV

War is composed of nothing but accidents, and, although holding to general principles, a general should never lose sight of everything to enable him to profit from these accidents; that is the mark of genius.

In war there is but one favourable moment; the great art is to seize it.

MAXIM XCVI

A general who retains fresh troops for the day after a battle is almost always beaten. He should, if helpful, throw in his last man, because on the day after a complete success there are no more obstacles in front of him; prestige alone will insure new triumphs to the conqueror.

MAXIM XCVII

The rules of fighting require that a part of an army should avoid fighting alone against an entire army that has already been successful.

MAXIM XCVIII

When a general has laid siege to a place by surprise and has gained a few days on his adversary, he should profit from this by covering himself with lines of circumvallation; from this moment, he will have improved his position and will have acquired a new element of power and a new degree of force in the general framework of affairs.

MAXIM IC

In war the commander of a fortress is not a judge of events; he should defend the fortress to the last; he deserves death if the surrenders it a moment before he is forced to.

MAXIM C

Agreements to surrender made by surrounded bodies, either during a battle or during an active campaign, are contracts with all the advantageous clauses in favour of the individuals who contract them, and all the onerous clauses against the prices and the other soldiers of the army. To avoid peril oneself, while making the position of the rest more dangerous, is an act of cowardice.

MAXIM CI

Defensive war does not exclude attacking, just as offensive war doe sot exclude defending, although its aim may be to force the frontier and invade the enemy's country.

MAXIM CII

The art of war indicates that it is necessary to turn or envelop a wing without separating the army.

MAXIM CIII

When they are thoroughly understood, field fortifications are always useful and never injurious.

MAXIM CIV

An army can march anywhere and at any time of the year, wherever two men can place their feet.

MAXIM CV

Conditions of the ground should not alone decide the organisation for combat, which should be determined from consideration of all circumstances.

MAXIM CVI

Flank marches should be avoided, and when they must be undertaken, they should be as short as possible and made with the greatest speed.

MAXIM CVII

Nothing can be designed better to disorganize and destroy an army than pillage.

MAXIM CVIII

Praise from enemies is suspicious; it cannot flatter an honourable man unless it is given after the cessation of hostilities.

MAXIM CIX

Prisoners of war do not belong to the power for which they have fought; they all are under the safeguard of honour and generosity of the nation that has disarmed them.

MAXIM CX

Conquered provinces should be maintained in obedience to the conquerors by moral means, such as the responsibility and administration. Hostages are among the most powerful means; but to be effective, they should be many and chosen from the preponderant elements, and the people must be convinced that immediate death of the hostages will follow violation of their pledges.

MAXIM CXI

The geographical conditions of a country, life in plains of mountains, education or discipline, have more influence than climate on the character of the troops.

MAXIM CXII

All great captains have done great things only by conforming to the rules and natural principles of the art; that is to say, by the wisdom of their combinations, the reasoned balance of means with consequences, and efforts with obstacles. They have succeeded only by thus conforming, whatever may have been the audacity of their enterprises and the extent of their success. They have never ceased to make war a veritable science. It is only under this title that they are our great models, and it is only in imitating them that one can hope to approach them.

MAXIM CXIII

The first law of naval tactics should be that as soon as the admiral has given the signal that he is going to attack, each captain should the necessary movements to attack an enemy ship, take part in the combat and support his neighbours.

MAXIM CXIV

War on land, in general, consumers more men than naval warfare; it is more dangerous. The sailor in a fleet fights but once during a campaign; the ground soldier fights every day. The sailor, whatever may be the fatigues and dangerous of the sea, suffers much less than the soldier; he is never hungry nor thirsty; he always has a place to sleep, his kitchen, his hospital and his pharmacy. There are fewer sick in the English and French fleets, where discipline maintains cleanliness and experience has discovered all the means of preserving health, than in armies. Besides the perils, of battle, the sailor risks those of tempests; but seamanship has so much diminished the latter that it cannot be compared with those on land, such as popular uprisings, partial assassinations and surprises by hostile light troops.

MAXIM CXV

An admiral commanding a fleet and a general commanding an army are men who need different qualities. One is born with the qualities proper to command an army, while the necessary qualities to command a fleet are acquired only by experience.

The art of war on land is an art of genius, of inspiration. On the sea everything is definite and a matter of experience. The admiral needs only one science, navigation. The general needs all or a talent equal to all, that of profiting by all experience and all knowledge. An admiral needs to divine nothing; he knows where his enemy is and he knows his strength. A general never knows anything with certainty never sees his enemy clearly and never knows positively where he is. When armies met, the least accident of the terrain, the smallest wood, hides a portion of the army. The most experienced eye cannot state whether he sees the entire enemy army or only three quarters of it. It is by the eyes of the mind, by reasoning over the whole, by species of inspiration that the general sees, knows and judge. The admiral needs only an experienced glance; nothing of the enemy force is hidden from him. What makes the general's function difficult is the necessity of nourishing so many men and animals; if he permits himself to be guided by administrators, he will never budge and his expeditions will fail. The admiral is never bothered since he carries everything with him. An admiral has neither reconnaissance to make, terrain to examine nor fields of battle to study. Indian Ocean, American Ocean or North Sea – it is always a liquid plain. The most skillful will have no advantage over the least, except for his knowledge of prevailing winds in such and such coastal waters, by foresight of those which should prevail or by atmospheric signs; qualities which are acquired by experience and by experience only.

The general never knows the field of battle on which he may operate. His understanding is that of inspiration; he has no positive information; data to reach knowledge of localities are so contingent on events that almost nothing is learned by experience. It is a faculty to understand immediately the relations of the terrain according to the nature of different countries; it is, finally, a gift, called a *coup de oeil militaire* (the ability to take in the military situation at a glance) which great generals have received from nature. However, the observations that can be made from topographic maps and the facility which education and habit give in reading maps, can be of some assistance.

An admiral depends more on the captains of his ships than a general on his generals. The latter has the opportunity to take direct command of the troops himself, to move to any point and to repair false movements. An admiral can influence personally only the men on the vessel on which he finds himself; smoke prevents signals from being seen and winds change or vary over the space occupied by his line. It is thus of all professions that in which subalterns should use the largest initiative.

CHAPTER 6

CARL VON CLAUSEWITZ: PRINCIPLES OF WAR

"Theory cannot equip the mind with formulas for solving problems, nor can it mark the narrow path on which the sole solution is supposed to lie by planting a hedge of principles on either side. But it can give the mind insight into the great mass of phenomena and of their relationships, then leave it free to rise into the higher realms of action. There the mind can use its innate talents to capacity, combining them all so as to seize on what is right and true as though this were a single idea formed by their concentrated pressure-as though it were a response to the immediate challenge rather than a product of thought."

— Carl von Clausewitz

Carl Philip Gottlieb von Clausewitz (1780-1831), was a Prussian general and theorist of war. His posthumously published work **On War** (1832) is the most important general treatment of its subject yet produced. Carl von Clausewitz has long been recognized as one of the greatest and most original writers on the subject of war. Clausewitz' life was that of a soldier. It was rarely happy, never easy, and it did not see the fulfilment of his fondest hope: to gain a position of sufficient influence that he might translate into reality his ideas on the theory and conduct of war. Born in 1780, a son of a retired Prussian officer, he joined the army when he was only 12 years old. After participating in the war against France in 1793-94, he spent several years in a small garrison town, Neuruppin, which he spent studying the writings of Frederick the Great, whose concept of duty he particularly admired. In 1801 he entered the 'War School' (*Kreigsschule)* in Berlin. Financial hardship made life difficult and added an element of pessimism to his over-sensitive character. However, one of his instructors, Scharnhorst, recognized his brilliance and outstanding ability and gave him the encouragement he needed.

In 1803, on Scharnhorst's recommendation, he became aide-de-camp to Prince August of Prussia. He accompanied his royal master in the campaign of 1806 against Napoleon, and was taken prisoner by the French. On his return to Germany in 1807, he worked in collaboration with Scharnhorst, whose ideas on military theory and on the necessity of reforming the Prussian army he shared. In 1810, again on Scharnhorst's recommendation, he was attached to the Prussian General Staff in the 'General War School'. He was also appointed military instructor of the Prussian Crown Prince, Frederick William (later King Friedrich Wilhelm IV, r.1840-58).

Clausewitz was scarcely the first to see that wars arise from political quarrels, or that they answer to purposes beyond themselves – that they are about something. But he was the first to recognize the analytic power that these perceptions possessed when rigorously applied to all aspects of war.

For Clausewitz, the subordination and permeation of war by politics meant that there could be no purely military solution to any military problem. It also exemplified a kind of complex tension that always attracted him. War, he famously proposed, was a remarkably trinity whose essential elements – primordial violence and passion, the free play of chance and creativity on the battlefield, and intelligent political purpose – could never be fixed in any arbitrary relationship. War's subordination to politics was logically necessary, and the norm in practice. Yet it was never perfect or absolute. War always threatened to escape its political restraints, and often did succeed in modifying the course of policy to some extent. The violence of war and the rationality of politics were thus theoretical opposites whose real existence was nevertheless marked not by mutual repulsion or exclusion, but by intense and continuous interaction.

Violence and reason, genius and friction, attack and defence, risk and decisiveness, ends and means, fear and courage, victory and defeat – such dualities weave their way throughout the narrative, that may sometimes startle or disconcert us, but which finally provide the work with an intellectual integrity that transcends it superficial incongruities. In a note written towards what proved to be the end of his life, Clausewitz openly feared that his work would be liable to endless misinterpretation and much half baked criticism, an apprehension that has been borne out more than once. Yet his ultimate ambition – to write a book that would not be forgotten after two or three years – would also be amply fulfilled. Few comparably demanding works in any field have so thoroughly withstood the test of time.

Clausewitz's writings reveal a mind constantly engaged by questions of the broadest military and political significance. In October 1806, when the forces of Napoleonic France crushed those of Prussia at the battles of Jena and Auerstadt, Clausewitz was present as tutor to the king's nephew. In the retreat that followed he assumed command of part of the rear guard—the only time he commanded troops in combat and eventually spent seven months interned in France. Upon his return he became involved in the movement to reform the Prussian state and army. In 1812 following Prussia'a acceptance of a French alliance which Clausewitz found politically and emotionally intolerable, he resigned his commission and, along with some 30 other Prussian officers, went to serve in Russia. There he witnessed the epic campaign that would break Napoleon's hold on Europe, a process to which Clausewitz made a modest personal contribution as negotiator, on the Russian side, the convention of Tauroggen, by which the Prussian contingent of the Grande Armee withdrew from the war.

As the war moved back into central Europe, Clausewitz worked to raise provincial militia and other irregular forces against the French, activity that was judged as treason by some since, like the Convention of Tauroggen, it was done without the king's consent. He regained his Prussian commission in April 1814, and was chief of staff to a corps during the Waterloo campaign. In 1818 he became superintendent of the Allgemeine Kriesggshule (War College) in Berlin, a purely administrative post that did not require him to teach, but did afford time for historical and theoretical work. In 1831 he set his studies aside when the outbreak of civil war in Poland caused Prussia to mobilize part of its army. Clausewitz was chosen as chief of staff of the forces deployed to observe the conflict. He died in Breslau of cholera, a few months later.

Clausewitz had his own ideas about the best way to conduct military operations, and much of his writing is devoted to strategic and tactical analysis intended to appeal to the practical instincts of other professional soldiers. For Clausewitz, one requirement for clear thinking was an unflinching respect for war's physical, psychological, and historical reality. He disdained bold strategizing that took no account of how difficult the simplest action becomes in the resistant medium of war. He recognized the impact of fear, danger, confusion, and fatigue on men in battle, and wrote about them with unusual candour. Clausewtz's recognition of the theoretical significance of limited war was both a consequence and a source of his insight into war's political and instrumental character.

Before Clausewitz left Prussia in 1812 to join the Russian army and resist Napoleon, he prepared an essay on war to leave with the sixteen year-old Prussian Crown Prince. This essay was called "The most important principles of the art of war to complete my course of instruction for his Royal Highness the Crown Prince" ["*Die wichtigsten Grundsätze des Kriegführens zur Ergänzung meines Unterrichts bei Sr. Königlichen Hoheit dem Kronprinzen*"]. This essay is usually referred to as the "Principles of War." It represented Clausewitz' theoretical development up to that point, translated into a form suitable for his young student. Unfortunately, it has often been treated as a summary of Clausewitz' mature theory—which it most emphatically is not. Rather, it is only a primitive precursor to his later *magnum opus* - **On War** (which was published in 1832). Its subject matter is largely tactical. While some of the more important theoretical concepts of *On War* are fairly well-developed ("friction," for example), many are embryonic and others entirely absent. In particular, and in great contrast to the later work, "Principles of War" is not notably sophisticated in historical terms. It is based almost entirely on the experience of Frederick the Great and the wars with revolutionary France and Napoleon prior to 1812.

Clausewitz was basically a codifier. He did not really propose any strikingly new or progressive ideas as strategy or tactics. He carried forward the rationale of pure logic to many of his writings. As a result, his arguments often went to the extreme, not that he was not aware of the dangers of such postulation. He wrote that, "Reasoning in the abstract, the mind cannot stop short of an extreme.... But everything takes a different shape when it passes from abstraction to reality". In fact, the main intellectual appeal of Clausewitz's writing lies in the fact that he did not try to sell any theories.

Clausewitz went to great lengths towards formulating a theory of "military aim". According to him "All action in war is to disarm the enemy... If our opponent is to be made to comply with our will, we must place him in a situation which is more oppressive to him than the sacrifice we demand.... Every change in this position which is produced by a continuation of war must, therefore, be a change for the worse".

This formulation, and its elaboration, profoundly influenced the strategic thinking of not only the Prussians, but much later generations of military strategists. It is not difficult to discern the seeds of the strategy of Mutually Assured Destruction of the nuclear age in this postulation.

Clausewitz deliberated a great deal on battle as a means to the end of war. "There is only one single means, it is the fight". The idea of fighting must necessarily be at the foundation". [1] But he also summarized that "the object of combat is not always the destruction of the enemy's forces. It's object can often be attained as much without combat taking place at all".

Clausewitz also analysed theoretically the idea of "absolute" warfare, which lead to his most quoted postulate that war is only "a continuation of state policy by other means". However, his theoretical analysis again led him to extremes, such as, "To induce into the philosophy of war a principle of moderation would be an absurdity. War is an act of violence pushed to its utmost bounds".[2] But Clausewitz also qualified this principle of "utmost force" by the statement: "The political object, as the original motive of the war, should be the standard for determining both the aim of military force, and also the amount of efforts to be made".

The greatest dangers in war, and in life, come from the unexpected; when others do not respond in the manner that you thought they would. The course of events then disrupts your plans and produce confusion, and the changed circumstances become overwhelming. The idea of strategy is to create your own circumstances. A commander has to learn the art of looking beyond the battle and calculating ahead. On a philosophical plane, Clausewitz had analysed what may be called the structure of war, and the relationship between means and ends. Two other aspects which merit mention are his concept of the "centre of gravity" against which the strategic (or military) thrust must be directed, and his concepts or categorisation of attack and defence.[3]

This particular work has rarely aroused any enthusiasm among Clausewitz' more theoretically-oriented students, since it fails to reflect many of the most important of its author's later and deeper insights. *Principles of War* is nonetheless interesting in its own right, on two counts. It provides evidence of Clausewitz' astuteness and also affords a discussion of warfare in the Napoleonic era. Note, however, that the views Clausewitz expresses herein are not those of Napoleon—of whom he has often and erroneously been proclaimed the "High Priest." Rather, Clausewitz' conceptions are those of his mentor, General Gerhard von Scharnhorst, perhaps the most capable of Napoleon's enemies.

Clausewitz' work is the result of thought and observation, philosophy and experience. To back up his generalisations he refers continually to actual campaigns, many of which he had thoroughly studied and in some of which he had himself participated. He did have an originality of thought and flexibility of ideas. He was acute in his perception of the linkage between war and politics. "War is an act of violence, pushed to its utmost bounds." This act of violence, moreover, is not divorced from the political life of a nation; it is not an abnormal situation, but merely the forceful realisation of a political aim, "a mere continuation of policy by other means." Therefore, it must be dictated by political considerations, and military leadership of a state must be subordinated to its political leadership. In fact, even today there can be no discussion on warfare and its theory without invoking the name of Clausewitz.

Most parts of Clausewitz' essay on "Principles of War" still have current value, e.g. the influence of terrain on warfare. His advice: "Be audacious and cunning in your plans, firm and persevering in their execution, determined to find a glorious end," will never lose its significance.

Clausewitz was acutely aware of the dangers of imposing rules. The genius, he wrote, rises above all rules and laughs at them. Yet, he enunciated four principles: employ all available forces with the utmost energy; concentrate where the decisive blow is to be struck; lose no time and surprise the enemy; and, follow up success with the utmost energy. He also enunciated three general principles for defence, fourteen for offence, eight for troops and seventeen for use of terrain.

Some points of amplification and clarification on the text are necessary. The term "corps" as used by Clausewitz does not refer to a specific army unit (such as a modern army-corps), but is used simply to describe any section of the army.

The battles that Clausewitz alludes to as examples are explained at Footnotes to the original text.

NOTES

1. Clausewitz, like Sun Tzu, is eminently quotable. Few catch the subtlety of his logic, because Clausewitz cannot be understood without some understanding of Hegelian dialectics of thesis, anti-thesis and synthesis. Casual readers take the easier route by quoting phrases; e.g. " We have the only means of war—the battle"; "Only a great and general battle can produce great results"; "Let us not hear of generals who conquer without bloodshed".
2. According to Liddell Hart, this postulation, misread, misinterpreted and taken out of context, has lead to the modern definition of "total war". Liddell Hart maintains that the statement is a negation of statesmanship and intelligent strategy which serves the ends policy.
3. Clausewitz has been accused of being an advocate of defensive warfare, because of his statement that "defence is the stronger form of warfare". His assertion was,

however, to stress that even the weaker side has a good chance of winning a war because of the moral superiority he enjoys and the political (and thus material) sympathy that the attacker gathers. Moreover, Clausewitz also covers the dialectic relationship between the defensive and the offensive, and shows that the offensive has a positive object while the defensive is essentially negative.

THE MOST IMPORTANT PRINCIPLES FOR THE CONDUCT OF WAR

CARL VON CLAUSEWITZ

These principles, though the result of long thought and continuous study of the history of war, have nonetheless been drawn up hastily, and thus will not stand severe criticism in regard to form. In addition, only the most important subjects have been picked from a great number, since a certain brevity was necessary. These principles, therefore, will not so much give complete instruction to Your Royal Highness, as they will stimulate and serve as a guide for your own reflections.

I. PRINCIPLES FOR WAR IN GENERAL

1. The theory of warfare tries to discover how we may gain a preponderance of physical forces and material advantages at the decisive point. As this is not always possible, theory also teaches us to calculate moral factors: the likely mistakes of the enemy, the impression created by a daring action, ... yes, even our own desperation. None of these things lie outside the realm of the theory and art of war, which is nothing but the result of reasonable reflection on all the possible situations encountered during a war. We should think very frequently of the most dangerous of these situations and familiarize ourselves with it. Only thus shall we reach heroic decisions based on reason, which no critic can ever shake.

Any person who may present this matter differently to Your Royal Highness is a pedant, whose views will only be harmful to you. In the decisive moments of your life, in the turmoil of battle, you will some day feel that this view alone can help where help is needed most, and where a dry pedantry of figures will forsake you.

2. Whether counting on physical or moral advantages, we should always try, in time of war, to have the probability of victory on our side. But this is not always possible. Often we must act AGAINST this probability, SHOULD THERE BE NOTHING BETTER TO DO. Were we to despair here, we would abandon the use of reason just when it becomes most necessary, when everything seems to be conspiring against us.

Therefore, even when the likelihood of success is against us, we must not think of our undertaking as unreasonable or impossible; for it is always reasonable, if we do not know of anything better to do, and if we make the best use of the few means at our disposal.

We must never lack calmness and firmness, which are so hard to preserve in time of war. Without them the most brilliant qualities of mind are wasted. We must therefore familiarize ourselves with the thought of an honourable defeat. We must always nourish this thought within ourselves, and we must get completely used to it. Be convinced, Most Gracious Master, that without this firm resolution no great results can be achieved in the most successful war, let alone in the most unsuccessful.

Certainly this thought frequently occupied the mind of Frederick II during his first Silesian wars. Because he was familiar with it he undertook his attack near Leuthen, on that memorable fifth of December, and not because he believed that his oblique formation would very likely beat the Austrians.

3. In any specific action, in any measure we may undertake, we always have the choice between the most audacious and the most careful solution. Some people think that the theory of war always advises the latter. That assumption is false. If the theory does advise anything, it is the nature of war to advise the most decisive, that is, the most audacious. Theory leaves it to the military leader, however, to act according to his own courage, according to his spirit of enterprise, and his self-confidence. Make your choice, therefore, according to this inner force; but never forget that no military leader has ever become great without audacity.

II. TACTICS OR THE THEORY OF COMBAT

War is a combination of many distinct engagements. Such a combination may or may not be reasonable, and success depends very much on this. Yet the engagement itself is for the moment more important. For only a combination of successful engagements can lead to good results. The most important thing in war will always be the art of defeating our opponent in combat. To this matter Your Royal Highness can never turn enough attention and thought. I think the following principles the most important:

1. General Principles For Defence

1. To keep our troops covered as long as possible. Since we are always open to attack, except when we ourselves are attacking, we must at every instant be on the defensive and thus should place our forces as much under cover as possible.

2. Not to bring all our troops into combat immediately. With such action

all wisdom in conducting a battle disappears. It is only with troops left at our disposal that we can turn the tide of battle.

3. To be little or not at all concerned about the extent of our front. This in itself is unimportant, and an extension of the front limits the depth of our formation (that is, the number of units which are lined up one behind the other). Troops which are kept in the rear are always available. We can use them either to renew combat at the same point, or to carry the fight to other neighbouring points. This principle is a corollary of the previous one.

4. The enemy, while attacking one section of the front, often seeks to outflank and envelop us at the same time. The units which are kept in the background can meet this attempt and thus make up for the support usually derived from obstacles in the terrain. They are better suited for this than if they were standing in line and extending the front. For in this case the enemy could easily outflank them. This principle again is a closer definition of the second.

5. If we have many troops to hold in reserve, only part of them should stand directly behind the front. The rest we should put obliquely behind. From this position they in turn can attack the flank of the enemy columns which are seeking to envelop us.

6. A fundamental principle is never to remain completely passive, but to attack the enemy frontally and from the flanks, even while he is attacking us. We should, therefore, defend ourselves on a given front merely to induce the enemy to deploy his forces in an attack on this front. Then we in turn attack with those of our troops which we have kept back. The art of entrenchment, as Your Royal Highness expressed so excellently at one time, shall serve the defender not to defend himself more securely behind a rampart, but to attack the enemy more successfully. This idea should be applied to any passive defence. Such defence is nothing more than a means by which to attack the enemy most advantageously, in a terrain chosen in advance, where we have drawn up our troops and have arranged things to our advantage.

7. This attack from a defensive position can take place the moment the enemy actually attacks, or while he is still on the march. I can also, at the moment the attack is about to be delivered, withdraw my troops, luring the enemy into unknown territory and attacking him from all sides. The formation in depth—i.e., the formation in which only two-thirds or half or still less of the army is drawn-up in front and the rest directly or obliquely behind and hidden, if possible—is very suitable for all these moves. This type of formation is, therefore, of immense importance.

8. If, for example, I had two divisions, I would prefer to keep one in the

rear. If I had three, I would keep at least one in the rear, and if four probably two. If I had five, I should hold at least two in reserve and in many cases even three, etc.

9. At those points where we remain passive we must make use of the art of fortification. This should be done with many independent works, completely closed and with very strong profiles.

10. In our plan of battle we must set this great aim: the attack on a large enemy column and its complete destruction. If our aim is low, while that of the enemy is high, we will naturally get the worst of it. We are penny-wise and pound-foolish.

11. Having set a high goal in our plan of defence (the annihilation of an enemy column, etc.), we must pursue this goal with the greatest energy and with the last ounce of our strength. In most cases the aggressor will pursue his own aim at some other point. While we fall upon his right wing, for example, he will try to win decisive advantages with his left. Consequently, if we should slacken before the enemy does, if we should pursue our aim with less energy than he does, he will gain his advantage completely, while we shall only half gain ours. He will thus achieve preponderance of power; the victory will be his, and we shall have to give up even our partly gained advantages. If Your Royal Highness will read with attention the history of the battles of Ratisbon and Wagram, all this will seem true and important.[1]

In both these battles the Emperor Napoleon attacked with his right wing and tried to hold out with his left. The Archduke Charles did exactly the same. But, while the former acted with great determination and energy, the latter was wavering and always stopped half-way. That is why the advantages which Charles gained with the victorious part of his army were without consequence, while those which Napoleon gained at the opposite end were decisive.

12. Let me sum up once more the last two principles. Their combination gives us a maxim which should take first place among all causes of victory in the modern art of war: "Pursue one great decisive aim with force and determination."

13. If we follow this and fail, the danger will be even greater, it is true. But to increase caution at the expense of the final goal is no military art. It is the wrong kind of caution, which, as I have said already in my "General Principles," is contrary to the nature of war. For great aims we must dare great things. When we are engaged in a daring enterprise, the right caution consists in not neglecting out of laziness, indolence, or carelessness those

measures which help us to gain our aim. Such was the case of Napoleon, who never pursued great aims in a timid or half-hearted way out of caution.

If you remember, Most Gracious Master, the few defensive battles that have ever been won, you will find that the best of them have been conducted in the spirit of the principles voiced here. For it is the study of the history of war which has given us these principles.

At Minden, Duke Ferdinand suddenly appeared where the enemy did not expect him and took the offensive, while at Tannhausen he defended himself passively behind earthworks.[2] At Rossbach, Frederick II threw himself against the enemy at an unexpected point and an unexpected moment.[3]

At Liegnitz, the Austrians found the King at night in a position very different from that in which they had seen him the previous day. He fell with his whole army upon one enemy column and defeated it before the others could start fighting.[4]

At Hohenlinden, Moreau had five divisions in his front line and four directly behind and on his flanks. He outflanked the enemy and fell upon his right wing before it could attack.[5]

At Ratisbon, Marshal Davout defended himself passively, while Napoleon attacked the fifth and sixth army-corps with his right wing and beat them completely.

Though the Austrians were the real defenders at Wagram, they did attack the emperor on the second day with the greater part of their forces. Therefore Napoleon can also be considered a defender. With his right wing he attacked, outflanked and defeated the Austrian left wing. At the same time he paid little attention to his weak left wing (consisting of a single division), which was resting on the Danube. Yet through strong reserves *(i.e.,* formation in depth), he prevented the victory of the Austrian right wing from having any influence on his own victory gained on the Rossbach. He used these reserves to retake Aderklaa.

Not all the principles mentioned earlier are clearly contained in each of these battles, but all are examples of active defence.

The mobility of the Prussian army under Frederick II was a means towards victory on which we can no longer count, since the other armies are at least as mobile as we are. On the other hand, outflanking was less common at that time and formation in depth, therefore, less imperative.

2. General Principles For Offence

1. We must select for our attack one point of the enemy's position *(i.e.,* one section of his troops—a division, a corps) and attack it with great

superiority, leaving the rest of his army in uncertainty but keeping it occupied. This is the only way that we can use an equal or smaller force to fight with advantage and thus with a chance of success. The weaker we are, the fewer troops we should use to keep the enemy occupied at un-important points, in order to be as strong as possible at the decisive point. Frederick II doubtlessly won the battle of Leuthen only because he massed his small army together in one place and thus was very concentrated, as compared to the enemy.[6]

2. We should direct our main thrust against an enemy wing by attacking it from the front and from the flank, or by turning it completely and attacking it from the rear. Only when we cut off the enemy's line of retreat are we assured of great success in victory.

3. Even though we are strong, we should still direct our main attack against one point only. In that way we shall gain more strength at this point. For to surround an army completely is possible only in rare cases and requires tremendous physical or moral superiority. It is possible, however, to cut off the enemy's line of retreat at one point of his flank and thereby already gain great success.

4. Generally speaking, the chief aim is the certainty (high probability) of victory, that is, the certainty of driving the enemy from the field of battle. The plan of battle must be directed towards this end. For it is easy to change an indecisive victory into a decisive one through energetic pursuit of the enemy.

5. Let us assume that the enemy has troops enough on one wing to make a front in all directions. Our main force should try to attack the wing concentrically, so his troops find themselves assailed from all sides. Under these circumstances his troops will get discouraged much more quickly; they suffer more, get disordered—in short, we can hope to turn them to flight much more easily.

6. This encirclement of the enemy necessitates a greater deployment of forces in the front line for the aggressor than for the defender.

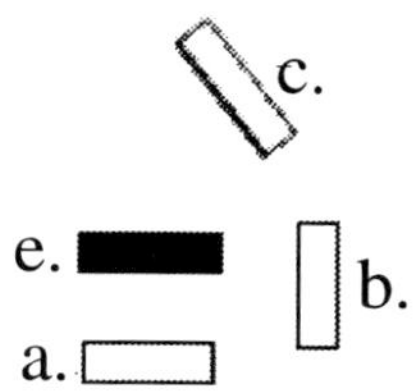

If the corps **a b c** should make a concentric attack on the section **e** of the enemy army, they should, of course, be next to each other. But we should never have so many forces in the front line that we have none in reserve. That would be a very great error which would lead to defeat, should the enemy be in the least prepared for an encirclement.

If **a b c** are the corps which are to attack section **e**, the corps **f** and **g** must be held in reserve. With this formation in depth we are able to harass the same point continuously. And in case our troops should be beaten at the opposite end of the line, we do not need to give up immediately our attack at this end, since we still have reserves with which to oppose the enemy.

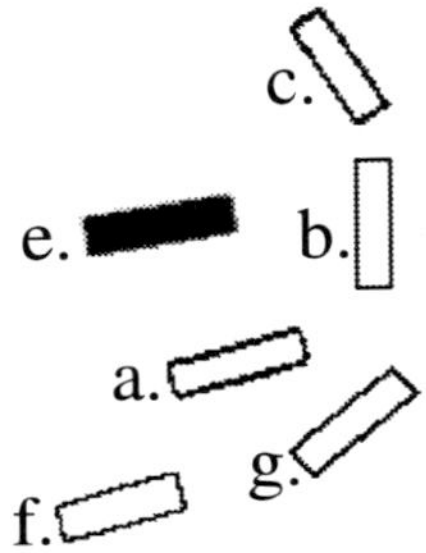

The French did this in the battle of Wagram. Their left wing, which opposed the Austrian right wing resting on the Danube, was extremely weak and was completely defeated. Even their centre at Aderklaa was not very strong and was forced by the Austrians to retreat on the first day of battle. But all this did not matter because Napoleon had such depth on his right wing, with which he attacked the Austrian left from the front and side. He advanced against the Austrians at Aderklaa with a tremendous column of cavalry and horse-artillery and, though he could not beat them, he at least was able to hold them there.

7. Just as on the defensive, we should choose as the object of our offensive that section of the enemy's army whose defeat will give us decisive advantages.

8. As in defence, as long as any resources are left, we must not give up until our purpose has been reached. Should the defender likewise be active, should he attack us at other points, we shall be able to gain victory only if we surpass him in energy and boldness. On the other hand, should he be passive, we really run no great danger.

9. Long and unbroken lines of troops should be avoided completely. They would lead only to parallel attacks, which today are no longer feasible.

Each division makes its attack separately, though according to the directions of a higher command and thus in agreement with each other. Yet one division (8,000 to 10,000 men) is never formed into one single line, but into two, three, or even four. From this it follows that a long unbroken line is no longer possible.

10. The concerted attacks of the divisions and army corps should not be obtained by trying to direct them from a central point, so that they maintain contact and even align themselves on each other, though they may be far apart or even separated by the enemy. This is a faulty method of bringing about cooperation, open to a thousand mischances. Nothing great can be achieved with it and we are certain to be thoroughly beaten by a strong opponent.

The true method consists in giving each commander of an army corps or a division the main direction of his march, and in pointing out the enemy as the objective and victory as the goal.

Each commander of a column, therefore, has the order to attack the enemy wherever he may find him and to do so with all his strength. He must not be made responsible for the success of his attack, for that would lead to indecision. But he is responsible for seeing that his corps will take part in battle with all its energy and with a spirit of self-sacrifice.

11. A well-organized, independent corps can withstand the best attack for some time (several hours) and thus can not be annihilated in a moment. Thus, even if it engaged the enemy pre-maturely and was defeated, its fight will not have been in vain. The enemy will unfold and expend his strength against this one corps, offering the rest a good chance for an attack.

The way in which a corps should be organized for this purpose will be treated later.

We therefore assure the cooperation of all forces by giving each corps a certain amount of independence, but seeing to it that each seeks out the enemy and attacks him with all possible self-sacrifice.

12. One of the strongest weapons of offensive warfare is the surprise attack. The closer we come to it, the more fortunate we shall be. The unexpected element which the defender creates through secret preparations and through the concealed disposition of his troops, can be counterbalanced on the part of the aggressor only by a surprise attack. Such action, however, has been very rare in recent wars, partly because of the more advanced precautionary measures, partly because of the rapid conduct of campaigns. There seldom arises a long suspension of activities, which lulls one side into security and thus gives the other an opportunity to attack unexpectedly.

Under these circumstances—except for nightly assaults which are always possible (as at Hochkirch)—we can surprise our opponent only by marching to the side or to the rear and then suddenly advancing again. Or, should we be far from the enemy, we can through unusual energy and activity arrive faster than he expects us.

13. The regular surprise attack (by night as at Hochkirch)[7] is the best way to get the most out of a very small army. But the aggressor, who is not as well acquainted with the terrain as the defender, is open to many risks. The less well one knows the terrain and the preparations of the enemy, the greater these risks become. In many instances, therefore, these attacks must be considered only as desperate means.

14. This kind of attack demands simpler preparations and a greater concentration of our troops than in the daytime.

3. Principles Governing the Use of Troops

1. If we cannot dispense with firearms (and if we could, why should we bring them along?), we must use them to open combat. Cavalry must not be used before the enemy has suffered considerably from our infantry and artillery. From this it follows:

(a) That we must place the cavalry behind the infantry. That we must not be easily led to use it in opening combat. Only when the enemy's disorder or his rapid retreat offer the hope of success, should we use our cavalry for an audacious attack.

2. Artillery fire is much more effective than that of infantry. A battery of eight six-pounders takes up less than one-third of the front taken up by an infantry battalion; it has less than one- eighth the men of a battalion, and yet its fire is two to three times as effective. On the other hand, artillery has the disadvantage of being less mobile than infantry. This is true, on the whole, even of the lightest horse-artillery, for it cannot, like infantry, be used in any kind of terrain. It is necessary, therefore, to direct the artillery from the start against the most important points, since it cannot, like infantry, concentrate against these points as the battle progresses. A large battery of 20 to 30 pieces usually decides the battle for that section where it is placed.

3. From these and other apparent characteristics the following rules can be drawn for the use of the different arms:

(a) We should begin combat with the larger part of our artillery. Only when we have large masses of troops at our disposal should we keep horse and foot-artillery in reserve. We should use artillery in great batteries massed against one point. Twenty to thirty pieces combined into one battery defend the chief part of our line, or shell that part of the enemy position which we plan to attack.

(b) After this we use light infantry—either marksmen, riflemen, or fusiliers—being careful not to put too many forces into play at the beginning. We try first to discover what lies ahead of us (for we can seldom see that clearly in advance), and which way the battle is turning, etc. If this firing line is sufficient to counteract the enemy's troops, and if there is no need to hurry, we should do wrong to hasten the use of our remaining forces. We must try to exhaust the enemy as much as possible with this preliminary skirmish.

(c) If the enemy should lead so many troops into combat that our firing line is about to fall back, or if for some other reason we should no longer hesitate, we must draw up a full line of infantry. This will deploy between 100 and 200 paces from the enemy and will fire or charge, as matters may be.

(d) This is the main purpose of the infantry. If, at the same time, the battle-array is deep enough, leaving us another line of infantry (arranged in columns) as reserve, we shall be sufficiently master of the situation at this sector. This second line of infantry should, if possible, be used only in columns to bring about a decision.

(e) The cavalry should be as close behind the fighting troops during battle as is possible without great loss; that is, it should be out of the enemy's grape-shot or musket fire. On the other hand, it should be close enough to take quick advantage of any favourable turn of battle.

4. In obeying these rules more or less closely, we should never lose sight of the following principle, which I cannot stress enough:

Never bring all our forces into play haphazardly and at one time, thereby losing all means of directing the battle; but fatigue the opponent, if possible, with few forces and conserve a decisive mass for the critical moment. Once this decisive mass has been thrown in, it must be used with the greatest audacity.

5. We should establish one battle-order (the arrangement of troops before and during combat) for the whole campaign or the whole war. This order will serve in all cases when there is no time for a special disposition of troops. It should, therefore, be calculated primarily for the defensive. This battle-array will introduce a certain uniformity into the fighting-method of the army, which will be useful and advantageous. For it is inevitable that a large part of the lower generals and other officers at the head of small contingents have no special knowledge of tactics and perhaps no outstanding aptitude for the conduct of war.

Thus there arises a certain methodism in warfare to take the place of art, wherever the latter is absent. In my opinion this is to the highest degree the case in the French armies.

6. After what I have said about the use of weapons, this battle-order, applied to a brigade, would be approximately as follows:

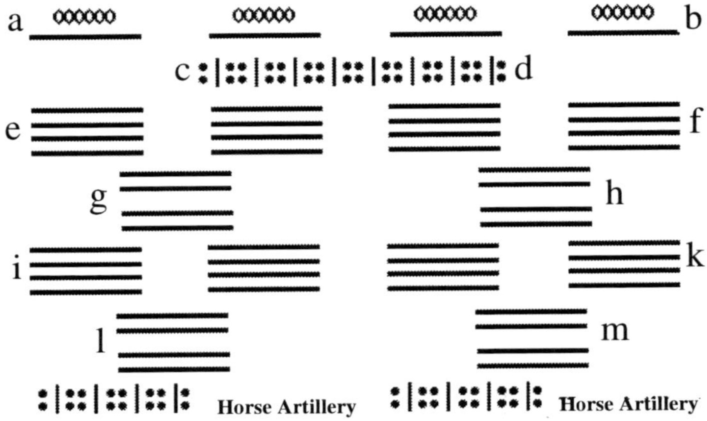

a-b is the line of light infantry, which opens combat and which in rough terrain serves to some extent as an advanced guard. Then comes the artillery, c-d, to be set up at advantageous points. As long as it is not set up, it remains behind the first line of infantry. e-f is the first line of infantry (in this case four battalions) whose purpose is to form into line and to open fire, and g-h are a few regiments of cavalry. i-k is the second line of infantry, which is held in reserve for the decisive stage of the battle, and l-m is its cavalry. A strong corps would be drawn up according to the same principles and in a similar manner. At the same time, it is not essential that the battle array be exactly like this. It may differ slightly provided that the above principles are followed. So, for instance, in ordinary battle-order the first line of cavalry g-h can remain with the second line of cavalry, l-m. It is to be advanced only in particular cases, when this position should prove to be too far back.

7. The army consists of several such independent corps, which have their own general and staff. They are drawn up in line and behind each other, as described in the general rules for combat. It should be observed at this point that, unless we are very weak in cavalry, we should create a special cavalry reserve, which, of course, is kept in the rear. Its purpose is as follows:

(a) To fall upon the enemy when he is retreating from the field of battle and to attack the cavalry which he uses to cover up his retreat. Should we defeat the enemy's cavalry at this moment, great successes are inevitable, unless the enemy's infantry would perform miracles of bravery. Small detachments of cavalry would not accomplish this purpose.

(b) To pursue the enemy more rapidly, if he should be retreating unbeaten or if he should continue to retreat the day after a lost battle. Cavalry moves faster than infantry and has a more demoralizing effect on the retreating troops. Next to victory, the act of pursuit is most important in war.

(c) To execute a great (strategic) turning move, should we need, because of the detour, a branch of the army which moves more rapidly than the infantry.

In order to make this corps more independent, we should attach a considerable mass of horse artillery; for a combination of several types of arms can only give greater strength.

8. The battle-order of troops described thus far was intended for combat; it was the formation of troops for battle.

The order of march is essentially as follows:

(a) Each independent corps (whether brigade or division) has its own advanced- and rear-guard and forms its own column. That, however, does not prevent several corps from marching one behind the other on the same road, and thus, as it were, forming a single column.

(b) The corps march according to their position in the general formation of battle. They march beside or behind each other, just as they would stand on the battle-field.

(c) In the corps themselves the following order is invariably observed: the light infantry, with the addition of one regiment of cavalry, forming the advanced and rear-guard, then the infantry, the artillery, and last the remaining cavalry.

This order stands, whether we are moving against the enemy—in which case it is the natural order— or parallel with him. In the latter case we should assume that those troops which in the battle formation were behind each other should march side by side. But when we have to draw up the troops for battle, there will always be sufficient time to move the cavalry and the second line of infantry either to the right or left.

4. Principles for the Use of Terrain

1. The terrain (the ground or country) offers two advantages in warfare.

The first is that it presents obstacles to the enemy's approach. These either make his advance impossible at a given point, or force him to march more slowly and to maintain his formation in columns, etc.

The second advantage is that obstacles in the terrain enable us to place our troops under cover.

Although both advantages are very important, I think the second more important than the first. In any event, it is certain that we profit from it more frequently, since in most cases even the simplest terrain permits us to place ourselves more or less under cover. Formerly only the first of these advantages was known and the second was rarely used. But today the greater mobility of all armies has led us to use the former less frequently, and therefore the latter more frequently. The first of these two advantages is useful for defence alone, the second for both offence and defence.

2. The terrain as an obstacle to approach serves chiefly to support our flank, and to strengthen our front.

3. To support our flank it must be absolutely impassable, such as a large river, a lake, an impenetrable morass. These obstacles, however, are very rare, and a complete protection of our flank is, therefore, hard to find. It is rarer today than ever before, since we do not stay in one position very long, but move about a great deal. Consequently we need more positions in the theater of war.

An obstacle to approach which is not wholly impassable is really no *point d'appui* for our flank, but only a reinforcement. In that case troops must be drawn up behind it, and for them in turn it becomes an obstacle to approach.

Yet it is always advantageous to secure our flank in this way, for then we shall need fewer troops at this point. But we must beware of two things: first, of relying so completely on this protection that we do not keep a strong reserve in the rear; second, of surrounding ourselves on both flanks with such obstacles, for, since they do not protect us completely, they do not always prevent fighting on our flanks. They are, therefore, highly detrimental to our defence, for they do not permit us to engage easily in active defence on either wing. We shall be reduced to defence under the most disadvantageous conditions, with both flanks, a d and c b, thrown back.

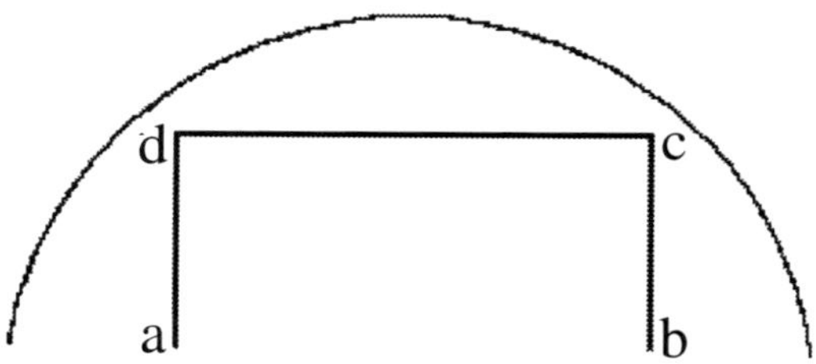

4. The observations just made furnish new arguments for the formation in depth. The less we can find secure support for our flanks, the more corps we must have in the rear to envelop those troops of the enemy which are surrounding us.

5. All kinds of terrain, which cannot be passed by troops marching in line, all villages, all enclosures surrounded by hedges or ditches, marshy meadows, finally all mountains which are crossed only with difficulty, constitute obstacles of this kind. We can pass them, but only slowly and with effort. They increase, therefore, the power of resistance of troops drawn up behind them. Forests are to be included only if they are thickly wooded and marshy. An ordinary timber-forest can be passed as easily as a plain. But we must not overlook the fact that a forest may hide the enemy. If we conceal ourselves in it, this disadvantage affects both sides. But it is very dangerous, and thus a grave mistake, to leave forests on our front or flank unoccupied, unless the forest can be traversed only by a few paths. Barricades built as obstacles are of little help, since they can easily be removed.

6. From all this it follows that we should use such obstacles on one flank to put up a relatively strong resistance with few troops, while executing our planned offensive on the other flank. It is very advantageous to combine the use of entrenchments with such natural obstacles, because then, if the enemy should pass the obstacle, the fire from these entrenchments will protect our weak troops against too great superiority and sudden rout.

7. When we are defending ourselves, any obstacle on our front is of great value.

Mountains are occupied only for this reason. For an elevated position seldom has any important influence, often none at all, on the effectiveness of arms. But if we stand on a height, the enemy, in order to approach us, must climb laboriously. He will advance but slowly, become separated, and arrive with his forces exhausted. Given equal bravery and strength, these advantages may be decisive. On no account should we overlook the moral effect of a rapid, running assault. It hardens the advancing soldier against danger, while the stationary soldier loses his presence of mind. It is, therefore, always very advantageous to put our first line of infantry and artillery upon a mountain.

Often the grade of the mountain is so steep, or its slope so undulating and uneven, that it cannot be effectively swept by gun- fire. In that case we should not place our first line, but at the most only our sharp-shooters, at the edge of the mountain. Our full line we should place in such a way that the enemy is subject to its most effective fire the moment he reaches the top and reassembles his forces.

All other obstacles to approach, such as small rivers, brooks, ravines, etc., serve to break the enemy's front. He will have to reform his lines after passing them and thus will be delayed. These obstacles must, therefore, be placed under our most effective fire, which is grape-shot (400 to 600 paces), if we have a great deal of artillery or musket-shot (150 to 200 paces), if we have little artillery at this point.

8. It is, therefore, a basic law to place all obstacles to approach, which are to strengthen our front, under our most effective fire. But it is important to notice that we must never completely limit our resistance to this fire but must hold ready for a bayonet-charge an important part of our troops (1/3 to 1/2) organized into columns. Should we be very weak, therefore, we must place only our firing-line, composed of riflemen and artillery, close enough to keep the obstacle under fire. The rest of our troops, organized into columns, we should keep 600 to 800 paces back, if possible under cover.

9. Another method of using these obstacles to protect our front is to leave them a short distance ahead. They are thus within the effective range of our cannon (1000 to 2000 paces) and we can attack the enemy's columns from all sides, as they emerge. (Something like this was done by Duke Ferdinand at Minden). In this way the obstacle contributes to our plan of active defence, and this active defence, of which we spoke earlier, will be executed on our front.

10. Thus far we have considered the obstacles of the ground and country primarily as connected lines related to extended positions. It is still necessary to say something about isolated points.

On the whole we can defend single, isolated points only by entrenchments or strong obstacles of terrain. We shall not discuss the first here. The only obstacles of terrain which can be held by themselves are:

(a) Isolated, steep heights.

Here entrenchments are likewise indispensable; for the enemy can always move against the defender with a more or less extended front. And the latter will always end up by being taken from the rear, since one is rarely strong enough to make front towards all sides.

(b) Defiles.

By this term we mean any narrow path, through which the enemy can advance only against one point. Bridges, dams, and steep ravines belong here.

We should observe that these obstacles fall into two categories: either the aggressor can in no way avoid them, as for example bridges across large rivers, in which case the defender can boldly draw up his whole force so as to fire upon the point of crossing as effectively as possible. Or we are not absolutely sure that the enemy can not turn the obstacle, as with bridges across small streams and most mountain defiles. In that case it is necessary to reserve a considerable part of our troops 1/3 to 1/2 for an attack in close order.

(c) Localities, villages, small towns, etc.
With very brave troops, who fight enthusiastically, houses offer a unique defence for few against many. But, if we are not sure of the individual soldier, it is preferable to occupy the houses, gardens, etc., only with sharp-shooters and the entrances to the village with cannons. The greater part of our troops (1/2 to 3/4) we should keep in close columns and hidden in the locality or behind it, so as to fall upon the enemy while he is invading.

11. These isolated posts serve in large operations partly as outposts, in which case they serve not as absolute defence but only as a delay to the enemy, and partly to hold points which are important for the combinations we have planned for our army. Also it is often necessary to hold on to a remote point in order to gain time for the development of active measures of defence which we may have planned. But, if a point is remote, it is *ipso facto* isolated.

12. Two more observations about isolated obstacles are necessary. The first is that we must keep troops ready behind them to receive detachments that have been thrown back. The second is that whoever includes such isolated obstacles in his defensive combinations should never count on them too much, no matter how strong the obstacle may be. On the other hand, the military leader to whom the defence of the obstacle has been entrusted must always try to hold out, even under the most adverse circumstances. For this there is needed a spirit of determination and self-sacrifice, which finds its source only in ambition and enthusiasm. We must, therefore, choose men for this mission who are not lacking in these noble qualities.

13. Using terrain to cover the disposition and advance of troops needs no detailed exposition.

We should not occupy the crest of the mountain which we intend to defend (as has been done so frequently in the past) but draw up behind it. We should not take our position in front of a forest, but inside or behind it; the latter only if we are able to survey the forest or thicket. We should keep our troops in columns, so as to find cover more easily. We must make use of villages, small thickets, and rolling terrain to hide our troops. For our advance we should choose the most intersected country, etc.

In cultivated country, which can be reconnoitered so easily, there is almost no region that can not hide a large part of the defender's troops if they have made clever use of obstacles. To cover the aggressor's advance is more difficult, since he must follow the roads.

It goes without saying that in using the terrain to hide our troops, we must never lose sight of the goal and combinations we have set for ourselves. Above all things we should not break up our battle-order completely, even though we may deviate slightly from it.

14. If we recapitulate what has been said about terrain, the following appears most important for the defender, i.e., for the choice of positions:

(a) Support of one or both flanks.
(b) Open view on front and flanks.
(c) Obstacles to approach on the front.
(d) Masked disposition of troops. And finally
(e) Intersected country in the rear, to render pursuit more difficult in case of defeat. But no defiles too near (as at Friedland), since they cause delay and confusion.[8]

15. It would be pedantic to believe that all these advantages could be found in any position we may take up during a war. Not all positions are of equal importance: the most important are those in which we most likely may be attacked. It is here that we should try to have all these advantages, while in others we only need part.

16. The two main points which the aggressor should consider in regard to the choice of terrain are not to select too difficult a terrain for the attack, but on the other hand to advance, if possible, through a terrain in which the enemy can least survey our force.

17. I close these observations with a principle which is of highest significance, and which must be considered the keystone of the whole defensive theory:

> NEVER TO DEPEND COMPLETELY ON THE STRENGTH OF THE TERRAIN AND CONSEQUENTLY NEVER TO BE ENTICED INTO PASSIVE DEFENCE BY A STRONG TERRAIN.

For if the terrain is really so strong that the aggressor cannot possibly expel us, he will turn it, which is always possible, and thus render the strongest terrain useless. We shall be forced into battle under very different circumstances, and in a completely different terrain, and we might as well not have included the first terrain in our plans. But if the terrain is not so strong, and if an attack within its confines is still possible, its advantages can never make up for the disadvantages of passive defence. All obstacles are useful, therefore, only for partial defence, in order that we may put up a relatively strong resistance with few troops and gain time for the offensive, through which we try to win a real victory elsewhere.

III. STRATEGY

This term means the combination of individual engagements to attain the goal of the campaign or war.

If we know how to fight and how to win, little more knowledge is needed. For it is easy to combine fortunate results. It is merely a matter of experienced judgment and does not depend on special knowledge, as does the direction of battle.

The few principles, therefore, which come up in this connection, and which depend primarily on the condition of the respective states and armies, can in their essential parts be very briefly summarized:

1. General Principles

1. Warfare has three main objects

(a) To conquer and destroy the armed power of the enemy;

(b) To take possession of his material and other sources of strength, and

(c) To gain public opinion.

2. To accomplish the first purpose, we should always direct our principal operation against the main body of the enemy army or at least against an important portion of his forces. For only after defeating these can we pursue the other two objects successfully.

3. In order to seize the enemy's material forces we should direct our operations against the places where most of these resources are concentrated: principal cities, storehouses, and large fortresses. On the way to these objectives we shall encounter the enemy's main force or at least a considerable part of it.

4. Public opinion is won through great victories and the occupation of the enemy's capital.

5. The first and most important rule to observe in order to accomplish these purposes, is to use our entire forces with the utmost energy. Any moderation shown would leave us short of our aim. Even with everything in our favour, we should be unwise not to make the greatest effort in order to make the result perfectly certain. For such effort can never produce negative results. Suppose the country suffers greatly from this, no lasting disadvantage will arise; for the greater the effort, the sooner the suffering will cease.

The moral impression created by these actions is of infinite importance. They make everyone confident of success, which is the best means for suddenly raising the nation's morale.

6. The second rule is to concentrate our power as much as possible

against that section where the chief blows are to be delivered and to incur disadvantages elsewhere, so that our chances of success may increase at the decisive point. This will compensate for all other disadvantages.

7. The third rule is never to waste time. Unless important advantages are to be gained from hesitation, it is necessary to set to work at once. By this speed a hundred enemy measures are nipped in the bud, and public opinion is won most rapidly.

Surprise plays a much greater role in strategy than in tactics. It is the most important element of victory. Napoleon, Frederick II, Gustavus Adolphus, Caesar, Hannibal, and Alexander owe the brightest rays of their fame to their swiftness.

8. Finally, the fourth rule is to follow up our successes with the utmost energy. Only pursuit of the beaten enemy gives the fruits of victory.

9. The first of these rules serves as a basis for the other three. If we have observed it, we can be as daring as possible with the last three, and yet not risk our all. For it provides us with the means of constantly creating new forces in our rear, and with fresh forces any misfortune can be remedied.

Therein lies the caution which deserves to be called wise, and not in taking each step forward with timidity.

10. Small states cannot wage wars of conquest in our times. But in defensive warfare even the means of small states are infinitely great. I am, therefore, firmly convinced that if we spare no effort to reappear again and again with new masses of troops, if we use all possible means of preparation and keep our forces concentrated at the main point, and if we, thus prepared, pursue a great aim with determination and energy, we have done all that can be done on a large scale for the strategic direction of the war. And unless we are very unfortunate in battle we are bound to be victorious to the same extent that our opponent lags behind in effort and energy.

11. In observing these principles little depends on the form in which the operations are carried out. I shall try, nevertheless, to make clear in a few words the most important aspects of this question.

In tactics we always seek to envelop that part of the enemy against which we direct our main attack. We do this partly because our forces are more effective in a concentric than in a parallel attack, and further because we can only thus cut off the enemy from his line of retreat.

But if we apply this to the whole theater of war (and consequently to the enemy's lines of communication), the individual columns and armies, which are to envelop the enemy, are in most cases too far away from each other to participate in one and the same engagement. The opponent will find himself in the middle and will be able to turn against the corps one by one and defeat them all with a single army. Frederick II's campaigns may serve as examples, especially those of 1757 and 1758.[9]

The individual engagement, therefore, remains the principal decisive event. Consequently, if we attack concentrically without having decisive superiority, we shall lose in battle all the advantages, which we expected from our enveloping attack on the enemy. For an attack on the lines of communication takes effect only very slowly, while victory on the field of battle bears fruit immediately.

In strategy, therefore, the side that is surrounded by the enemy is better off than the side which surrounds its opponent, especially with equal or even weaker forces.

Colonel Jomini was right in this, and if Mr. von Bülow has demonstrated the opposite with so much semblance of truth, it is only because he attributed too great an importance to the interruption of provisions and carelessly and completely denied the inevitable success of battle.

To cut the enemy's line of retreat, however, strategic envelopment or a turning movement is very effective. But we can achieve this, if necessary, through tactical envelopment. A strategic move is, therefore, advisable only if we are so superior (physically and morally) that we shall be strong enough at the principal point to dispense with the detached corps.

The Emperor Napoleon never engaged in strategic envelopment, although he was often, indeed almost always, both physically and morally superior.

Frederick II used it only once, in 1757, in his invasion of Bohemia.[10] To be sure, the result was that the Austrians could not give battle until Prague, and what good was the conquest of Bohemia as far as Prague without a decisive victory? The battle of Kolin forced him to give up all this territory again, which proves that battles decide everything. At the same time he was obviously in danger at Prague of being attacked by the whole Austrian force, before Schwerin arrived. He would not have run this risk had he passed through Saxony with all his forces. In that case the first battle would have been fought perhaps near Budin, on the Eger, and it would have been as decisive as that of Prague. The dislocation of the Prussian army during the winter in Silesia and Saxony undoubtedly caused this concentric manoeuvre. It is important to notice that circumstances of this kind are generally more influential than the advantages to be gained by the form of attack. For facility of operations increases their speed, and the friction inherent in the tremendous war-machine of an armed power is so great in itself that it should not be increased unnecessarily.

12. Moreover, the principle of concentrating our forces as much as possible on the main point diverts us from the idea of strategic envelopment and the deployment of our forces follows automatically. I was right, therefore, in saying that the form of this deployment is of little consequence. There is, however, one case in which a strategic move against the enemy's flank will lead to great successes similar to those of a battle: if in a poor country the enemy has accumulated with great effort stores of supplies, on whose preservation his operations absolutely depend. In this case it may be advisable not to march our main forces against those of the enemy, but to attack his base of supply. For this, however, two conditions are essential:

(a) The enemy must be so far from his base that our threat will force him into a considerable retreat, and

(b) We must be able to obstruct his advance in the direction followed by his principal force with only a few troops (thanks to natural and artificial obstacles), so that he cannot make conquests somewhere else which will compensate for the loss of his base.

13. The provisioning of troops is a necessary condition of warfare and thus has great influence on the operations, especially since it permits only a limited concentration of troops and since it helps to determine the theater of war through the choice of a line of operations.

14. The provisioning of troops is carried on, if a region possibly permits it, through requisitions at the expense of the region.

In the modern method of war armies take up considerably more territory than before. The creation of distinct, independent corps has made this possible, without putting ourselves at a disadvantage before an adversary who follows the old method of concentration at a single point (with from 70,000 to 100,000 men). For an independent corps, organized as they now are, can withstand for some time an enemy two or three times its superior. Then the others will arrive and, even if the first corps has already been beaten, it has not fought in vain, as we have had occasion to remark.

Today, therefore, the divisions and corps move into battle independently, marching side by side or behind each other and only close enough to take part in the same battle, if they belong to the same army.

This makes possible immediate provisioning without storehouses. The very organisation of the corps with their General Staff and their Commissariat facilitates this.

15. If there are no more decisive motives (as for example the location of the enemy's main army), we choose the most fertile provinces for our operations; for facility of provisioning increases the speed of our actions.

Only the situation of the enemy's main force which we are seeking out, only the location of his capital and the place of arms which we wish to conquer are more important than provisioning. All other considerations, such as the advantageous disposition of our forces, of which we have already spoken, are as a rule much less important.

16. In spite of these new methods of provisioning, it is quite impossible to do without any depots whatever. Therefore, even when the resources of the region are quite sufficient, a wise military leader does not fail to establish depots in his rear for unexpected emergencies and in order to be able to concentrate his forces at certain points. This precaution is of the sort which are not taken at the expense of the final goal.

2. Defensive

1. Politically speaking defensive war is a war which we wage for our independence. Strategically it is the kind of campaign in which we limit ourselves to fighting the enemy in a theater of war which we have prepared for this purpose. Whether the battles which we wage in this theater of war are offensive or defensive, makes no difference.

2. We adopt a strategic defensive mainly when the enemy is superior. Fortresses and entrenched camps, which constitute the chief preparations for a theater of war, afford, of course, great advantages, to which may be added the knowledge of the terrain and the possession of good maps. A smaller army, or an army which is based on a smaller state and more limited resources, will be better able to withstand the enemy with these advantages than without them.

In addition there are the following two reasons which can lead us to choose a defensive war.

First, when the regions surrounding the theater of war render operations extremely difficult because of lack of provisions. In this case we avoid a disadvantage which the enemy is forced to undergo. This is the case now (1812) with the Russian army.

Second, when the enemy is superior in warfare. In a theater of war which we have prepared, which we know, and in which all minor conditions are in our favour, war is easier to conduct, and we commit fewer mistakes. When lack of trust in our troops and generals forces us to wage defensive war, we often like to combine tactical with strategic defensive. In that case we fight battles in prepared positions because we are thus again exposed to fewer mistakes.

3. In defensive just as in offensive warfare, it is necessary to pursue a great aim: the destruction of the enemy army, either by battle or by rendering its subsistence extremely difficult. Thus we shall disorganize it and force it into a retreat, during which it will necessarily suffer great losses. Wellington's campaign in 1810 and 1811 is a good example.[11]

Defensive warfare, therefore, does not consist of waiting idly for things to happen. We must wait only if it brings us visible and decisive advantages. That calm before the storm, when the aggressor is gathering new forces for a great blow, is most dangerous for the defender.

If the Austrians after the battle of Aspern had increased their forces threefold, as they might have and as the Emperor Napoleon did, then and only then would they have made good use of the lull which lasted until the battle of Wagram. This they did not do, and consequently the time was lost. It would have been wiser to profit from Napoleon's disadvantageous position, and to gather the fruits of the battle of Aspern.

4. The purpose of fortifications is to keep a considerable part of the enemy's army occupied as siege troops, to give us an opportunity to defeat the rest of his army. Consequently, it is best to fight our battles behind our fortifications and not in front of them. But we must not stand by idly, while they are being conquered, as Bennigsen did during the siege of Danzig.[12]

5. Large rivers, across which it is difficult to throw a bridge (such as the Danube below Vienna and the Lower Rhine), offer a natural line of defence. But we should not distribute our forces evenly along the river bank in order to prevent any crossing whatsoever. That would be most dangerous. On the contrary, we should watch the river and fall upon the enemy from all sides the minute he crosses, while he has not yet reassembled his forces and is still restricted to a narrow space on the river bank. The battle of Aspern offers a good illustration.[13] At Wagram the Austrians had yielded to the French too much territory without the slightest necessity, so that the disadvantages inherent in a river crossing had disappeared.

6. Mountains are the second obstacle which offers a good line of defence. There are two ways of using them. The first is to leave them in front of us, occupying them only with light troops and considering them, so to speak, a river which the enemy will have to cross. As soon as his separated columns emerge from the passes, we fall upon one of them with all our force. The second is to occupy the mountains ourselves. In that case we must defend each pass with just a small corps and keep an important part of the army (1/3-1/2) in reserve, in order to attack with superior forces one of the enemy columns that succeed in breaking through. We must not divide up this large

reserve to prevent completely the penetration of any enemy columns, but must plan from the outset to fall only upon those columns which we suppose to be the strongest. If we thus defeat an important part of the attacking army, any other columns which have succeeded in breaking through will withdraw of their own accord.

In the midst of most mountain formations we find more or less elevated plains (plateaus) whose slopes are cut by ravines serving as means of access. Mountains, therefore, offer the defender a region in which he can move rapidly to the right or left, while the columns of the aggressor remain separated by steep, inaccessible ridges. Only mountains of this kind are well adapted for defensive warfare. If, on the other hand, their whole interior is rough and inaccessible, leaving the defender dispersed and divided, their defence by the bulk of the army is a dangerous undertaking. For under these circumstances all advantages are on the side of the aggressor, who can attack certain points with great superiority, and no pass, no isolated point is so strong that it cannot be taken within a day by superior forces.

7. In regard to mountain warfare in general, we should observe that everything depends on the skill of our subordinate officers and still more on the morale of our soldiers. Here it is not a question of skilful manoeuvring, but of warlike spirit and wholehearted devotion to the cause; for each man is left more or less to act independently. That is why national militias are especially suited for mountain warfare. While they lack the ability to manoeuvre, they possess the other qualities to the highest degree.

8. Finally, it should be observed that the strategic defensive, though it is stronger than the offensive, should serve only to win the first important successes. If these are won and peace does not follow immediately, we can gain further successes only through the offensive. For if we remain continually on the defensive, we run the great risk of always waging war at our own expense. This no state can endure indefinitely. If it submits to the blows of its adversary without ever striking back, it will very likely become exhausted and succumb. We must begin, therefore, using the defensive, so as to end more successfully by the offensive.

3. Offensive

1. The strategic offensive pursues the aim of the war directly, aiming straight at the destruction of the enemy's forces, while the strategic defensive seeks to reach this purpose indirectly. The principles of the offensive are

therefore already contained in the "General Principles" of strategy. Only two points need be mentioned more fully.

2. The first is constant replacement of troops and arms. This is easier for the defender, because of the proximity of his sources of supply. The aggressor, although he controls in most cases a larger state, must usually gather his forces from a distance and therefore with great difficulty. Lest he find himself short of effectives, he must organize the recruiting of troops and the transport of arms a long time before they are needed. The roads of our lines of operation must be covered constantly with transports of soldiers and supplies. We must establish military stations along these roads to hasten this rapid transport.

3. Even under the most favourable circumstances and with greatest moral and physical superiority, the aggressor should foresee a possibility of great disaster. He therefore must organize on his lines of operation strong points to which he can retreat with a defeated army. Such are fortresses with fortified camps or simply fortified camps.

Large rivers offer the best means of halting the pursuing enemy for a while. We must therefore secure our crossing by means of bridgeheads, surrounded by a number of strong redoubts.

We must leave behind us a number of troops for the occupation of these strong points as well as the occupation of the most important cities and fortresses. Their number depends on how much we have to be afraid of invasions or of the attitude of the inhabitants. These troops, together with reinforcements, form new corps, which, in case of success, follow the advancing army, but in case of misfortune, occupy the fortified points in order to secure our retreat.

Napoleon always took great care with these measures for the protection of the rear of his army, and therefore, in his most audacious operations, risked less than was usually apparent.

IV. APPLICATION OF THESE PRINCIPLES IN TIME OF WAR

The principles of the art of war are in themselves extremely simple and quite within the reach of sound common sense. Even though they require more special knowledge in tactics than in strategy, this knowledge is of such small scope, that it does not compare with any other subject in extent and variety. Extensive knowledge and deep learning are by no means necessary, nor are extraordinary intellectual faculties. If, in addition to experienced judgment, a special mental quality IS required, it would be, after all that has been said cunning or shrewdness. For a long time the contrary has been maintained, either because of false veneration for the subject or because of the vanity of the authors who have written about it. Unprejudiced reflection should convince us of this, and experience only makes this conviction stronger. As recently as the Revolutionary War we find many men who proved themselves able military leaders, yes, even military leaders of the first order, without having had any military education. In the case of Condé, Wallenstein, Suvorov, and a multitude of others it is very doubtful whether or not they had the advantage of such education.[14]

The conduct of war itself is without doubt very difficult. But the difficulty is not that erudition and great genius are necessary to understand the basic principles of warfare. These principles are within the reach of any well-organized mind, which is unprejudiced and not entirely unfamiliar with the subject. Even the application of these principles on maps or on paper presents no difficulty, and to have devised a good plan of operations is no great masterpiece. The great difficulty is this:

TO REMAIN FAITHFUL THROUGHOUT TO THE PRINCIPLES WE HAVE LAID DOWN FOR OURSELVES.

To call attention to this difficulty is the purpose of these closing remarks, and to give Your Royal Highness a clear idea of it I consider the most important object of this essay.

The conduct of war resembles the workings of an intricate machine with tremendous friction, so that combinations which are easily planned on paper can be executed only with great effort.

The free will and the mind of the military commander, therefore, find themselves constantly hampered, and one needs a remarkable strength of mind and soul to overcome this resistance. Many good ideas have perished because of this friction, and we must carry out more simply and moderately what under a more complicated form would have given greater results.

It may be impossible to enumerate exhaustively the causes of this friction; but the main ones are as follows:

1. Generally we are not nearly as well acquainted with the position and measures of the enemy as we assume in our plan of operations. The minute we begin carrying out our decision, a thousand doubts arise about the dangers which might develop if we have been seriously mistaken in our plan. A feeling of uneasiness, which often takes hold of a person about to perform something great, will take possession of us, and from this uneasiness to indecision, and from there to half measures are small, scarcely discernible steps.

2. Not only are we uncertain about the strength of the enemy, but in addition rumour (i.e., all the news which we obtain from outposts, through spies, or by accident) exaggerates his size. The majority of people are timid by nature, and that is why they constantly exaggerate danger. All influences on the military leader, therefore, combine to give him a false impression of his opponent's strength, and from this arises a new source of in- decision.

We cannot take this uncertainty too seriously, and it is important to be prepared for it from the beginning.

After we have thought out everything carefully in advance and have sought and found without prejudice the most plausible plan, we must not be ready to abandon it at the slightest provocation. On the contrary, we must be prepared to submit the reports which reach us to careful criticism, we must compare them with each other, and send out for more. In this way false reports are very often disproved immediately, and the first reports confirmed. In both cases we gain certainty and can make our decision accordingly. Should this certainty be lacking, we must tell ourselves that nothing is accomplished in warfare without daring; that the nature of war certainly does not let us see at all times where we are going; that what is probable will always be probable though at the moment it may not seem so; and finally, that we cannot be readily ruined by a single error, if we have made reasonable preparations.

3. Our uncertainty about the situation at a given moment is not limited to the conditions of the enemy only but of our own army as well. The latter can rarely be kept together to the extent that we are able to survey all its parts at any moment, and if we are inclined to uneasiness, new doubts will arise. We shall want to wait, and a delay of our whole plan will be the inevitable result.

We must, therefore, be confident that the general measures we have adopted will produce the results we expect. Most important in this connection is the trust which we must have in our lieutenants. Consequently, it is important to choose men on whom we can rely and to put aside all other considerations. If we have made appropriate preparations, taking into account all possible misfortunes, so that we shall not be lost immediately if they occur, we must boldly advance into the shadows of uncertainty.

4. If we wage war with all our strength, our subordinate commanders and even our troops (especially if they are not used to warfare) will frequently encounter difficulties which they declare insurmountable. They find the march too long, the fatigue too great, the provisions impossible. If we lend our ear to all these difficulties, as Frederick II called them, we shall soon succumb

completely, and instead of acting with force and determination, we shall be reduced to weakness and inactivity.

To resist all this we must have faith in our own insight and convictions. At the time this often has the appearance of stubbornness. But in reality it is that strength of mind and character which is called firmness.

5. The results on which we count in warfare are never as precise as is imagined by someone who has not carefully observed a war and become used to it.

Very often we miscalculate the march of a column by several hours, without being able to tell the cause of the delay. Often we encounter obstacles which were impossible to foresee. Often we intend to reach a certain place with our army and fall short of it by several hours. Often a small outpost which we have set up achieves much less than we expected, while an enemy outpost achieves much more. Often the resources of a region do not amount to as much as we expected, etc.

We can triumph over such obstacles only with very great exertion, and to accomplish this the leader must show a severity bordering on cruelty. Only when he knows that everything possible is always being done, can he be sure that these small difficulties will not have a great influence on his operations. Only then can he be sure that he will not fall too far short of the aim which he could have reached.

6. We may be sure that an army will never be in the condition supposed by someone following its operations from an armchair. If he is sympathetic to the army he will imagine it from a third to a half stronger and better than it really is. It is quite natural that the military commander will make the same mistake in planning his first operations. Consequently, he will see his army melt away as he never thought it would, and his cavalry and artillery become useless. What appeared possible and easy to the observer and to the commander at the opening of a campaign is often difficult and even impossible to carry out. If the military leader is filled with high ambition and if he pursues his aims with audacity and strength of will, he will reach them in spite of all obstacles; while an ordinary person would have found in the condition of his army a sufficient excuse for giving in.

Masséna proved at Genoa and in Portugal the influence of a strong-willed leader over his troops. At Genoa, the limitless exertion to which his strength of will, not to say his harshness, forced people, was crowned with success. In Portugal he at least retreated later than anyone else would have.[15]

Most of the time the enemy army is in the same position. For example, Wallenstein and Gustavus Adolphus at Nuremberg,[16] and Napoleon and

Bennigsen after the battle of Eylau.[17] But while we do not see the condition of the enemy, our own is right before our eyes. The latter, therefore, makes a greater impression on ordinary people than the first, since sensuous impressions are stronger for such people than the language of reason.

7. The provisioning of troops, no matter how it is done, whether through storehouses or requisitions, always presents such difficulty that it must have a decisive influence on the choice of operations. It is often contrary to the most effective combination, and forces us to search for provisions when we would like to pursue victory and brilliant success. This is the main cause for the unwieldiness of the whole war machine which keeps the results so far beneath the flight of our great plans.

A general, who with tyrannical authority demands of his troops the most extreme exertions and the greatest privations, and an army which in the course of long wars has become hardened to such sacrifices will have a tremendous advantage over their adversaries and will reach their aim much faster in spite of all obstacles. With equally good plans, what a difference of result!

8. We cannot stress the following too much:

Visual impressions gained during actual combat are more vivid than those gained beforehand by mature reflection. But they give us only the outward appearance of things, which, as we know, rarely corresponds to their essence. We therefore run the risk of sacrificing mature reflection for first impression.

The natural timidity of humans, which sees only one side to everything, makes this first impression incline toward fear and exaggerated caution.

Therefore we must fortify ourselves against this impression and have blind faith in the results of our own earlier reflections, in order to strengthen ourselves against the weakening impressions of the moment.

These difficulties, therefore, demand confidence and firmness of conviction. That is why the study of military history is so important, for it makes us see things as they are and as they function. The principles which we can learn from theoretical instruction are only suited to facilitate this study and to call our attention to the most important elements in the history of war.

Your Royal Highness, therefore, must become acquainted with these principles in order to check them against the history of war, to see whether they are in agreement with it and to discover where they are corrected or even contradicted by the course of events.

In addition, only the study of military history is capable of giving those who have no experience of their own a clear impression of what I have just called the friction of the whole machine.

Of course, we must not be satisfied with its main conclusions, and still less with the reasoning of historians, but we must penetrate as deeply as possible into the details. For the aim of historians rarely is to present the absolute truth. Usually they wish to embellish the deeds of their army or to demonstrate the concordance of events with their imaginary rules. They invent history instead of writing it. We need not study much history for the purpose we propose. The detailed knowledge of a few individual engagements is more useful than the general knowledge of a great many campaigns. It is therefore more useful to read detailed accounts and diaries than regular works of history. An example of such an account, which cannot be surpassed, is the description of the defence of Menin in 1794, in the memoirs of General von Scharnhorst. This narrative, especially the part which tells of the sortie and break through the enemy lines, gives Your Royal Highness an example of how to write military history.

No battle in history has convinced me as much as this one that we must not despair of success in war until the last moment. It proves that the influence of good principles, which never manifests itself as often as we expect, can suddenly reappear, even under the most unfortunate circumstances, and when we have already given up hope of their influence.

A powerful emotion must stimulate the great ability of a military leader, whether it be ambition as in Caesar, hatred of the enemy as in Hannibal, or the pride in a glorious defeat, as in Frederick the Great.

Open your heart to such emotion. Be audacious and cunning in your plans, firm and persevering in their execution, determined to find a glorious end, and fate will crown your youthful brow with a shining glory, which is the ornament of princes, and engrave your image in the hearts of your last descendants.

NOTES

1. The battles of Ratisbon and Wagram were part of Napoleon's campaign against Austria in 1809. At Eckmühl, near Ratisbon in Southern Germany, a French army under Napoleon and his Marshal Davout defeated a strong Austrian army on April 22. This paved the way for Napoleon's invasion of Austria, where at the village of Wagram, near Vienna, he succeeded in beating the Archduke Charles so thoroughly (July 5-6) that Austria had to ask for an armistice shortly afterwards.
2. At the Battle of Minden in Westphalia, Duke Ferdinand of Brunswick, one of Frederick the Great's generals during the Seven Years' War, won a significant victory over the French under Marshal Contades. He had planned to attack the French positions in the early hours of 1 August 1759, when he received word that the French in turn were getting ready to attack him. He went through with his plans for

mobilisation, thus completely upsetting Contades' preparations for a surprise attack. In the ensuing battle the allied Prussian, English, and Hanoverian troops won a decisive victory, which resulted in the withdrawal of the French beyond the Rhine and Main rivers. At the same time, about one-third of Ferdinand's army, organized as an independent corps under General von Wangenheim, was stationed to the left of the main army, near the village of Tannhausen. This corps had not been informed of the impending French attack. An enemy corps under Broglie opened fire on Wangenheim's entrenchments around 5 A.M. It failed to follow up its surprise attack, thus enabling Wangenheim to draw up his troops and resist Broglie until the defeat of the main army under Contades forced the French to retreat.

3. At Rossbach, on 5 November 1757, Frederick the Great's army of 22,000 men defeated a combined French and German army twice its size, under the leadership of the incompetent Princes of Soubise (France) and Hildburghausen (Saxony). While his opponents, thinking he was beating a hasty retreat, began their pursuit, Frederick's excellently trained cavalry under General von Seydlitz suddenly attacked their right flank. The enemy, with no time to draw up in battle-formation, was completely dispersed and defeated. The moral effect of Frederick's victory was tremendous both inside and outside of Germany. It reestablished his reputation, which had suffered considerably after his defeat at Kolin.
4. The Battle of Liegnitz, like those of Rossbach and Leuthen earlier, shows Frederick the Great's skill in defeating a superior force by using his highly mobile army in a concentrated attack, keeping the enemy as much in the dark about his intentions as possible. Finding himself surrounded near Liegnitz (Saxony) by several Austrian armies numbering close to 100,000, he planned a careful withdrawal. During the night of 14-15 August 1760, he broke camp, leaving his fires burning, however, to deceive the enemy, who had planned a three-cornered attack for the morning of 15 August. At dawn the Prussian King surprised one section of the Austrian army under Laudon on the river Katzbach, and defeated 30,000 men with an army half this size.
5. During Napoleon's campaign against the Second Coalition (Great Britain, Austria, and Russia), the French General Moreau had concentrated his forces at the village of Hohenlinden, situated in the midst of a great forest on a plateau east of Munich. Despite the warnings of his generals, Archduke John of Austria entered the forest on 2 December 1800, to seek the French. Meanwhile Moreau, hidden by the forest, moved part of his forces, outflanked the Austrians, and caught them between two fires. The Austrian army was thoroughly beaten, losing more than 20,000 men, and Moreau was free to continue his advance toward Vienna.
6. Frederick the Great achieved the necessary concentration of his forces by a peculiar battle-order known as "Schiefe Schlachtordnung" (oblique formation). Though by no means new (it had been used occasionally since antiquity), it was Frederick who first applied this formation consistently in almost all his battles. In his General Principles of Warfare, written in 1748, Frederick described it as follows: "We `refuse' one of our wings to the enemy and strengthen the wing with which we plan to attack." This would make possible the defeat of a vastly superior enemy: "An army of 100,000

men, thus attacked on its flank, can be beaten by 30,000 men." The most successful example of Frederick's use of this formation "in echelon" was the battle of Leuthen.

7. At Hochkirch, a village in Saxony, the Austrian army of Marshal Daun delivered a serious defeat to Frederick the Great's forces on 14 October 1758. Attacking at the crack of dawn, the Austrians caught the over-confident King of Prussia unprepared, and with a force of 78,000 they defeated his army of 40,000, inflicting heavy losses on the Prussians. About 9,000 men were lost and several of Frederick's generals were killed or wounded. Most of the rules dealing with this cavalry reserve, though no longer valid in modern warfare, can be applied almost word for word to mechanized units.
8. At Friedland, in East Prussia, a Russian army under Bennigsen was defeated by Napoleon, on 14 June 1807, during the War of the Third Coalition against France. The Russians were withdrawing along the right bank of the river Alle, towards Königsberg, when they met a single French corps under the command of Marshal Lannes. Bennigsen thought this an excellent chance for an attack, but Lannes held out until Napoleon arrived with his main army. The Emperor concentrated his main attack on the Russian left wing, which was separated from the right wing by a ravine, and whose only possible retreat was through a narrow outlet between this ravine and the river. Napoleon's artillery, concentrating on this point, inflicted heavy losses on the Russians before they succeeded in gaining the other bank of the Alle.
9. During the Seven Years' War, Prussia found herself surrounded by enemies: Saxony and Austria to the south, France to the west, Sweden to the north, and Russia to the east. Frederick the Great overcame his difficult position by making full use of the advantages which fighting on "interior lines" offers to a highly mobile army led by a commander who does not shrink from taking the initiative: Without waiting to declare war he seized Saxony in 1756. His invasion of Bohemia in 1757 was checked by the Austrians at Kolin and he had to fall back upon his own territories. From there he advanced with lightning speed, first into Central Germany to defeat the French at Rossbach and from there back to Silesia, where he beat the Austrians at Leuthen. On 25 August 1758 he defeated the Russians near Zorndorf. Eventually, however, the numerical superiority of his opponents became too great and Frederick was forced to limit himself to a more defensive strategy, while his tactics remained offensive.
10. In the spring of 1757 Frederick the Great invaded Bohemia with three separate armies. Two of these advanced from Saxony (one led by the King himself) and a third from Silesia, under the command of the seventy-two year old Marshal Schwerin. The Austrian army under Prince Charles retreated before the invaders and took up a strong position near Prague. Schwerin's army was late in arriving, and when it finally did, the Prussians defeated the Austrians (6 May 1757), but allowed a large part of the Austrian forces to withdraw. On 18 June, Frederick, though outnumbered, once more attacked the Austrian army, this time under Marshal Daun, near Kolin. He was thoroughly beaten, largely because of the numerical superiority of the Austrians and the ability and courage of Marshal Daun.

11. Wellington's Campaign of 1810-11 was part of the Peninsular War (1808-13) to free Spain and Portugal from the domination of Napoleon. Just as in Russia during Napoleon's campaign of 1812, the inhabitants of the Peninsula voluntarily destroyed their possessions and stores of supplies, to make provisioning of the enemy impossible and to hasten his defeat. This policy of "scorched earth," as it is called today, was eminently successful in both cases.
12. During the spring of 1807, Napoleon ordered Marshal Lefebvre to lay siege to the city of Danzig. The siege, beginning in March, lasted into May. The Russian commander-in-chief, Ben- Nigsen, who was stationed in the vicinity, remained passive throughout, even though the capitulation of Danzig gave Napoleon a valuable base and released a number of his troops, which he used to great advantage shortly afterwards in the battle of Friedland.
13. In the vicinity of Aspern and Essling, two villages near Vienna, Napoleon suffered a great military defeat on 21-22 May 1809. After winning against the Austrians near Ratisbon, he had made his entry into Vienna on 13 May. The enemy's army, under Archduke Charles, had withdrawn to the north bank of the Danube, and Napoleon, in order to attack it, had to cross the river. In a murderous battle Charles defeated the French, who lost one of their ablest leaders, Marshal Lannes. After receiving vast reinforcements, Napoleon attempted another crossing on 4 July. This time he was successful, and on 5-6 July he won the battle of Wagram, thus terminating Austria's premature war of liberation.
14. Louis II of Bourbon, Prince of Condé (1621-86), known as the "Great Condé," started on a brilliant military career in 1640, towards the end of the Thirty Years' War (1618-48). In 1643 he was made commander of the French forces against the Spaniards in northern France and won the decisive victory of Rocroi, which, at the age of 22, established him as one of the great military figures of history.

    Albrecht von Wallenstein (1583-1634), a Bohemian nobleman, was one of the outstanding military leaders of the Imperial Catholic party during the Thirty Years' War, though his military education, according to Clausewitz's and our own standards, was brief and superficial. He saw two years of armed service (1604-06) against the Turks and Hungarians, and from 1617 on he was commander of an increasing number of mercenaries (mostly hired at his own expense from a rapidly growing fortune), which he put at the disposal of the Emperor Ferdinand II.

    Count Alexander Suvorov (1729-1800) won fame as commander of the Russian forces during Catherine the Great's wars with Turkey (1768-74, 1787-92). In 1799, he was given supreme command over the Italian armies of the Second anti-French Coalition and succeeded in driving the French out of Italy.
15. Andre Masséna, Prince of Essling, a distinguished French General and Marshal during the Revolutionary and Napoleonic Wars. In the spring of 1800, during the war of the Second Coalition, he was ordered by Napoleon to defend the Italian city of Genoa against the Austrians. The latter suddenly attacked, cut his army in two, and forced him to withdraw into the town with his remaining right wing. The Austrian general Ott laid siege to the city, and Masséna kept him occupied by constant sorties.

In spite of the growing shortage of food he held out until June 4, enabling Napoleon to win the battle of Marengo. In 1810 Masséna was made commander-in-chief of a French army of 70,000 invading Portugal to drive the English under Wellington "into the sea." Again he had to pitch his will-power and determination against the terrible enemy of hunger. The British troops withdrew into the interior, leaving behind them a mountainous country bare of provisions. Only one major battle was fought and lost by the French (at Busaco). Most of the French losses of 25,000 men were due to sickness and starvation. It is largely because of Masséna's skilful retreat that not more troops were lost.

16. During the period of Swedish intervention (1630-32) in the Thirty Years' War, Albrecht von Wallenstein, the leader of the Catholic and Imperial forces (see note 20) and King Gustavus Adolphus of Sweden occupied positions opposite each other near Nuremberg in Southern Germany. After Wallenstein had several times refused battle, the Swedes attacked his camp on 3 September 1632. Fighting lasted into the night, inflicting heavy losses on both sides, but Gustavus Adolphus did not succeed in driving out Wallenstein.
17. Near Eylau in East Prussia, a French army under Napoleon and his Marshals Davout and Ney claimed a victory over the Russians, led by Bennigsen, on Feb. 8, 1807. The success of both armies changed frequently during battle, due to the various reinforcements they received, and at nightfall neither of them had won a decisive victory; but the French losses exceeded those of the Russians, who had lost more than a third of their men. Bennigsen, however, realizing the exhaustion of his troops and fearing further reinforcement of the French army, withdrew, leaving Napoleon to claim victory.

CHAPTER 7

REFLECTIONS

"There is no fate worse than being continuously under guard, for it means you are always afraid"

— Julius Caesar, 100-44 BC

Merely to use the term 'the military art' is to enter directly into the debate as to whether warfare is indeed an art, and thus the sphere of unquantifiable qualities such as given ability and inspiration (not to mention the luck about which Napoleon enquired when considering an officer for senior rank), or a science in which every military situation can be reduced to a number of variables which, if the correct formula is identified and applied, must inevitably lead to victory.

Strategy is the application of sound human sense to the conduct of war; its teachings go little beyond the requirement of common sense. Its value lies entirely in concrete application. The main point is to correctly estimate the situation and then to do the simplest and most natural things with firmness and caution. Thus war becomes an art – an art, of course, which is served by many sciences. In war, as in art, we find no universal forms; in neither can a rule take the place of talent.

This is an area where there has been little agreement amongst military thinkers over the centuries. Some, like Jomini, have tended towards the prescriptive, arguing that war has rules whose application brings success and whose breach courts failure. Others, like Clausewitz, have been more descriptive, emphasizing that war is the realm of chance and uncertainty, and the pure light of reason glows darkly through its fog. A study of the history of warfare shows that new ideas emerge during periods of revolutionary change or at times of crisis, and these ideas remain dominant until they themselves are rendered inadequate by new paradigmatic changes.

Even the most descriptive have recognized that even if war has no rules, it certainly possesses broad principles, and a proper grasp of its purpose, function, and scale is crucial to understanding it. Tactics make the steps from which operational moves are assembled; strategy points out the path. An understanding of these levels and what is required to be achieved by each lies at the heart of the military art. For example, any successful defensive strategy will need to embrace counter offensive operations; often an offensive strategy will need to include defensive operations in order to guard flanks, rear areas, and borders with countries not involved in any given conflict. Various fighting techniques, or tactics, are required for each type of operations. Achieving the right balance of effort between offensive and defensive operations; determining where to seek a decision in battle and how much of the force to retain uncommitted in the form of reserves are some of the most important considerations a commander must face in developing his tactical or higher level campaign plan. In answering such questions a commander must rest on his knowledge of the military art tempered by his operational experience and the advice offered by his staff. The capability to make keenly judged and timely decisions, combined with the ability to motivate the troops under his command and the resolution to overcome the frictions and inevitable setbacks of war, constitute that rare and elusive quality of generalship.

Yet the management and conduct of war requires more than the adoption of tactical or operational schemes of manoeuvre in order to meet some strategic design. While the amount of resources allocated to conflict remains critical, much is also determined by the society, culture, and history of the armed groups or states concerned. Further, the organisational structure, weapons and equipment, doctrine, level of training and not least efficiency and morale of the forces involved, all contribute to military effectiveness. Non-military influences as well as organisational and technological matters help shape the military art. While an analysis of the practice by an army of the military art will not necessarily reveal its detailed equipment list, it should indicate the force's view of conflict and suggest what military strategies, operational methods and tactics it might employ.

The fate of all civilisations has been linked to their military means. The ancient Egyptians, Greeks, Persians, Carthaginians and Romans developed well organized standing armies and fleets to wage war against their foes in pursuit of policy ends. The Roman way of war, for example, capitalized on tough, highly disciplined, and well trained units of manpower that could be committed flexibly over a wide geographical area and for long duration. Few nations could resist Rome's power, in the long term, as long as she possessed the necessary economic and social means to maintain her military forces and to sustain the will to fight. Yet ultimately, less well organized but more numerous, brutal, and committed peoples overwhelmed the Roman Empire. In view of the economic effort (finance), social commitment (blood), and political stakes (survival) involved, writers began to record the lessons from past conflict and to investigate the enduring dynamics of war. Early military historians such as Herodotus and Xenophon give us detailed insights into how man fought in ancient times, giving us rich descriptions of battles, tactics, and weaponry. Thucydides not only tells us why Athens and Sparta waged the Peloponnesian wars, but also explains why he wrote his famous history: "My work is not a piece of writing designed to meet the taste of an immediate public, but is done to last forever".

Military literature expanded in the Roman period, reflecting a fascination in the art of war and its impact on political and social development. Polybius composed his Histories in order to inform his Greek compatriots about the way in which Rome had sought and achieved power. In their treatment of the Punic wars, there is little doubt that Polybius wrote as much to explain as to narrate the rise of Rome's military prowess while Livy stood to glorify it. But of all the Greek or Roman works on war, perhaps, Vegetius' De re Militari was the most influential in the longer term. Although largely neglected at the time of writing—a misfortune of many military philosophers down the ages—Vegetius was well read during the Renaissance. While Machiavelli in his *Arte della Guerra* (The Art of War) based much of his work on Vegetius, he provided more than a mere historical study.

Although based on classical thought, Machiavelli's general rules for commanders were of considerable contemporary significance. Yet well before Machiavelli had begun to study classical military history, Europe in the 13th century had been surprised by the sudden rise of Asian military might. Genghis Khan had spread fear and terror through the western world. Mongol military power rested on thorough preparation, organisation, training and harsh discipline. Its advantage in battle largely depended on the shock action delivered by its body of fierce and highly skilled horsemen. More subtle methods were employed in achieving operational and strategic success. Genghis Khan used a combination of surprise, deception, and psychological operations to put his opponents off balance, both mentally and physically. These techniques remain very much relevant today. Above all, the Mongols – a nomadic race of some three to four million only – developed various methods to convince their enemies that they were more numerous than was the case. Frugal methods of supply (what we might now term lean logistics) improved the Mongols strategic mobility as did their ruthless rape of subjugated peoples and their territory. By the mid-13th century the Mongols had attacked successfully Russia, Poland, and Hungary and dominated most of Asia. Perhaps one of the most formidable armies in history, the Mongols presented a unified force who exploited their opponent's military weaknesses and political differences. The Mongol art of war that successfully synchronized time, space, and forces was essentially one of manoeuvre, and not without lasting influence and was not lost on modern military thinkers. In Great Captains Unveiled (1926), "Liddell Hart declared that the tank and the airplane were natural heirs and successors to the Mongol horsemen.

The earliest known treatise on the conduct of war – the Art of War, written by Sun Tzu, was not accessible in Europe until a translation into French appeared in the late 18th century. By this time a series of European writers already had begun to codify the nature and principles of war in an attempt to provide the keys to military success. The birth of the modern military art is usually attributed to the French Revolutionary Napoleonic wars. The period's pre-eminent writers, Clausewitz and Jomini, remain the subject of detailed study and scrutiny today. If early 19th century tactics have become overtaken by modern technology, strategy, logistics, and command remain highly relevant elements of the military art. In this respect the enigmatic Clausewitz has more to tell us of contemporary significance in *Vom Kriege* (On War), published posthumously in 1832, than the prolific Jomini whose General Principles (1816) and Principal Maxims (1830) now seem outdated. That said, his influence in Europe and notably in America and Russia was far greater than that of Clausewitz during the 19th century.

The whole science of war may be briefly defined as the art of placing in the right position, at the right time, a mass of troops greater than your enemy can there oppose you. But faith in such simple truisms is not universal nor can they always be applied readily. There are few short cuts in the military art, as a series of long and bloody conflicts since ancient times indicates. For example, success in the American Civil War had as much to do with the North's superior strategic position with her richer industrial and manpower resources as with any dominant weaponry or battlefield tactics.

The general principles of the war are deduced from the rules and methods used by those generals who are known as great and eminent in the practice of the profession. In the art of war, as in all experimental sciences, observations made upon the actual occurrences precede the theories. It is, therefore, evident that an intimate connection exists between the history of military operations and the art of war, and that a course of military history is indispensable as an introduction to the teaching of the science of war. The conduct of war is an art, a free creative activity based on a scientific (disciplined) foundation.

Traditionally, Russian and Soviet theorists have taken a broader view of military science and art, and the term military doctrine has meaning and emphasis unparalleled in the West. For the Soviets, military doctrine represented a politico-military frame work and instrument for formulating the state's views on war, its preparations, conduct and prevention. Ideologically-influenced military science formed the theoretical basis for military doctrine, which was politically endorsed. In turn, the most important component of military science was the study and practice of the military art which encompassed strategy, operational art, and tactics. All this study was underpinned by research and development into weapons technology and the establishment of mathematical norms for the employment of forces to achieve decisive results.

Science and technology have continued to drive weaponry and tactics at an accelerating rate, particularly over the past two centuries, and the military art has developed on more enduring lines. If tactics belong in drill books or doctrine manuals, strategy better lends itself to study through historical example. In illustration, if descriptions of ancient or medieval weapons are irrelevant in the conduct of war today, the works of Sun Tzu, Clausewitz, and Jomini or strategy are certainly not. Likewise, it is highly likely that 20th century writings on the military art will remain topical for many more decades and the subject of detailed investigation. For example, Liddell Hart's strategy of the indirect approach underwrites contemporary manoeuvre warfare.

Success in war demands hard training and continual practice. For centuries, commanders have recognized that military proficiency requires prior study and exercise. In the history of the Decline and Fall of the Roman Empire, Edward Gibbon remarks: "In the midst of peace, the Roman troops familiarized themselves with the practice of war; and it is prettily remarked by an ancient historian who had fought against them, that the effusion of blood was the only circumstances which distinguished a field of battle from a field of exercise. It was the policy of the ablest generals, and even of the emperors themselves, to encourage these military studies by their presence and example".

If the art of generalship has developed from direct leadership to more indirect methods of command, then the responsibility of those in command to train their subordinates in the military art remains. In sum, while it is relatively easy to gain a superficial picture of the art of war, perhaps through the media of popular fiction and film, such are the complexities of its dynamics and subtleties of its texture that war demands serious study. Like a language, the military art has its own lexicon, grammar, and syntax. Any picture of war must be viewed in relation to its constituent parts: strategy, operations, tactics, logistics, personnel, and command. As with religion, the conduct of war requires a doctrine to ensure coherence and consistency of teaching. In most cases training, judgement, confidence, and an element of intuition are fundamental prerequisites of success in the application of force. It requires balancing theory with practice, and a flexibility of mind to learn from past experience. But for those military commanders who ignore war's unforgiving realities and who are overconfident, unwarranted risk taking may lead to deadly gambles. For, unlike any other human activity, the costs of failure in war can be catastrophic for individuals, units, military formations, societies, and whole nations alike.

Therefore, it is wise to take a wide perspective – and here military history must play its part in order to learn about war, to view it from a number of angles, and, above all, to stand sufficiently well back in order to place any given conflict or particular operation into proper focus. For the future, a study of the military art may point out the path ahead. If neglected, the strategic overview, a balanced analysis of a plan of campaign together with its likely consequences, may be lost in a mass of tactical and technical detail.

A study of military history provides a backdrop to the examination of some facets of the word 'strategy'. In the first instance, one should see where the use of stratagem started. It is nearly impossible now to trace any intelligible or authentic account of warfare before the Greco-Persian wars (5th century BC). Normally this is taken to be the start point of military history. During this period tactics and strategy were more or less synonymous. But a clear example of a strategic move can be found when Darius invaded Greece in 490 BC. Half his infantry and cavalry laid siege to the city of Eriteria; whereon Athens sent all her forces rushing to the help of the sister city. But the balance of the Persian force suddenly landed at Marathon, cutting off the Greek force from Athens. The Persian plan was to defeat the armies of the two cities in detail, before they could join together, an excellent strategic move. Unfortunately, the Persians lost the tactical battle of Marathon, and failed to reap the benefits of a well conceived strategy.

This strategy of keeping the enemy forces divided and falling on them one after the other was successfully employed by Frederick the Great. Frederick had to fight five powers simultaneously – France, Austria, Russia, Sweden and the Empire. However, Austria and Russia were his main antagonists. Once both his enemies were near the frontier, he manoeuvred with great energy, concentrating against each in turn. Even after the terrible defeat by the Russians at the battle of Kunendrof (1759), where his defeat was mainly due to the enemy superiority of numbers, he did not totally give up and was ultimately able to push back the Russians. Throughout the Seven Years War, which opened in August 1756, when Frederick invaded Saxony in order to forestall the plans of the coalition (today it could be termed as a preemptive attack), Frederick marched and counter-marched his army so as to deal with one of his enemies at a time.

Philip of Macedon used excellent strategy to manoeuvre his forces behind the Athenic Army and then defeat them in the Battle of Charonea (338 BC) and establish Macedonian supremacy over Greece. His son, Alexander, one of the most enduring romantic military heroes, besides a great Captain of war, carried on with the work started by his father. A study of the campaigns of Alexander shows the zigzag fashion of his advance through Asia Minor into Egypt, and thence to Persia. His goal was to unify the scattered Greek colonies and thus carve out a great empire for Greece. That he succeeded in such a short span of time, speaks volumes for his stratagem. As a general, Alexander initiated many practices that are followed even today e.g. forced marches, relentless pursuit, winter campaigns, methods of maintaining a force far removed from its home base. He was also probably the first commander to realize that the proper function of a general is not to fight himself but to direct others. More than anything else, Alexander perceived the necessity of economy of force and correct application of the force at the right time and place. His invading army consisted of 30,000 to 40,000 foot soldiers and 1,000-5,000 horses and he could not afford to squander any of it.

If Alexander strode like a giant in the 4th century BC, so did Napoleon much later. His Italian campaign and campaigns in Europe are well known. He formulated a definite plan of campaign, manoeuvred suitably (though not always successfully) to position his armies in a superior manner before striking. The best example of his planning can be found in the first Italian campaign , where making the best use of the terrain features, he planned to strike at the point of junction of the Austrian and Sandinian armies and defeat them in detail. That he was helped a great deal by foolish moves and division of force by Beauliu (the Austrian commander) does not detract from the brilliancy of his plans. Strategy of similar nature was extensively used by

Napoleon in his later campaigns. One could even say that by about 1800 AD Napoleonic strategy had become fixed. When he was stronger he attempted an enveloping movement; when weaker, he operated on interior lines and dealt with one force after the other.

What does strategy seek to achieve? It should seek to achieve a superior position or advantageous position or offset some kind of inferiority vis-a-vis the enemy prior to the commencement of battle. But, superior strategy does not inevitably bring success in battle, or even a decisive campaign. One could then postulate that a perfect strategy should be that which can bring about decision without even any fighting, or serious fighting. Thus Liddell Hart maintains that "true aim is to seek a strategic situation so advantageous that, if it does not of itself produce the decision, its continuation by a battle is sure to achieve this".

And finally, what exactly is the study of strategy? Is there a continuum, a thread which connects the thoughts of many thinkers on the subject of strategy, military history and the entire gamut of the social phenomenon known as war? Strategy has a history, which develops, changes, and where parallels can be found. But, there is also an essence, a set of universal truths or some permanent elements which have remained unaffected throughout history. These universal truths or permanent elements or essence has sought to be codified as "Principles of War". Different armies have different ones but most agree on some common ones, though expressed in slightly different language. Thus "maintenance of aim, economy of effort, concentration of force, offensive action, logistics, and surprise", would be found common to almost all armies. But strategy is also history – the history of warfare, study of which leads to the crystallisation of ideas, which would lead to victory. In the ultimate analysis, armies exist to ensure victory over the adversary.

Jomini is probably the first thinker to have discerned that there are "principles". Jomini had stated that the essential object of his book was "to demonstrate there is a fundamental principle in all operations of war, a principle which should preside over all measures adopted so that they may be successful". Having experimented with many formulations, Jomini decided that the fundamental principle of strategy consisted of:

(a) Bringing, by strategic measures, the major part of an army's forces successively to bear upon the decisive areas of a theatre of war and as far as possible upon enemy's communication without compromising one'

(b) Manoeuvring in such a manner as to engage one's major forces against parts of those of the enemy.

(c) Furthermore, in battle, by tactical manoeuvres, bringing one's major forces to bear on the decisive area of the battlefield or on part of the enemy's lines which it is important to overwhelm.

(d) Arranging matters in such a fashion that these masses of men be not only brought to bear at the decisive place but that they be put into action speedily and together, so that they make a simultaneous effort. There has been considerable debate over the relevance of old fashioned "strategy" in these days of nuclear war and enlarged concepts of national security. Indeed, this is a new field – a field where there are no past precedents to go by. The evolutionary approach does not help us in understanding a nuclear battlefield or what might be the political (for that matter the ultimate) result of a nuclear explosion. Hence, the evolution of an entirely new set of strategic concepts mostly developed by academicians in various universities and "think tanks". But that is a subject which requires separate study. Suffice to conclude that conventional war of the Second World War pattern would remain even when there is a threat of nuclear war. And as long conventional war remains, study of strategy would remain relevant.

From strategy devolves a military doctrine i.e. an approved set of principles and methods, intended to provide large military organisations with a common outlook and a uniform basis for action. It makes explicit ideas or assumptions that in earlier times were conveyed by cultural means, or directly by commanders to their subordinates. When Sparta's hoplites advanced slowly and in step, shield in the left hand, spear in the right, or when the English archers at Agincourt shot their arrows in volleys they were acting on the basis of rules that would today be regarded as doctrinal in character, but which at the time could be adequately conveyed from one unit to another, and from one generation to the next, without benefit of official codification. As armies have grown larger, and their weapons and tactics more complex, more formal means of harmonizing their actions have become necessary. The introduction of firearms was an important impetus to the formalisation of doctrine, since their use required the orchestration of complex, learned procedure by hundreds or even thousands of individuals. 17th century picture books designed to show musketeers the many intricate steps required to load and fire their weapons, or the many 18th century works intended to demonstrate the optimum means of besieging a fortress, organizing an encampment, or deploying infantry from column to line and back again, are recognizably the forerunners of modern doctrinal publications.

Military doctrine is the basis of military training and indirectly, of command and control. At the tactical level, its character is largely perspective. Doctrine cannot dissipate the fog of war, and but it can simplify the decisions that have to be made under the duress of combat, by limiting the range of choices that are deemed relevant to given circumstances. It also helps ensure that all elements of an army will view similar situations in similar ways, thus conferring a degree of predictability upon the inherently chaotic actions of dispersed forces. The significance of this latter function should not be underestimated. In the absence of real time tactical communications, the promulgation of effective common doctrine is one of the few means by which senior commanders can influence the conduct of the tactical battle. Tactical doctrine is also on a foundational element of the military planning process, most especially in the case of what is sometimes called adaptive planning – the improvisation of solutions to problems not foreseen at the outset of hostilities.

The value of doctrine at what is now called the operational level of war is more complex. Doctrine achieves its clarifying effects by a judicious narrowing of the intellectual horizons of those making decisions. As the value of creativity and spontaneous insight increases, the pertinacity of prescriptive doctrine declines. At the same time, senior commanders can easily become more dependent upon doctrinal solutions than their subordinates, because they have less opportunity to practice their wartime roles; commands above a corps usually exist only on paper in peacetime, and actual manoeuvres employing such large formations are exceedingly rare. Frederick the Great, whose approach to tactics was, broadly, that no one reasons, everyone executes (General Principles of War, 1746) nevertheless recognized that general officers required a different kind of guidance. His instructions for Generals Commanding Detachments, Wings, Second Lines, and Prussian Armies (1753) was an early attempt to formulate doctrine in a way that conveyed overall intentions and requirements, while simultaneously insisting upon the obligation of senior officers to exercise independent judgement and personal initiative. Most military doctrine presents itself as authoritative but not directive, and leaves it to the reader to ponder the difference.

Modern military doctrine is markedly technocratic in character. This is a reflection of the enormous influence that technological systems exert on the conduct of war, and also of the belief that doctrine itself should have a scientific basis, which is usually summarized in terms of a small number of principles of war. The fact that the fighting doctrines of most armies have tended, at any given moment, to resemble each other provides some vindication for this point of view. Differences may, of course, remain significant. Among military victories of recent times, those by Germany over France in 1940, and by Israel over its Arab neighbours in 1967, the Bangladesh campaign of 1971, or the recent Gulf wars, are the ones in which the doctrinal superiority of one side is conceded to have carried the greatest weight, if only because the adversaries appear otherwise to have been so evenly matched. Technological change has made military doctrine subject to constant revision, to the point where assimilating such change to the conduct of war has become one of its core functions. At the same time, military doctrine always reflects the social conditions, cultural preferences, and historical experiences of those who promulgate it. Here again there is a fine balance to be struck between the use of doctrine to enforce innovation and its more conservative function as the bearer of professional values and institutional memories.

"It is not the same when a fighter moves because he wants to move, and another when he moves because he has to"

— Joe Frazier